ETHNIC GROUPS OF AMERICA: THEIR MORBIDITY, MORTALITY AND BEHAVIOR DISORDERS

Volume II - The Blacks

ETHNIC GROUPS OF AMERICA: THEIR MORBIDITY, MORTALITY AND BEHAVIOR DISORDERS

Volume II - The Blacks

Edited by

AILON SHILOH

Professor of Anthropology
in Public Health
Graduate School of Public Health
Professor and Director
Graduate Studies
Department of Anthropology
University of South Florida
Tampa, Florida

and

IDA COHEN SELAVAN

Lecturer
College of Arts and Sciences
University of Pittsburgh
Pittsburgh, Pennsylvania

CHARLES C THOMAS • PUBLISHER
Springfield • Illinois • U.S.A.

Published and Distributed Throughout the World by
CHARLES C THOMAS ● PUBLISHER
Bannerstone House
301-327 East Lawrence Avenue, Springfield, Illinois, U.S.A.

© *1974, by* CHARLES C THOMAS ● PUBLISHER
ISBN 0-398-03022-7 (cloth)
ISBN 0-398-03023-5 (paper)
Library of Congress Catalog Card Number: 72–81717

With THOMAS BOOKS *careful attention is given to all details of
manufacturing and design. It is the Publisher's desire to present books that
are satisfactory as to their physical qualities and artistic possibilities and
appropriate for their particular use.* THOMAS BOOKS *will be true to those
laws of quality that assure a good name and good will.*

Printed in the United States of America

BB-14

Library of Congress Cataloging in Publication Data

Shiloh, Ailon.
  Ethnic groups of America.

  CONTENTS: v. 2. The Blacks.
    1. Minorities—Health and hygiene—United States.
  2. Minorities—Medical care—United States.
  I. Selavan, Ida Cohen, joint editor II. Title.
  [DNLM: 1. Ethnic groups—U.S. 2. Morbidity—U.S.
  3. Mortality—U.S. WA300 S556e]
  RA448.4.S54   362.8'4   72–81717
  ISBN 0–398–03022–7
  ISBN 0–398–03023–5 (pbk.)

CONTRIBUTORS

CYNTHIA BANDFIELD, M.S.
Department of Psychiatry
Columbia University College of
  Physicians and Surgeons
New York, New York

THEODORE M. BAYLESS, M.D.
Associate Professor of
  Medicine
  and Gastroenterology
The Johns Hopkins School of
  Medicine
Baltimore, Maryland

D.M. BERKSON, M.D.
Northwestern University
  Medical School
Chicago, Illinois

ANN F. BRUNSWICK, M.A.
Columbia University School of
  Public Health and
  Administrative Medicine
New York, New York

FRED BURBANK
Stanford University
  Medical Center
Department of Psychiatry
Adult Out-Patient Clinic
Stanford, California

WILLIAM M.
CHRISTOPHERSON,
  M.D.
Department of Pathology
University of Louisville
  School of Medicine
Health Sciences Center
Louisville, Kentucky

PAUL B. CORNELY, M.D.,
  Dr. P.H., F.A.P.H.A.
Professor and Head, Department
  of Preventive Medicine and
  Public Health
Howard University College of
  Medicine
Washington, D.C.

CLEMENT A. FINCH, M.D.
Division of Hematology
Department of Medicine
University of Washington
  School of Medicine
Seattle, Washington

FRANK A. FINNERTY, JR.,
  M.D.
Georgetown University Medical
  Division
D.C. General Hospital
Washington, D.C.

MAYER FISCH, M.D.
11 East 75th Street
New York, New York

JOSEPH F. FRAUMENI, JR.,
  M.D.
Epidemiology Branch
National Cancer Institute
National Institutes of Health
Public Health Service
U.S. Department of HEW
Bethesda, Maryland

v

GEORGE C. GRAHAM, M.D.
Professor of Human Nutrition
and
Associate Professor of
Pediatrics
The Johns Hopkins School of
Hygiene and Public Health
Baltimore, Maryland

ERNEST M. GRUENBERG, M.D.,
Dr. P.H., F.A.P.H.A.
Professor of Psychiatry
Department of Psychiatry
Columbia University College
of Physicians and Surgeons
New York, New York

Y. HALL, M.S.
Northwestern University
Medical School
Chicago, Illinois

MILTON HELPERN, M.D.
Professor and Chairman
Department of Forensic
Medicine
New York University School of
Medicine
New York, New York

DOLORES E. JACKSON
316 Beach 56th Street
Arverne, New York

ERIC JOSEPHSON, PH.D.
Columbia University School of
Public Health and
Administrative Medicine
New York, New York

H.A. LINDBERG, M.D.
Department of Medicine
Northwestern University
Medical School
Chicago, Illinois

W. MILLER, M.P.H.
Northwestern University
Medical School
Chicago, Illinois

GEORGE E. MURPHY, M.D.
Associate Professor of
Psychiatry
Washington University School
of Medicine
St. Louis, Missouri

ROBERT M. NALBANDIAN, M.D.
Associate Pathologist,
Blodgett Memorial Hospital
Grand Rapids, Michigan

SHIN JOONG OH, M.D.
Assistant Professor of
Neurology
University of Alabama Medical
Center
Birmingham, Alabama

DAVID M. PAIGE, M.D.,
M.P.H.
Assistant Professor of
Maternal and
Child Health
The Johns Hopkins School of
Hygiene and Public Health
Baltimore, Maryland

JAMES E. PARKER, M.D.
Department of Pathology
University of Louisville
School of Medicine
Louisville, Kentucky

ANN HALLMAN PETTIGREW,
M.D.
Teaching Fellow
Tufts University School of
Medicine
Medford, Massachusetts

THOMAS F. PETTIGREW
Professor of Social Psychology
Harvard University
Department of Psychology and
  Social Relations
Cambridge, Massachusetts

LEE N. ROBINS, PH.D.
Research Professor of
  Sociology in Psychiatry
Washington University School
  of Medicine
St. Louis, Missouri

GEOFFREY ROSE, D.M.,
  M.R.C.P.
Lecturer in Epidemiology
London School of Hygiene and
  Tropical Medicine
Senior Registrar in Medicine
St. Mary's Hospital
London, England

MAURICE V. RUSSELL,
  M.S.W., ED.D.
Professor of Preventive
  Medicine
New York University
  Medical Center and Director,
Social Service,
New York, New York

ROBERT B. SCOTT, M.D.
Department of Medicine
Medical College of Virginia
Health Sciences Center
Virginia Commonwealth
  University
Richmond, Virginia

VICTOR W. SIDEL, M.D.
Chief, Division of Social
  Medicine
Montefiore Hospital;
Professor of Community Health
Albert Einstein College of
  Medicine
Bronx, New York

GEORGE A. SILVER, M.D.
Professor of International
  Health
Yale University School of
  Medicine
New Haven, Connecticut

JEREMIAH STAMLER, M.D.
Professor and Chairman,
  Department of Community
  Health and Preventive
  Medicine
Northwestern University
  Medical School
Chicago, Illinois

ROBERT STRAYER, M.S.W.
Director, Psychiatric Social
  Service
Bridgeport Clinic
Connecticut Division on
  Alcoholism
Bridgeport, Connecticut

GORDON F. SUTTON, PH.D.
Department of Sociology
University of Massachusetts
Amherst, Massachusetts

M.M. VITOLS, M.D.
1500 Westbrook Avenue
Richmond, Virginia

This work is dedicated to the pioneers in the delivery of effective health services to the black people.

FOREWORD

This volume represents a self-contained contribution concerning black health and health services. It is hoped that this work will provoke and stimulate more comprehensive studies, both in depth and range, of the problems at hand, and that future editions of this volume or works of similar nature will reflect this improved research.

The question as to whether America's blacks constitute a race, ethnic group, or socio-cultural population, or a mix of these and other variables, is finally under serious study. At this time we consider it useful to include the Negroes as one population in our report of the morbidity, mortality and behavior disorders of America's ethnic groups.

ACKNOWLEDGMENT

This volume would not have been possible without the professional assistance and responsibility of Miss Barbara Beck, of the University of Pittsburgh, and Mrs. Barbara E. Hawkins, of the University of South Florida, who proceeded with us in seeing this manuscript through from original development to final publication. We would also like to acknowledge the evaluation of our developing manuscript made by Dr. Paul B. Cornely, Professor and Head, Department of Preventive Medicine and Public Health, Howard University College of Medicine.

CONTENTS

Page

Contributors— v

Dedication— ix

Foreword— xi

Acknowledgment— xiii

PART ONE

MORBIDITY PATTERNS

Chapter

1. THE HEALTH STATUS OF THE NEGRO TODAY AND IN THE FUTURE—Paul B. Cornely 5

2. ASSESSING MORTALITY AND MORBIDITY DISADVANTAGES OF THE BLACK POPULATION OF THE UNITED STATES—Gordon F. Sutton 18

3. RACE, DISEASE AND DESEGREGATION: A NEW LOOK—Ann Hallman Pettigrew and Thomas F. Pettigrew 36

PART TWO

STRESS

4. CEREBRO VASCULAR DISEASES IN NEGROES—Shin Joong Oh 67

5. CARDIOVASCULAR MORTALITY AMONG AMERICAN NEGROES— Geoffery Rose 78

6. RACIAL PATTERNS OF CORONARY HEART DISEASE—J. Stamler, D.M. Berkson, H.A. Lindberg W. Miller, and Y. Hall 84

7. HYPERTENSION IS DIFFERENT IN BLACKS—Frank A. Finnerty, Jr. 100

PART THREE

THE GENETIC FACTOR

8. PATHOPHYSIOLOGIC ASPECTS OF SICKLE CELL ANEMIA—Clement A. Finch 107

9. SICKLE CELL ANEMIA—Robert M. Nalbandian 117

10. HEALTH CARE PRIORITY AND SICKLE CELL ANEMIA—Robert B. Scott 121

11. SICKLE CELL DISEASE: MEETING A NEED—Delores E. Jackson 129

PART FOUR

CANCER

12. U. S. CANCER MORTALITY: NONWHITE PREDOMINANCE—Fred Burbank, and Joseph F. Fraumeni, Jr. 149

13. A STUDY OF THE RELATIVE FREQUENCY OF Carcinoma of the CERVIX IN THE NEGRO—William M. Christopherson, and James E. Parker 163

PART FIVE

ALCOHOLISM AND DRUG ADDICTION

14. STUDY OF THE NEGRO ALCOHOLIC—Robert Strayer 171

15. CULTURE PATTERNS OF DRINKING IN NEGRO AND WHITE ALCO-HOLICS—M.M. Vitols 186

16. DRUG USE IN A NORMAL POPULATION OF YOUNG NEGRO MEN— Lee N. Robins, and George E. Murphy 195

17. FATALITIES FROM NARCOTIC ADDICTION IN NEW YORK CITY— Milton Helpern 215

PART SIX

MENTAL ILLNESS

18. MENTAL ILLNESS AMONG NEGROES—Maurice V. Russell . 225

19. THE EPIDEMIOLOGY OF PSYCHIATRIC EMERGENCIES IN AN URBAN HEALTH DISTRICT—Mayer Fisch, Ernest M. Gruenberg, and Cynthia Bandfield 231

PART SEVEN

TOWARDS THE DELIVERY OF EFFECTIVE HEALTH SERVICES

20. HEALTH ATTITUDES AND BEHAVIOR OF ADOLESCENTS IN HARLEM—Ann F. Brunswick, and Eric Josephson 243

21. MILK PROGRAMS: HELPFUL OR HARMFUL TO NEGRO CHILDREN?— David M. Paige, Theodore M. Bayless, and George G. Graham 252

22. CAN MORE PHYSICIANS BE ATTRACTED TO GHETTO PRACTICE?—Victor W. Sidel 259

23. WHAT HAS BEEN LEARNED ABOUT THE DELIVERY OF HEALTH CARE SERVICES TO THE GHETTO?—George A. Silver 271

Author Index 281

Subject Index 289

ETHNIC GROUPS OF AMERICA: THEIR MORBIDITY, MORTALITY AND BEHAVIOR DISORDERS

Volume II - The Blacks

PART ONE
MORBIDITY PATTERNS

As Paul B. Cornely demonstrates in the first chapter, there has been a widening gap between the mortality and morbidity rates of whites and blacks. There have been indications of a high rate of mental retardation, there is a shortage of medical manpower, racial discrimination and other unfavorable patterns which affect the health of Negro Americans. Cornely makes some suggestions to rectify the situation, among which is the need for improved research and collection of data on mortality and morbidity.

This point is also emphasized by Gordon F. Sutton in Chapter Two. Adequate reliable data are just not available. Furthermore, it seems clear in many instances that what were once considered racial variables, may really have been socioeconomic differences. (One of the more significant findings of recent years, Sutton believes, is the demonstration of how blacks encounter disability at relatively younger ages.)

Ann H. Pettigrew and Thomas F. Pettigrew review what is known about Negro American health from a comparative point of view. They consider many aspects of Negro morbidity, e.g., rates of mental illness, communicable diseases, hereditary illnesses and others, indicating where data are unreliable and pointing up areas of Negro resistance to certain kinds of diseases. Their study is designed to counteract arguments that Negro Americans are innately less healthy than whites.

Chapter 1

THE HEALTH STATUS OF THE NEGRO TODAY AND IN THE FUTURE

PAUL B. CORNELY

INTRODUCTION

The first nationwide conference on the health status of the Negro, held on March 13 and 14, 1967, during the Centennial Observance of Howard University, was called for the purpose of having a group of knowledgeable and experienced scholars, researchers, educators, and providers of health services consider the major health problems of this segment of the population, and to suggest guidelines which would be helpful to governmental and voluntary agencies at the local, state, and national levels. Financial support for this conference came from the Public Health Service and the Milbank Fund; about 200 persons from 20 states were in attendance. It should be made clear that this two-day conference was not called for the purpose of finding instant solutions to the many health and welfare problems which beset the Negro.

I have been asked to summarize what occurred at this conference. This is being presented under the following three headings: (a) major health problems of the Negro, (b) possible solutions for selected health problems, and (c) the urgency of the situation.

Reprinted with permission from the *American Journal of Public Health*, April, 1968.

The writer is greatly indebted to the authors of the addresses, and the chairmen and co-chairmen who prepared preconference summaries for the Workshop Sessions of the Conference on the Health Status of the Negro Today and in the Future.

Health Problems of the Negro in the United States

The major health problems of the Negro were discussed at length at one of the workshops. Although I shall not go through all of them, nevertheless, it is well to mention three of the many health problems with which the conference struggled so that none of us will entirely forget what is happening to our fellow Americans.

1. *The Widening Gap.* Any objective look at the available data comparing Negro and white mortality and morbidity shows that the gap between the two is getting wider. This is true for most of the important public health indexes used in this country.

2. *Mental Retardation.* The prevalence of inferior intellectual functioning among the Negro community is illustrated by recent studies of Negro school-age children. Eighth grade pupils in Central Harlem were found to have a mean I.Q. of 87.7, while the average I.Q. for New York City eighth graders was 100.1.[1] A normative study of 1,800 Negro elementary school children in five southern states yielded a mean I.Q. of 80.7.[2] According to the most recent classification system accepted by the American Association of Mental Deficiency,[3] which is also used by the US Public Health Service, the average child in the latter study is "borderline retarded." These data do not present any particularly new information; such findings have been reported for over 50 years.[4,5] The precursors of, and factors associated with, mental retardation abound in the Negro community. Mental retardation has been found to be associated with prematurity, complications of pregnancy, low socio-economic status, as well as lower occupational levels, lower educational attainment, and broken homes. Yet, little has been done to alleviate these conditions.

3. *Health Concerns of the Unskilled and Semiskilled Worker.* The unskilled and semiskilled workers have the most serious health problems and receive the least adequate health care. Because of segregation and discrimination, the great majority of Negroes fall into these occupational groups, and their health problems stem mainly from this fact. The health services received by them tend to be obtained from two

sources: (1) charity wards and clinics and (2) private care by overworked and harried general practitioners.

Another factor has to do with injury and compensation. Negroes who are largely concentrated in unskilled and heavy labor occupations are often subjected to greater risk of injury and consequent potential loss of health.

Because these workers are largely unskilled, poorly educated, and Negro, even union activity, significant in protecting the workmen's interest in these areas in the past, is largely waning and in some areas has tragically disappeared.

There is a growing tendency in many industries to contest all claims made by injured workmen, particularly where disability results. This kind of activity on the part of industry forces the claimant in many instances to require legal services to establish the merit of his claim or forfeit, through ignorance and inadequate education, the very benefit for which the law originally came into being. The Negro is the greater sufferer.

These three examples are sufficient. The others are indeed known only too well—discriminatory health patterns, shortage of health manpower, organization, delivery and utilization of health services, and so on.

Possible Solutions for Selected Health Problems

Each of the workshops of the Howard University Conference attempted to develop possible solutions and recommendations for many of the health problems which beset the Negro. An effort will be made here to summarize the more salient approaches which came to the fore.

What Can Be Done About the Unfavorable Morbidity and Mortality Patterns of the Negro?

The unfavorable morbidity and mortality experiences of the Negro population are not due to any genetic differences, but rather to the socioeconomic and environmental deficiencies, such as poverty, housing, unemployment, nonavailability, and/or inaccessibility of health services facilities, discrimination and segregation, and inadequate family structure. Therefore, the major thrust to improve the health of the Negro must be directed at these factors along the following lines:

a. A massive, coordinated, and comprehensive attack on the nation's social, economic, and health problems sponsored by the federal government is critically and urgently needed. A recent press release in Washington reported that Argentina recently sent six Peace Corps volunteers to help in poverty areas in our affluent society. It is possible that after a brief exposure here, these volunteers will ask their country to send surplus beef to feed the starving children in Mississippi.

b. Much of the mental retardation in the Negro community can be alleviated by positive, significant, and lasting improvement in the over-all standard of living. The high incidence of borderline mental retardation among the deprived is acutely susceptible to available remedies. A comprehensive plan of effective action for the Negro community as a whole, and for the functionally retarded individual in particular, is necessary if a notable decline in the incidence of mental retardation in the Negro community is to be observed.

c. Research is urgently needed to determine the many factors which affect the full utilization of health services by the poor, and to find ways and means to develop a health care system which will reach and be accepted by the poor.

d. Negro health professionals should become actively interested in the correction of factors which promote homicide, drug addiction, illegitimacy, and other behavior problems with high incidence among Negro youth. Currently there appears to be considerable apathy among this group.

e. Small regional conferences financed by the federal government or foundations should be developed to consider some of the health problems of the Negro. These conferences could bring together specialists in the field for a more careful consideration of these problems. Hopefully these would stimulate an increase in research in many neglected areas.

Government-Financed Health Care and the Negro

The role of the federal government in the organization, financing, and delivery of health services had been a relatively passive one until President Johnson and the 89th Congress caused the federal structure's concern with health to be propelled into the 20th century. It is well known that this country does not have a delivery system that provides high quality medical care for every citizen. The deficiencies in some areas are serious, in others, shocking. How can government-sponsored programs, such as Medicare and Medicaid, be altered so that the Negro can receive maximum benefits? There are presently two important deterring factors which must be faced and must be resolved. These are poverty and discrimination.

The effects of poverty need not be amplified, but the ills of discrimination must continue to be recognized. Discrimination is an additional senseless and un-Christian burden for the American Negro poor. If one looks at statistical data from public health clinics, one wonders where do poor whites receive their care, since public health clinics are generally filled with Negro clients. In the report of the US Commission on Civil Rights, entitled "Title VI—One Year After," one finds the statement:

> In 1963 (in Selma, Alabama, where there were equal numbers of white and Negro families with incomes below $3,000), 1,600 babies were born to residents of the county. All but four of the 600 white babies were born in hospitals with physicians in attendance, but only 300 of the 1,000 Negro babies were delivered in hospitals with physician care. Seven hundred babies were born outside hospitals—most attended by midwives.
>
> Although it is not known how poor white women receive prenatal care in Selma (as stated by the County Health Officer), it was apparent that the care they received outside the public health programs resulted in the birth of their babies in hospitals, with a physician in attendance. On the other hand, the federally assisted public health programs which provide care only for Negroes, resulted primarily in the birth of babies outside hospitals attended only by untrained midwives.

Thus, if medical and health care financed by the federal government is to reach the Negro, urgent social action is necessary. Social action in this instance is implementing Title VI, the Civil Rights Act passed by Congress in 1964. The Department of Health, Education, and Welfare has been given the task. But, seriously, what can it accomplish with a budget of 4.5 million dollars for 1967, and a request for 1968 of $5,434,000 in a country which is not a melting pot, but a collectivity of ethnic and economic groups?

Aside from alleviation of poverty and discrimination, everyone admits that if government-financed health programs are to reach the Negro poor, there must be innovation to meet the needs of the ghetto. This is certainly true for new programs, but it is even more applicable to old programs which have missed the mark. School health services which have held a prominent place in public health practice in this country during the past 50 years are a case in point. These services represent an annual expenditure in excess of $250,000,000. Thousands of nurses are employed in this service system on a full-time basis, and thousands of physicians spend part of their professional time working in these programs. School health services have steadfastly steered a course that did not include medical care, except for an occasional program which provided ophthalmic examinations and eyeglasses. Should such limited programs be continued in the face of huge gaps in facilities and manpower in the medical care aspects of comprehensive services? The artificial dichotomy of preventive and curative services that is so widely evident in school health service programs should be abolished. They should be integrated into the mainstream of medical and health programs. Is there any reason for not offering medical care in the school and utilizing available school health staffs in these activities? Schools located in inner cities and in other areas of poverty should become identified as sites for delivering curative medical care.

Health Manpower and the Negro Community

The problem of health manpower is two-faced in its dimensions as far as the Negro is concerned. We know there are tremendous shortages in all health professions, which damage the health of all, and particularly the Negro poor. Conversely, this shortage in trained and skilled personnel badly affects the economic base of the Negro community and maintains it in a welfare posture. Since much has been written about shortages concerning doctors, dentists, and other professional personnel, and what needs to be done, this section will be devoted to the nonprofessional health aides. However, it is mandatory that attention be called to the plight of the Negro dentist. He is becoming a vanishing American. Dr. Joseph Henry, dean of the Dental School at Howard University, states that in 1940 the proportion of Negro dentists in this country was 4 percent; in 1950, 3 percent; and in 1965, this had been reduced to 2 percent. Of the 375 applicants to the Dental School, less than 70 were Negroes, so that for the first time in its history, the freshman class at Howard University Dental School will have a majority of white students. This is indeed a critical situation.

The training and use of nonprofessional health aides or health services aides are of great import for the Negro community. Development and expansion of needed neighborhood community health services have been handicapped by increasing shortage of trained personnel, and the major difficulties of reaching, motivating, and involving the people in the neighborhood who need services. At the same time, disadvantaged residents of these communities lack realistic employment, training, and career opportunities in all but the most menial or dead-end entry levels of the job market.

A significant answer to this complex problem has been the development of experimental programs for the training and employment of local residents in nonprofessional jobs with career possibilities in community health service programs. Several training centers in the country, including Howard University in Washington, Lincoln Hospital in New York, and the California State Department of Health, have developed such nonprofessional positions on a variety of entry levels in health services, and have successfully trained and employed disadvantaged persons for these positions.

As with the professional programs, counseling and recruitment must become more extensive and more aggressive. High schools and junior community colleges should develop more effective programs to guide students' attention to possibilities and gratification inherent in health careers. Various health agencies, like hospitals and health departments in Negro communities, should be used as educational media for health careers. Part-time or summer jobs in these agencies should be made available to both Negro and white youths. Extensive promotional activities should be carried out through the radio, television, and newspapers which cater to and are used by certain segments of the population.

Health agencies can also help solve this problem by making provisions to take Negroes of minimal educational background, give them on-the-job training, and, subsequently, as they improve, provide them with the opportunity for formal education while at work, and so allow them to move up the occupational ladder. Of course, it is obvious that there must be parallel efforts to raise salaries and improve working conditions of health aides, thus allowing health agencies to compete with industry in attracting Negro youths. By the same token, boards of education should approve such training and certify the training centers. Licensing boards must also come to grips with some of the questions raised, and be willing to revise their regulations to give more recognition to on-the-job training.

Health Attitudes and Behavior of Negro and White Individuals Which Affect Health Care and Utilization of Services

The attitudes and behavior of people—the donors and recipients of health care—adversely or favorably affect the utilization of health services. The professionals—the donors of health care—can be helpful in many ways, and some of these can be mentioned. A major difficulty in the reception of health care is the social distance between the provider and the recipient of health care. Inasmuch as the former is in possession of the information which the recipient requires for the care of his health, this must be transmitted adequately. Professionals should be more aware of this and be alert to the need to modify their presentation to assure and insure acceptability and understanding. This involves the attitude which middle-class professionals have toward the poor: the usual professional tendency to treat disease and not the patient, and to leave his way of life, environment, problems, and emotions out of the picture. All too often it is the professional who is "hard-to-reach" and not the patient. There is, therefore, a need for training programs to include study units which will aid professionals in understanding their own prejudices and altering them. Professionals must also be taught how to communicate effectively with low-income persons; how to develop satisfactory interpersonal relationships; and how to work with others in the community.

Attention must also be called to the fact that most health education material continues to be geared to middle-class vocabulary and attitudes. An experiment worthy of wider application has been made whereby a group of lower socioeconomic individuals prepared their own health education materials. The drawings were a bit crude and the words different from the usual professional language, but the information was effectively transmitted. Another is the approach which the Health Education Division of the District of Columbia Department of Public Health has used. Selected materials, before being published, were submitted to a group of neighborhood health aides for criticisms and suggested changes in the format and wording, and then pretested among a group of the families with which they were working.

Just as professionals have impediments, so do low-income Negro consumers of health services. A study by Cornely and Bigman[6] has emphasized some of these and need not be repeated here. However, it must be reiterated that these differences in the health attitudes and behavior of low-income Negro families must be taken into consideration in any program for improvement.

Health of the Worker

What can be done about the health problems of the unskilled and semiskilled Negro workers and their families? First of all, there seems to be a suspicion that neither Medicare nor Medicaid will accomplish the objective of providing a single system of medical care for all citizens and, therefore, the time has come to adopt a new abolition movement —"Abolish Charity Medicine." All minority groups, be they Negro, Puerto Rican, or Indian, are the unwilling victims of the present charity system of medical care. The abolition of charity medicine can only be implemented with the passage of legislation establishing a national health insurance scheme dedicated to the principle that every individual in the United States has a right to medical care.

Second, there are presently many inadequacies in workmen's compensation legislation in every state and continuing efforts must be made to improve these laws. However, the inequities of each state program, as well as those existing between the states, make it imperative to consider the feasibility of a national workmen's compensation law which would assure a minimum level of benefits throughout the nation.

Third, the deplorable condition of occupational health programs at the local, state, and federal level is a reflection of the almost total lack of national leadership. Although there has been a marked increase in funds appropriated by Congress for occupational health, there is no genuine federal commitment for the improvement and expansion of these services. Consequently, there is little effort being made to coordinate occupational health with comprehensive community health programs. This only intensifies the existing fragmentation of the health of the worker. Moreover, little attention is being devoted to increasing the number of workers covered by in-plant programs. This is a further manifestation of the economic restrictions imposed on occupational health programs by organized medicine. It must also be noted that occupational health programs are making no effort to overcome the illiteracy of many unskilled and semiskilled workers. It is difficult to implement health and safety programs if the worker is unable to read or understand educational materials. The rehabilitation of the injured worker should be closely coordinated with workmen's compensation programs. In many states there is little cooperation and no coordination between these two programs.

Urgency of the Situation

The salient deliberations and discussions of the Howard University Conference have been summarized above. The Negro revolution and protestations occuring throughout the United States underscore the importance of the health problems of the Negro, and all Americans must be concerned about their urgency. This urgency must be viewed in the light of the following four considerations which repeatedly come into clear focus.

1. Our affluent society is allowing a widening gap to develop between the health of the white and nonwhite population. This adds fuel to the smoldering Negro revolution which explodes intermittently. Those concerned with health care can contribute their skills to the resolution of these conflicts and frictions which are being intensified daily, particularly in our large metropolitan communities.

2. The health of the Negro is both an expression and the result of the social and economic burdens imposed upon him. His health is inseparably connected with poor housing, unemployment, and inadequate education. But the health problems of the Negro are also the health problems of the poor. There is, therefore, a tremendous justification for setting aside ethnic considerations and making the health of all the poor our major concern. This is the desideratum, but it is impossible to achieve today, or in the immediate future, because of the burdens of a long existent cultural pattern. There is a basic difference between the black and white poor because of discrimination and segregation which continue in our midst. Both the consumer and the providers of health services suffer. This is not a mere physical barrier. More importantly, it is emotional and it alters the attitude and behavior of those who seek health and those who dispense it. The health provider, if he is to serve and aid the black poor, must himself undergo a revolution or conversion in his own thinking. Only in this way will he be able to meet and understand the major changes which are occuring in the attitude of the Negro community. This has tremendous importance to universities and colleges engaged in training members of the health team.

3. Health agencies, whether federal, national, or local, must realize that the health problems of the Negro poor are extremely urgent, and financial support for a nationwide "man in his home" program should equal that of the "man on the moon" project. Unless this is done with dispatch, our communities, particularly the urban centers, will continue to grow into black jungles of unmanageable proportions. The resolution of this is a challenge to the federal government, particularly Congress. This government has not been willing to establish certain social objectives and goals to be accomplished within stated periods of time. Neither has it been willing to face up to the problems of black America because the mentality of the majority of the leaders of this country is still polluted with the miasma of prejudice.

4. The health problems of the Negro poor are many, and have been known for a long time. Yet there is insufficient data, as well as a paucity of studies, designed to answer many of the questions confronting us. How can these problems be attacked if the epidemiology is woefully inadequate? The Public Health Service, the universities, and foundations should address themselves to these problems and stimulate interest in finding answers.

The urgency of the situation is of grave importance to all health workers, and particularly to the leaders of the profession. The American Public Health Association itself has just recently accepted the challenge and the urgency by committing itself to the employment of a staff person who will be concerned with the problems of discrimination and segregation in health matters. But solid achievements in this area cannot take place unless there is the commitment of the almost 20,000 members of this organization, and particularly those of the two Sections (Medical Care and Health Officers) assembled here today. The time has come for the Councils of these two Sections to come together and initiate the procedure whereby they can become an effectively strong unit in order to accomplish three major tasks.

a. Determine and delineate the nature and function of the type of health agency at the local, state, or federal level, which this country needs now and for the future, in order to provide each one of us with the health and medical services which are needed.

b. Define the social objectives and goals which must become part of the political structure of our country.

c. Formulate an approach whereby the APHA can become the effective spokesman for whatever consumer group today or tomorrow is denied the health care which our technology has made possible.

The task which our country faces today is urgent.

REFERENCES

1. Moynihan, D.P.: *The Negro Family: The Case for National Action.* U.S. Department of Labor, Office of Policy Planning and Research, 1965.

2. Kennedy, W.A., et al: A normative sample of intelligence and achievement of Negro elementary school children in the southeastern United States. *Monogr Soc Res Child Dev, 28,* No. 6 Ser. No. 90, 1963.

3. Heber, R.: A Manual of Terminology and Classification in Mental Retardation, 2nd ed. *Am J Ment Defic Monogr Suppl,* April, 1961.

4. Peterson, J.: The Comparative Abilities of White and Negro Children. *Comp Psychol Mongr, 5:*1–141, 1923.

5. Shuey, A.M.: *The Testing of Negro Intelligence.* Lynchburg, Va., Bell, 1958.

6. Cornely, P.B., and Bigman, S.K.: Some considerations in changing health attitudes. *Children, 10,1:*23–28, January-February, 1963.

Chapter 2

ASSESSING MORTALITY AND MORBIDITY DISADVANTAGES OF THE BLACK POPULATION OF THE UNITED STATES

Gordon F. Sutton

A description of mortality and morbidity differentials by race in the context of social and economic inequalities is hard to come by. This is true because the kinds of statistics that might be most useful for this purpose are not usually available. Changes in the character of mortality and morbidity over the last hundred years may have had some important influence regarding why this is so.

A review of mortality trends since 1800, from data for areas such as New York City which have such historical series, is instructive. Such a series displays a pronounced raggedness over the nineteenth century which is replaced by a smoother figure associated with a monotonic reduction in mortality in the twentieth century. In this later period, pronounced variability in mortality rates is less striking across time and more striking in the group differences in risk of death.

As this shift in the pattern of variability has occurred, the frame of reference for examining mortality has required new criteria of social valuation which would permit distinctions as to which differences, or changes in differences, are impor-

Abridged and reprinted with permission from *Social Biology*, December, 1971.

tant and which are not.[22] The mortality literature has been slow to respond to this need.

Suppose we are concerned with comparing two populations for current mortality experience. If the comparison is made with an eye to a purely demographic concern for survivorship, then deaths may be related to populations at risk and adjusted for differences in age, sex composition, or other selected characteristics thought to obscure the comparison. However, if the mortality experience for comprehensive survivorship is of less interest than the impact of mortality on subject populations in relation to its effect upon the long-run social and economic well-being of the population, then the standard procedures are less useful. Trends in the age-adjusted mortality differentials by race are less telling than those which describe changing costs of mortality in the lifeways of the populations; mortality in the economically active components of the population, for instance may be a more useful target than mortality at ages which account for most deaths.

In this paper, I should like to explore mortality and morbidity in the black population by comparison with the nonblack (actually, white) population. But I propose to carry forth this examination in the context of a concern for the manifest social and economic inequalities in the society which are such that black men and women are at a clear disadvantage.[4,6,25] Thus, the problem of the measurement of mortality is complicated to the extent to which it is necessary to weight some deaths more than others. Other complications arise in the need to focus upon white-black differences in mortality which comprise major components in the mortality experience of significance in the framework of social and economic inequalities of blacks; by the same token, some large *relative* black-white differences must be accorded less emphasis. The corresponding analysis in the case of morbidity statistics is impeded by other obstacles. Data on morbidity are less often available for the population by race than data on mortality. Moreover, those data which are available are not readily interpreted, especially in any attempt to combine both mortality and morbidity into a single index.[18,31]

SOCIAL DIFFERENTIALS
IN MORTALITY

The analysis of morbidity and mortality has historically focused heavily upon biomedical conditions in the interests of searching out relevant determinants. Today, however, the social and economic conditions which prevail in the instances of illness and death are of growing significance in the United States. The reason is found in the perceived relatively low level of mortality which has been attained here. The seemingly irresistible and immutable processes of aging which are the deserts of all who survive to later life stand on one side while on the other the genetic defects and accidents contributing to the losses among the very young as well as the middle-aged now loom large.[18] So there remain fields of battle for medicine.

But more striking now are the differential patterns of morbidity and death which afflict the population not through medical ignorance but rather through our ignorance of the differences in the way the social order impinges on different human groupings. Medicine and social welfare concerns join hands here in calling for further explication of these differences.

Differential mortality is hardly a new field of study. Many works in the literature for hundreds of years attest to this. However, the progress of understanding differences from a social and economic standpoint appears less well-advanced. And more importantly, the condition of certain population aggregates remains particularly obscure because the study of differentials themselves do not necessarily depict the social and cultural conditions which may accompany the lifeways of specific subpopulations. As examples of subpopulations, one may consider persons in poverty and persons who are black, Mexican-American, or American Indian in the United States.

Evidence to the support of the argument of slow progress in developing social and economic insights is found in the paucity of adequate statistical material for such disadvantaged subpopulations on a national basis. For the Spanish-descent population, as an example, no national data were available until 1969. For all such groups, uncertainty attends the adequacy of data which are available. Both census and vital data are plagued with under-reporting or misreporting of characteristics and events for such groups.[3,8,13] The comparability of data among such groups, and even within groups across time, is hazardous. Measures of mortality of American Indians have again only recently been subject to question as the 1960 census appears to have generated an unusual affinity of persons to this population when compared with earlier censuses.[26] Census undercounts among so-called hard-to-enumerate areas have been of concern to demographers for some years and have recently become notorious as the more militant black population has looked for evidence of racialism in a new and vital perspective.

As we address the problems of disease, disability, and loss of life among those in poverty, another barrier to understanding arises in the absence of a widely agreed upon and analytically adequate definition of poverty. As interest in poverty developed in the early part of the last decade, an economic definition of poverty was conceived which could be rationalized by determining income levels corresponding to costs of a marginal diet and by describing the relationship between food costs and other expenses.[19] This definition does not, however, deal with the institutional population. More importantly, perhaps, it does not throw light on the relationship between illness and poverty as to the direction of causation. For these reasons, findings which show higher risks of death or higher morbidity rates among the poor are difficult to interpret. Does poverty provide the milieu for reduced life chances, or is poverty a state frequently attained in the short run by the failure of disabled persons, say in the year prior to death, to sustain gainful employment, and thus non-poverty status.[14]

In many respects, the relationship between health and poverty is poorly understood. Although it might be conjectured that a strong negative relationship exists between the extent of poverty and the extent of health and well-being, statistical evidence on this point is not consistently in support of this contention.[16,28,32-34] At the same time, there are specific relationships in which poverty status shows more evidence of morbidity and higher risks of mortality. Certain ethnic and racial groups show similar evidence of ill health which in part is associated with socioeconomic status and attendant health differentials, but which is also in part associated with biological and social conditions which affect the members of these ethnic groups.[10-12] Studies of poverty and race on other than health matters have shown, for example, relationships with socioeconomic background on the one hand, and discrimination on another, as partly independent antecedents in affecting current status.[6]

MORTALITY AND
DISADVANTAGED STATUS

That differentials exist as to the force of mortality according to social status has long been recognized.[1] For much of this time, up until quite recently, these differentials were accepted as inevitable, as inevitable as poverty itself. Although comprehensive studies of occupational differentials date back at least to the turn of this century,[29] the apparent focus of concern in such studies has been more often with occupational hazards rather than with those associated with class and status differences.

Unusual difficulties attend the analysis of mortality by socioeconomic status. Since death tends to occur in disproportion among those who have retired from the labor force and since information provided on death records comes from persons other than the decedent, simple inquiries as to occupation are not thought to yield data of adequate quality for routine presentation and analysis.[17]

Obstacles attending occupational coding have led to its elimination in the preparation of machine-readable records, further obstructing the analysis of such data. These and other obstacles which relate to the interpretation of data on occupation in mortality studies have been described by Guralnick.[29]

Mortality records in the past have not contained information on educational attainment or on family income. These data, particularly data about schooling, are thought to have important advantages regarding problems of interpretation of occupational data. However, recent additions to the standard certificate of death have not included inquiries concerning educational attainment of the decedent.[17]

By far the most significant study in recent years designed to overcome many of these problems has been conducted by Kitagawa and Hauser.[15] This study is based upon a sample of records of deaths in 1960 matched against corresponding 1960 census records, thus bringing a wealth of information concerning population characteristics from persons who were still alive at the time of the census. It is from this study of some 62,400 decedents whose death records were successfully matched with 25 percent sample census records (since it is the sample census which contained the needed social and economic characteristics) that much of the following discussion of mortality dealing with race and with social and economic status is based.

RACE AND MORTALITY

We are concerned with the relationship between measures of health and with poverty and associated conditions of disadvantage. Two racial groups—there are more but data are not readily available—clearly exhibit disadvantaged status in the aggregate and can be examined as to their mortality experience. These are the blacks and the American Indians. Moreover, it is also instructive to examine data by color for the United States, since nine in ten in the nonwhite population are black and since there is a richer collection of statistics available for white-nonwhite comparison than there is for the comparison of Negro and white. But since some nonwhites fare better as a group than whites—for example, the Japanese and Chinese in viewing population distributions by family income—this category does not identify the clearly disadvantaged groups as sharply as do specific racial categories.

TABLE 2–I

DEATH RATES PER 1,000 FOR WHITE AND NONWHITE PERSONS
BY AGE AND SEX: UNITED STATES, 1900–1960

Age Groups By Sex	Whites					Nonwhites				
	1900–1902	1919–1921	1939–1941	1949–1951	1960	1900–1902	1919–1921	1939–1941	1949–1951	1960
Males										
Under 1	159.7	93.8	55.1	34.7	26.9	349.1	152.1	99.5	60.4	51.9
1–4	18.1	9.0	2.9	1.4	1.0	39.3	14.3	5.4	2.7	2.1
5–14	3.6	2.7	1.1	0.7	0.5	7.4	3.6	1.7	1.0	0.8
15–24	5.5	4.1	2.0	1.5	1.4	11.6	9.8	5.0	2.9	2.1
25–34	7.9	5.7	2.8	1.9	1.6	13.0	11.9	8.5	4.9	8.9
35–44	10.5	7.5	5.1	3.9	3.3	15.8	14.3	13.1	8.7	7.3
45–54	15.4	11.8	11.3	9.9	9.3	25.1	19.5	24.0	18.7	15.5
55–64	28.5	23.7	24.8	23.2	22.3	42.7	30.2	36.7	34.3	31.5
65–74	58.2	52.3	52.9	48.3	48.5	69.5	56.6	58.9	57.1	56.6
75–84	126.1	116.2	120.0	105.2	103.0	127.1	110.6	103.8	88.5	86.6
85 & over	262.4	242.6	242.0	218.3	217.5	231.4	227.6	188.9	151.8	152.4
Females										
Under 1	129.1	73.0	42.7	26.3	20.1	286.6	120.7	77.2	47.4	40.7
1–4	16.7	8.2	2.4	1.2	0.9	37.9	13.3	4.7	2.3	1.7
5–14	3.4	2.3	0.8	0.5	0.3	8.3	3.9	1.4	1.4	0.5
15–24	5.3	4.1	1.4	0.7	0.5	11.3	10.7	5.0	2.2	1.1
25–34	7.6	6.0	2.2	1.1	0.9	11.7	13.1	7.3	3.9	2.6
35–44	9.3	6.8	3.6	2.4	1.9	15.4	15.5	11.6	7.5	5.5
45–54	13.4	10.5	7.5	5.5	4.6	23.8	22.6	20.7	15.6	11.4
55–64	25.0	20.9	16.8	13.0	10.8	39.0	34.9	33.5	27.3	24.1
65–74	52.0	47.9	40.7	32.3	27.8	63.5	57.5	49.1	45.8	39.8
75–84	115.9	110.2	103.3	84.8	77.0	104.5	99.9	80.4	71.5	67.1
85 & over	246.7	235.6	224.9	196.4	194.8	205.4	206.4	149.8	126.9	128.7

Sources: Spiegelman, 1968, p. 90, Table 4.1; U.S. National Center for Health Statistics, 1963, Table 1-E.

Table 2-I presents death rates by sex, age, and color for selected decades since the turn of the century. Persistent differentials in survivorship favoring whites are seen to prevail over this period, except at ages 75 and over. Farley's discussion of trends in mortality and health conditions among blacks in the twentieth century points up two significant phenomena. First, the improvements in life chances and in income in the black population are dramatic in a relatively short period of time, from the decade of the Depression up to 1955. Second, there has been little improvement in mortality since 1955, although a significant drop in infant mortality is present.[8]

In the analysis of social and economic factors affecting mortality, mortality experience at the working ages (i.e., at ages associated with low mortality risks) is of considerable importance. Mortality among the aged does not tend to promote poverty-engendering conditions; more likely, the higher loss rates among the elderly might reduce somewhat the burden of survival upon families near or in conditions of poverty. Thus, arguing that the smaller the dependency ratio of persons in the younger or older age ranges to persons in the working ages—say ages 18 to 64 years—the better the long-run welfare conditions of the impoverished populations. The primary focus here is upon (1) the conditions of mortality at those working ages and (2) mortality among the newborn, although more generally including mortality experience up through attainment of maturity.

Mortality, morbidity, and poverty are apparently linked in such a way that it is possible to suggest, and not be far wrong, that ill-health and high mortality risks are inversely related to measures of individual or family income and affluence. In attempting to understand this nexus, it is especially important to give only secondary attention to mortality in exactly those ages which account most heavily for the attrition of successive generations of man. This is because of the nature of the relationship of sustenance and survival, and hence of the relationship of economic and social security to one's ties to the labor force and to gainful employment.

Thus, high mortality rates among the elderly might reduce somewhat the burden of survival upon families in and near conditions of poverty. Central questions within this framework become: (1) What are the chances of survival through the working years of those who attain maturity where concern is with the returns to the black segment of society following the investment in the raising of the child? (2) Viewing the experiences of the newborn and those in subsequent ages prior to the ages of labor force entry, what is the capacity of the population to sustain the effective force of population replacement at the working ages?

The lesser interest in the differentials among the aged is also encouraged by difficulties encountered in interpreting data for Negroes at the older ages. Age misreporting is certainly an important factor but it is not, according to Kitagawa (personal communication), possible to clearly establish whether the reversal in differentials at the very older ages is attributable to problems with the data or whether some other process is at work. On the other hand, Thornton and Nam have made a case for differential selection of a Darwinist order which accounts for the relatively high survival potential of many nonwhites at the older ages.[21,23]

No official life tables exist for the black population. Separate tables have been prepared for whites and nonwhites, however.[27] Using these tables, another way of looking at differences by color in mortality for the working ages is to compare survivorship values. This was done by determining the relative loss in the life table radix from age 20 to age 65. In the white population in 1960, 32 per cent of the survivors to age 20 do not survive to age 65, whereas the corresponding figure for nonwhites is 45 per cent.

MORTALITY AMONG BLACKS

Kitagawa has also reported that blacks had the highest mortality among racial groups for which national data are published—whites, American Indian, Japanese, Chinese, and other races. Her comparisons among races do not reflect corrections for under-enumeration since such calculations are not available by race. The black mortality indexes for population 5 years old and over are 28 per cent higher than whites for males and 47 per cent higher than whites for females.[13] For American Indians, by contrast, the levels are 24 per cent and 37 per cent above those for white males and females, respectively.

Narrowing to our main interest in those in the age range of 35 to 64 years, Kitagawa provides the following age-adjusted differentials (per cent by which each index exceeds that for whites of the corresponding sex):

	Male	*Female*
Negro	66	145
American Indian	28	69

INFANT AND CHILDHOOD
MORTALITY AND RACE

We know that in the 1950's, a leveling-off in the long-term decline in infant mortality occurred in the United States. That the leveling occurred before infant mortality rates were reduced to the levels found in a number of other countries has caused students of this phenomenon to refuse to consider the then existing levels as approaching an irreducible minimum.[18] Shapiro, Schlesinger, and Nesbitt have also reported that since 1950, this reduction in the rate of decline of this mortality measure was much more pronounced for nonwhites:

Between 1951 and 1953 substantial decreases in mortality in the first day of life were scored by the white group; among non-white infants the decrease in the rate of loss under 1 day stopped in 1943. More recently—since 1952—the rate of increase in mortality at this age has been greater for the nonwhite than the white infants.[20]

A shift in the timing of loss of life and wastage from the prenatal to the postnatal period is one possible explanation. A contention that these changes might be attributable to problems in the reliability of data for nonwhites is not thought to be warranted because similar patterns have been reported for nonwhites in areas known to have long approached adequate levels of reporting as to completeness and accuracy.[20]

Geographic variations in infant mortality rates permit the generalization that an area with a comparatively low rate among white infants will have a low rate among nonwhite infants; similarly this relationship between color groups holds for rates in the higher ranges. Infant mortality rates among white population have been higher in urban than in rural areas since the early 1950's. In contrast, nonwhite rates, at least since the late 1940's have been higher in rural areas. But the more notable relationship between color groups in the context of geographic variability "is that infant mortality is far greater everywhere among nonwhite children."[20]

MORBIDITY AND RACE

Considerable difficulty is encountered in contrasting populations as to morbidity experience given the diversity of diseases, injuries, and other pathological states which afflict man. A simplifying assumption in dealing with morbidity is taken when the focus of the analysis is on the social and economic consequences of such ill health and disability rather than on morbidity itself. Several appropriate measures of the consequences of morbidity have been developed for the population of the United States at the National Center for Health Statistics.

Table 2-II presents standardized morbidity ratios for three such measures by color and income for population under age 65.[32] These ratios relate actual morbidity to that expected when the effects of sex, age, and farm-nonfarm residence are removed. Thus, for acute conditions, the white population in families with less than $3,000 has a standardized morbidity ratio (SMR) of 103, indicating a level some 3 per cent higher than the total population controlling for the effects of sex, age, and farm-nonfarm residence; the corresponding SMR for nonwhites is 79, indicating a level substantially lower than the norm for the prevalence of acute conditions.

As can be seen in the table, nonwhites have the advantage over whites as to acute conditions, family income (using a two-way break at the $3,000 line) making little difference in either color group. By contrast, SMR's for hospital days

TABLE 2-II
STANDARDIZED MORBIDITY RATIOS
FOR SELECTED MEASURES OF
MORBIDITY FOR PERSONS UNDER 65
YEARS OF AGE, BY COLOR AND INCOME:
UNITED STATES, 1962–1963

Selected Measures Of Morbidity	Family Income	
	Under $3,000	$3,000 and Over
Acute Conditions		
White	103	105
Nonwhite	79	72
Hospital Days		
White	129	94
Nonwhite	102	97
Bed days		
White	133	91
Nonwhite	154	98

Source: U.S. Public Health Service, 1967, p. 3 and 8.
* Standardized morbidity ratio is the ratio of actual to expected events adjusted for age, sex, and farm-nonfarm residence.

and bed days are importantly affected by differences in family income, although color differences are comparatively minor.

Chronic illness which limits a person's major activity—for persons aged 45 and 64 years— afflicts some 12 percent of the total population. However, such affliction is much more common among those in the lower income classes than those with moderate or high income. As Guralnick points out, "It is evident from these . . . data that a sizeable proportion of the middle-aged 'poor' population suffer serious physical limitations in their ability to work" (U.S. Public Health Services, 1967, p. 6).

Using a somewhat different approach, Bauer[33] has described the population by color and income according to numbers of disability days per person. These data, which unfortunately include persons 65 years of age and over, show results similar to those of Guralnick[32] that color differences are on the whole not dramatic. Moreover, even when the relatively large color differences in work loss of females in the "less than $3,000" family income class are considered in the context of the work year—say of 50 five-day weeks—the impact seems small. A work loss of 6.3 days for white and 7.8 days for nonwhite is a difference of some 24 percent; but this difference is less than a one percent variation placed against a year's work. Thus, although it may be said that the disadvantage of nonwhite relative to white is quite large, the disadvantage expressed in terms of its apparent impact upon work is small.[33]

Bauer concludes in her study, "Analysis of the data showed that observed differences in health characteristics were related more to socioeconomic factors of the two population groups than to color."[33]

DISCUSSION

The problem addressed by Sullivan[31] in his study of the integration of mortality and morbidity experience into a health index takes on a somewhat different aspect when consideration of social and economic welfare is introduced to constrain the definition of the problem. For example, the classic approach to the dependency ratio, expressing the proportion of the population in the "dependent" ages to that in the working ages is, in cross-section in time, concerned with the implications of demographic processes for population survival and for productive potential in the population.

A somewhat more attractive approach, suggested by Dublin and Lotka[5] and more recently elaborated upon by Miller[24] and by Spiegelman[21] considers the "money value of a man." In this approach, both cross-section income data and accumulated savings over a working lifetime can be considered, but, in addition, changes in the earnings experiences of birth cohorts in the working ages over intercensal periods can be assessed.

Suppose we adopt such an approach. By carrying forth the contrast of earnings of the population aged 25 and 34 at the time of the census with the population aged 35 to 44 at the next, we might attempt to deal with the losses to earnings associated with morbidity experience and mortality, thereby explicating the consequences of health differentials in terms which make understandable movements toward social welfare objectives. Health measures are not unambiguous; some means of translating these for the appraisal which can distinguish between one kind of health benefit and another must be accomplished if any intelligible discussion of progressive health trends is to occur.

INTERRELATIONS
OF THE CONSEQUENCES
OF MORBIDITY AND MORTALITY

Statistics showing the mortality experience of Disability Insurance Benefits recipients under the Social Security Act, provides convincing evidence that the effect of mortality upon disabled persons has important consequences for data on morbidity since disabilities arising from serious acute and chronic conditions are associated with loss of life which is sufficiently large to affect the quality of reporting of such morbid conditions. It has been shown by Sirken[30] that the loss of morbidity experience from survey data in groups with high mortality risks—the aged, or, here, the disabled Social Security beneficiaries—is substantial.

Data from a 1966 survey of noninstitutionalized disabled adults[2] show that the mortality experience of disabled persons roughly corresponds to the cell "disability beneficiaries" of which there were nearly one million in 1966. Although disability definitions will vary (those with major activity limitations aged 17 to 64 in 1968 was just under 10 million[35]), it is reasonable for us to assume that a much more sizeable population is subject to mortality risks which are higher than normal for corresponding sex and age classes. Moreover, it should be clear that Disability Insurance beneficiaries are probably—in the context of our concern for black and low-income groups—somewhat better off than are many disabled persons not covered by disability insurance. Those disabled persons who are receiving public assistance payments—1.268 million in 1966—may well even more severely feel the force of mortality than the OASDHI* beneficiaries. Thus, the inter-

* Old Age Survivors Disability and Health Insurance

relation of mortality and morbidity brings us to propose that a crucial problem which must be addressed is the integration of these interdependent phenomena.

EFFECTS OF DEATH AND DISABILITY UPON DEPENDENTS

An additional problem in the appraisal of the survival conditions and the well-being of the black population in the United States is found in attempting to ascertain the effect of mortality and morbidity upon family organization. The social costs of such experiences, as in the case of direct economic costs, are better appraised in a family context where the realities of the burden of disabled family members as well as the social consequences of the economic loss are found in the death or disability of the breadwinner.

SUMMARY AND CONCLUSIONS

A review of recent data concerning morbidity and mortality differences between the white and black population is presented to reflect upon the contribution of these data to the relative well-being of the black population. Crude death rates and even age-adjusted mortality rates obscure important mortality differences between blacks and whites. These differences are found particularly at those ages which are of most significance in considering the problem of the social welfare of the population. The black-white differentials are greatest where they have the greatest impact. Morbidity data do not demonstrate such effects; however, it is apparent that mortality and morbidity experiences are closely interdependent and that an integration of these effects, which has not yet been successfully carried out, would be of considerable utility.

Data currently published do not lend themselves to simple interpretation of black-white differences related to welfare implications. The size of the mortality differential by race in the working ages is more appropriate to the concerns of the social welfare of blacks as a population in the aggregate than differentials taken more broadly as to general mortality. Even so, once we have established the relative level, the question remains: What is the calculus of well-being such that it is possible to sort out significant gains in the analysis of trends in the well-being of blacks in the United States?

REFERENCES

1. Antonovsky, Aaron: Social class life expectancy and overall mortality. *Milbank Mem Fund Q*, 95:31–73, 1967.

2. Brehm, Henry P.: The disabled on public assistance. *Soc Security Bull*, October, 1970, pp. 26–30.

3. Demeny, Paul, and Gingrich, Paul: A reconsideration of Negro-white mortality differentials in the U.S. *Demography, 4:*820–837, 1967.

4. Drake, St. Clair: The social and economic status of the Negro in the United States. In Parsons, T., and Clark, K.B. (Eds.): *The Negro American*. Boston, HM, 1966.

5. Dublin, Louis I., and Lotka, A.J.: *The Money Value of a Man*, rev. ed. New York, Ronald, 1946.

6. Duncan, Otis Dudley: Discrimination against Negroes. *Ann Amer Acad Polit Soc Sci*, May, 1967, pp. 85–103.

7. ———: Inheritance of poverty or inheritance of race? In Moynahan, D.P. (Ed.): *On Understanding Poverty*. New York, Basic, 1969.

8. Farley, Reynolds: The quality of demographic data for nonwhites. *Demography*, 5:1–10, 1968.

9. ———: *Growth of the Black Population: A Study of Demographic Trends*. Chicago, Markham, 1970.

10. Fuchs, Victor R.: Some economic aspects of mortality in the United States. Processed, 1965.

11. Goldstein, Marcus S.: Longevity: Health status of the Negro-American. *J Negro Educ*, Fall, 1963, pp. 337–348.

12. Kadushin, C.: Social class and the experience of ill health. *Sociol Inq*, 34:67–80, 1964.

13. Kitagawa, Evelyn: Race Differentials in Mortality in the United States, 1960. Paper presented at annual meetings of the Population Association of America, Boston, April, 1968.

14. ———: Social and economic differentials in mortality in the United States, 1960. In *Proceedings of the General Conference of International Union for Scientific Study of Population*. London, 1969.

15. Kitagawa, Evelyn, and Hauser, Philip M.: Methods used in a current study of social and economic differentials in mortality. In *Emerging Techniques of Population Research*. Annual Conference of the Milbank Memorial Fund, New York, 1962.

16. Lefcowitz, Myron J.: *Poverty and Health: A Critical Examination*. Madison, Wis., Institute for Research on Poverty, 1970.

17. Lunde, Anders S., and Grove, Robert D.: Demographic implication of the new United States certificates. *Demography*, 3:566–573, 1966.

18. Moriyama, Iwao M.: *Problems in the Measurement of Health Status: Indicators of Social Change,* Sheldon, Eleanor Bernert and Moore, Wilbert E., Eds. New York, Russell Sage, 1968.

19. Orshansky, Mollie: Counting the poor: Another look at the poverty profile. *Soc Security Bull,* January, 1965, pp. 3–29.

20. Shapiro, Sam, Schlesinger, Edward R. and Nesbitt, Robert E.L., Jr.: *Infant, Perinatal, Maternal, and Childhood Mortality in the United States.* Cambridge, Mass., Harvard U Pr, 1968.

21. Spiegelman, Mortimer: *Introduction to Demography,* rev. ed. Cambridge, Mass., Harvard U Pr, 1968.

22. Taeuber, Irene B.: Change and transition in the black population. *Population Index, 34:*121–151, 1968.

23. Thornton, Russell G., and Nam, Charles B.: The lower mortality rates of nonwhites at the older ages: An enigma in demographic analysis. Research Reports on Social Science, Gainesville, Fla., Fla St U, 1968, pp. 1–8.

24. Miller, Herman: *Income Distribution in the United States.* Washington, D.C., U.S. Bureau of the Census, Govt Print Off, 1966.

25. Livingston, Rockwell: *Trends in Social and Economic Conditions in Metropolitan and Nonmetropolitan Areas.* U.S. Bureau of the Census, Current Population Reports, series P-23, no. 33, Washington, D.C., Govt Print Off, 1970.

26. U.S. National Center for Health Statistics: *Vital Statistics of the United States, Mortality: 1960.* Washington, D.C., Govt Print Off, 1963, vol. II, pt. A.

27. ———: *United States Life Tables, 1959–61.* Public Health Services publ. 1252. Washington, D.C., Govt Print Off, 1964, vol. 1, no. 1.

28. Querec, Linda: *Relations Between Health Interview Survey Measures, Education, and Income.* U.S. National Center for Health Statistics, Office of Health Statistics Analysis. Processed, 1970.

29. Guralnick, Lillian: *Mortality by Occupation and Industry Among Men 20 to 64 Years of Age: United States, 1950.* U.S. Public Health Service, Vital Statistics Special Reports. Washington, D.C., Govt Print Off, 1962, vol. 53, no. 2.

30. Sirken, Monroe G.: *Hospital Utilization in the Last Year of Life.* U.S. Public Health Service, publ. 1000, series 2, no. 10. Washington, D.C., Govt Print Off, 1965.

31. Sullivan, Daniel: *Conceptual Problems in Developing an Index of Health.* U.S. Public Health Service, publ. 1000, series 2, no. 17. Washington, D.C., Govt Print Off, 1966.

32. Guralnick, Lillian: *Selected Family Characteristics and Health Measures.* U.S. Public Health Service, publ. 1000, series 3, no. 7. Washington, D.C., Govt Print Off, 1967.

33. Bauer, Mary Lou: *Differentials in Health Characteristics by Color.* U.S. Public Health Service, publ. 1000, series 10, no. 56. Washington, D.C., Govt Print Off, 1969.

34. Lawrence, Philip S., Gleeson, Geraldine A., White, Elijah L., Fuchsberg, Robert P., and Wilder, Charles S.: *Medical Care, Health Status, and Family Income: United States*. U.S. Public Health Service, series 10, no. 9. Washington, D.C., Govt Print Off, 1969.

35. Bauer, Mary Lou: *Current Estimates from the Health Interview Survey: United States, 1968*. U.S. Public Health Service, publ. 1000, series 10, no. 60. Washington, D.C., Govt Print Off, 1970.

Chapter 3

RACE, DISEASE AND DESEGREGATION: A NEW LOOK

Ann Hallman Pettigrew and Thomas F. Pettigrew

CLAIMS THAT the Negro American is innately less healthy than other Americans have gained new attention in the controversy over desegregation. Surely, argue many segregationists, the Supreme Court could not have meant that whites must associate with "diseased Negroes." The Mississippi legislature even resolved to use health criteria as a possible means of preventing school desegregation.[1] But are such claims and fears justified by available medical evidence? To answer this question, this paper takes a new look at the relationship between race and disease in the United States.

RACE AND THE NEGRO AMERICAN

Before discussing "race differences" in health, we should recognize that in a strict biological sense we are not comparing races at all. Rather, we are comparing groups socially defined as "races" in the United States.

Anthropologists agree that there is only one human species; but there are many varieties of this one species. These subspecies, or races, evolved thousands of years ago through genetic isolation brought about by geographic barriers. Thus, the many races, though all variations on a common theme, grew apart in some physical traits. But there are no pure races. All the major subspecies of mankind share in their gene pools some of the genes once considered racially distinctive. Indeed, as scholars learn more about prehistoric times, it becomes apparent that cultural and genetic interchange

Reprinted with permission from *Phylon*, Winter, 1963.

has been far more continuous and extensive than previously envisaged.

The United States is no exception to these trends, for it is as much a biological as a cultural melting pot. In fact, Negro Americans are often cited by anthropologists as an example *par excellence* of a cross-racial group. Geneticists estimate that roughly 25 percent of the Negro American gene pool is Caucasian in origin.[2] Moreover, the Negro and Caucasian strains giving rise to today's Negro American came from a great variety of African and European peoples; consequently, Negro Americans evidence an unusually wide range of physical traits. Despite this heterogeneity, a curious definition of "Negro" has developed in the United States. No matter how Caucasian one's genes may be in origin, one known trace of Negro ancestry makes one "Negro." To speak of such a people as a homogeneous "race" does obvious violence to any precise biological and anthropological meaning of the term.

This social conception of race, in spite of its severe limitations, is employed in this paper for two compelling reasons. First, for reasons of practicality, the pertinent medical literature has typically used the concept in this loose fashion. Second, the real-life problem of health and desegregation is also posed in these terms. Nonetheless, we should not forget that "race" and "racial differences" as employed here and throughout our culture are relative, not absolute, concepts.

MENTAL ILLNESS

The mental illness rates of Negro Americans have been a subject of considerable interest and debate. But there are formidable methodological problems to be overcome before any reasonably accurate estimate can be made of the true amount of psychosis and neurosis existing in the general population. For many years, investigators merely counted the number of people detained at any one time in mental institutions. This procedure is obviously inadequate. Such a rate not only reflects the existing prevalence of mental illness, but also the duration of detainment, the availability and quality of the treatment facilities, and a host of additional factors unrelated to the immediate problem. Consequently, later investigators have employed rates of first admission to psychiatric facilities over a specified time period. Though a marked improvement in technique, serious problems remain. Generally, only the data from public institutions are secured, causing an underestimation of mental illness among those who can afford private treatment. And even studies which carefully include both public and private patients leave uncounted the many mentally ill people who never seek treatment. Finally, complications arise from a dependence on psychiatric diagnoses, judgments that are often unreliable.

Keeping in mind these methodological qualifications, a few broad generalizations can be ventured on the basis of available evidence. Consider first the most severe mental aberrations, the psychoses. Repeated studies of first admissions of hospitals in a variety of states consistently show the occurrence of psychoses in the population to be about twice as great among Negroes[3-10],* Particular psychoses contribute disproportionately to the inflated ratio. Schizophrenia, the bizarre condition of social withdrawal and personality disorganization, has a significantly higher rate among Negroes. Two organic diagnoses—paresis and alcoholic psychoses—are also relatively more frequent among Negro first admissions. But this research sharply underestimates the amount of white psychoses. Allowances must be made for the fact that whites are much more able to afford private treatment and thus miss being enumerated in these studies of public facilities.

To correct this, Jaco, in his investigation of mental illness in Texas, made a strenuous effort to include private as well as public first admissions for treatment over a two-year period. The results are surprising. Rates among Negro Americans for psychoses, even schizophrenia, tended to fall below those of the white Anglo-Americans.[11] Technical prob-

---

* For methodological criticisms of such studies, see reference 10.

lems mar these results, too; [Δ] and before they can be relied upon the assumption must be made that roughly the same percentages of Negro and white psychotics are treated. There are good reasons for believing that this assumption is unjustified and that more Negro psychotics go untreated. Poorly educated Negroes often view psychiatry as white man's trickery, and consequently they are less likely to seek professional aid. And throughout the South virtually all private facilities are closed to Negroes and the public facilities open to them are symbolic instruments of white supremacy state governments, segregated, inferior, and grossly overcrowded. Such conditions suggest that Negro institutions not only do less for their patients but admit only the most serious cases. Thus Jaco's estimate of psychoses among Negro Americans in Texas is probably too low.

On balance, we can tentatively conclude that psychoses rates for Negroes, especially for schizophrenia and some organic psychoses, are higher than rates for whites. The definitive epidemiological research on this question is yet to be performed. Meanwhile, personality test investigations support this conclusion. Two studies independently conducted on diverse populations noted that Negro males scored significantly higher than comparable white males on scales measuring schizoid and manic trends.[15,16]

If group data on psychoses are difficult to decipher, group data on neuroses are even more confusing. Most of these less serious mental abnormalities do not require institutionalization; particularly among lower-status Negroes, neurotic symptoms are often ignored.[17] Not surprisingly, then, comparative group data on neuroses are somewhat contradictory. First admission rates for neuroses to state hospitals are generally much higher for whites than Negroes,[8] though this may just reflect that only the most incapacitated Negroes are accepted. Many neurotics receive treatment from private

---

[Δ] See reviews of Jaco's volume.[12,13] A study of a nonhospitalized population in Baltimore reached a similar conclusion to that of Jaco and is likewise limited by methodological difficulties.[14]

sources, and these individuals are predominantly white. Service studies provide conflicting data. Two Navy investigations report less neuroticism among Negroes,[18,19] whereas an Army investigation reports more frequent "minor psychiatric illness" among Negroes.[20] Personality test results on neurotic measures generally do not reveal racial differentials comparable to those obtained on measures of psychotic trends. In fact, two of these studies found samples of white males scored significantly higher than comparable Negro males on a character disorder scale of psychopathic personality trends.[15,16] All told, we can tentatively conclude that between Negroes and whites the ratio of neuroticism is not as great as for the psychoses, and for certain conditions, like character disorders, the incidence among Negroes may actually be less than among whites.

Comparative data on other symptomatology is somewhat more definite. Negroes apparently suffer less from psychosomatic difficulties. One World War II Selective Service Board study recorded a peptic ulcer rate for whites ten times that of Negroes.[21,*] Negroes also commit suicide less frequently. The national nonwhite death rate from suicide, 1949 through 1951, was only 42 percent of the white rate.[22]

What lies behind these "racial differences" in mental illness? Authorities agree that innate factors are not involved. † Rather, distinctions of social class and poverty, on the one hand, and racial restrictions, on the other, account for the differentials. Witness first the importance of class. Hollingshead and Redlich, in their research on *Social Class and Mental Illness,* found the patterns of mental illness among white lower-class patients in New Haven closely resembled those just described for Negro patients.[25,‡] Psychoses, par-

---

*However, the national death rates for ulcers of the stomach and duodenum during 1949 through 1951 were approximately the same for the two groups.[22]

† This is not to deny the existence of genetic factors in mental disorders. Twin studies have provided evidence which strongly suggests the operation of genetic factors in many of the psychoses; but the family lines involved have not been shown to be related to race.[23,24]

‡ Only 6 percent of the two lowest classes analyzed in this study[25] were Negro.

ticularly schizophrenia, were more prevalent among the poor than among the prosperous. By contrast, neuroses rates did not differ by class, though the type of diagnosis did. Lower-status patients more often "acted out" their problems—in anti-social and hysterical reactions; while upper-status patients more often "acted in"—in depressive and obsessive-compulsive reactions and character disorders.

Chicago data from the Faris-Dunham project of the 1930's indicated that social classes within the city's Negro population had markedly diverse mental disorder rates.* The reported incidence of schizophrenia, in particular, varied; the Negro area nearest the downtown business district had a rate over 60 percent greater than a more middle-class Negro area. Frumkin confirms these findings in a study of first admissions to the state mental hospitals of Ohio.[3] Analyzing each racial group separately, he noted that higher rates exist for both the white and Negro lower classes. Frumkin concluded that the higher admission rates of Negroes were "a function of the low status of the Negro rather than some biological or genetic difference due to 'race.'"

But social class is only part of the explanation. As early as 1913, one American psychiatrist, Arrah Evarts, pointed out how the behavior of three Negro schizophrenics was directly related to their racially restricted experiences.[27] These observations have been repeated often during the past half century. Ripley and Wolf, for example, traced the higher incidence of mental illness among Negro enlisted men on an isolated Pacific island to, among other factors, the dissatisfaction of the Negroes with their white officers and their strong sense of being the victims of racial discrimination.[20] The majority of the psychotic breakdowns among the Negroes in this situation were diagnosed paranoid schizophrenia, a fact which

*Compared with whites, Negroes have significantly larger rates of schizophrenia than manic-depression. This coincides with the fact that the New Haven and Chicago investigations found less of a relation between class and manic-depression than class and schizophrenia. Moreover, twin studies reveal a smaller genetic component for schizophrenia than for manic-depression.[24] In short, environmental factors are more important for the condition which reveals the greater racial differential.[26]

recalls the admonition of Kardiner and Ovesey against hasty application of the term "paranoid" to Negro patients. For Negroes "to see hostility in the environment is a normal perception. Hence, we must guard against calling the Negro paranoid when he actually lives in an environment that persecutes him."[28,]*

The destruction of mental health through the combination of poverty and persecution is not limited to Negro Americans. The marginal Peruvian mestizo, barely managing to survive on the outskirts of Lima, presents a case in point.[31] Mental illness, alcoholism, and family disorganization are widespread, as well as the familiar personality syndrome of inferiority feelings, insecurity, and hostility. The human species reacts to crushing oppression in much the same way the world over.

It is also instructive to compare these data of Negro Americans with those of Jewish Americans. Rather than the near-total rejection long experienced by Negroes, Jews have generally faced a more subtle, ambiguous rejection. This more uncertain, shadowy form of discrimination, together with the Jews' higher social status and closer group and family bonds, has led to a mental illness pattern strikingly different from that of Negroes. Whereas Negroes suffer from psychoses relatively more than neuroses, Jewish Americans have fairly low psychoses rates but especially high neuroses rates.[32]

These data of Jewish Americans suggest a laboratory analogy. In his famous conditioning research on dogs, Pavlov established what appeared to be a type of "experimental neurosis."[33] First, he trained a dog to distinguish between a circle and an ellipse by presenting food each time the circle appeared and withholding food each time the ellipse appeared. Then Pavlov began gradually altering the shape of the ellipse till it more and more resembled the circle.

---

*One of the ways persecution can lead to greater mental illness is the necessity to migrate long distances with few job skills. There has been considerable controversy over this point; it now seems that certain waves of particularly poor Negro migrants did have unusually high rate (*e.g.* 1930's), but that better educated recent arrivals to the North no longer evidence this phenomenon.[29,30]

Suddenly, at a point when the hungry animal could no longer differentiate one object from the other, the dog's behavior drastically changed. To speak anthropomorphically, the dog rejected the whole situation, became aggressive toward the experimenter, and in other ways tried to defend himself from intolerable anxiety. Other investigators, using an assortment of animals ranging from goats to chimpanzees, have replicated Pavlov's results.* The *experimental neuroses* created by these researchers often have the long-term effects and stubborn resistance to therapy characteristic of serious human neuroses.

The subtleties of anti-Semitic discrimination often blur the cues for the victim. Discovering whether a cool reception represents bad manners or prejudice can be as difficult as distinguishing the circle from the modified ellipse. With legal desegregation, this anxious uncertainty increases for Negro Americans. The clear-cut rejection of the past contributed to such conditions as the excessive withdrawal of schizophrenia; the ambiguous, discreet rejection of the future may well lead to the Jewish pattern of more neuroses. This possibility, combined with the rising economic position and growing group and family bonds of Negroes, suggests an hypothesis of future mental illness trends: among Negro Americans, psychoses rates will begin to recede while neuroses rates steadily climb.△

COMMUNICABLE DISEASE

Poverty, family disorganization, and slum living are even more critical factors in communicable disease than mental illness. Four categories of these conditions assume special significance for Negro American health: pulmonary tuberculosis, venereal disease, childhood disease, and parasitic disease.

---

*For a summary of earlier work, see reference 34.

△ Support for this hypothesis can be inferred from the findings of Myers and Roberts in differentiating the development of neurotics from that of schizophrenics in two social classes. They found that neurotics had been more rebellious, more often came from a stable home, and had loving and affectionate parents.[35]

Exposure to pulmonary tuberculosis was virtually universal in the nineteenth century; it struck members of all "races" and social classes throughout the nation. But a general attack upon the disease, through improved sanitation, nutrition, and treatment, has now localized it to specific groups which have benefited least from these advances. The spread of tuberculosis is now largely restricted to crowded, lower-class urban areas, "where the presence of individuals with tuberculosis in communicable form makes the dissemination of infection inevitable."[36] The further reduction of tuberculosis from its present localized distribution to a rare, sporadic condition is possible with the wider application of the same techniques which have already proven effective—improved standards of living, nutrition, and therapy.

In the meantime, lower-status Negro Americans are one of the underprivileged groups still evidencing high rates of pulmonary tuberculosis. Death rates for the disease are roughly four times higher for Negroes;* and incidence rates for active cases are about three times higher for Negroes.[37] Segregationists who employ these data to argue that biracial schools in the South present a health hazard, however, greatly oversimplify the problem. For example, the age group most resistant to the disease is between five and fourteen years old, the same age range most affected by educational desegregation.[37] Furthermore, the Negro-white differential in the incidence of active cases is smallest in the South. While the ex-Confederate states had among whites a median incidence rate for the years 1957 to 1959 slightly above the national figure for whites, they had among Negroes a median rate only about half the national rate for nonwhites.[37,38] Thus, instead of incidence rates among nonwhites four to six times those of whites, found in such colder, highly urban states as Illinois, Michigan, New Jersey, New York, and Pennsylvania, incidence rates for Southern Negroes average out less than twice the rates of whites. Consequently, the spread of

---

*These rates are for the period 1949–1951; rates called "Negro" are actually for nonwhites, 95.5 percent of whom are Negro.[22]

active tuberculosis, a most complex process in itself,[△] offers a feeble argument against the desegregation of Southern schools. Besides, if the segregationist were truly frightened by such a prospect, he would not allow Negroes to prepare his food and tend his home and children—situations that potentially raise a more realistic threat of tubercle transmission.

Beyond immediate concerns of desegregation is the question of innate racial resistance to pulmonary tuberculosis. Group constitutional predispositions to tuberculosis have never been proven; indeed, no definitive answer can be rendered until the various subspecies of mankind attain approximately the same standards of living. Meanwhile, the Negrowhite differences in the United States appear to be largely a function of exposure and socioeconomic factors.[36,40] In 1945, for example, the death rate for Negroes from the disease in cities of over a million people was almost twice that of Negroes in cities from 100,000 to 200,000 people.[41] It is in the most desperate slums of the huge ghettoes where overcrowding, wretched sanitation, and inadequate nutrition take their greatest toll. Nonetheless, the improved standard of living and better health facilities enjoyed by many Negroes in recent decades have brought about a dramatic decrease in tuberculosis mortality and incidence. In Manhattan, between 1910 and 1950, the death rate for nonwhites from the infection dropped from 445.5 to 62 per 100,000.[42] From 1955 to 1960, the national rates of new active cases among nonwhites dropped almost a third.[38]

Consider, too, the operation of these same factors in the tuberculoses rates of particular Caucasian groups. Celtic peoples in France, Wales, Ireland, and Scotland long had such elevated mortality rates from the disease that some observers regarded them as inherently less resistant. But general improvement of living conditions and active efforts to combat

---

[△] "Thus, while exposure to the tubercle bacillus is one necessary factor for the development of tuberculosis, there are many poorly understood accessory factors which, taken together, determine whether the disease will develop in the exposed person and which might be thought of as etiologic in one sense."[39]

the infection have brought declines in recent years. All nations experiencing the onset of industrialization, the devastation of war, or the deprivations of economic depression have suffered sharp increments in deaths from tuberculosis—"the white plague."[39,40] In the United States today, mortality among whites from the disease is still elevated among workers exposed to toxic dusts (e.g. coal miners), undernourished mountain folk, poor migrants, the institutionalized, and elderly, indigent males.[36,40,43]

The importance of sheer exposure in contracting the disorder is demonstrated by the high rates of positive tuberculin skin tests of white medical students and nurses.[44] And when exposure and social class are roughly equated between the racial groups, differences diminish. One North Carolina study of lower-status white female hospital employees and Negro student practical nurses noted virtually the same percentage of negative reactions to tuberculin skin tests.[45] Such data led May to conclude that "cultural factors play a predominant role in the distributional pattern" of pulmonary tuberculosis.[40]

Despite these findings, some believe that Negroes have a generalized respiratory weakness. Evidence against this contention is provided by another infectious respiratory condition, histoplasmosis, which in contrast to tuberculosis strikes whites in a fulminating form more often than Negroes.[46,*]

Pulmonary tuberculosis death rates, then, are steadily declining in the United States for both races, and there is every reason to expect that this trend will continue as treatment and environmental conditions improve. Among Negroes death and incidence rates from the disease are still considerably higher than for whites; however, evidence from many sources suggests that this is a function not of *race* but of exposure and socioeconomic differentials between the two groups. Even if there were a *racial* difference in resistance to the infection, it is virtually irrelevant since the disease

---

*Of similar interest is the resemblance between the leprosy bacillus and tubercle bacillus, yet some feel that the Negro is innately more resistant to severe leprosy than Caucasians and Mongoloids.[40]

can be, for all practical purposes, eliminated. "Tuberculosis is a totally unnecessary disease," writes Perkins. "It can be prevented. It can be cured. . . ."[47]

Venereal disease, particularly syphilis, is a second serious communicable infection disturbing Negro American health. Unlike tuberculosis, reporting problems make it difficult to estimate accurately the Negro-white differential in the incidence of a disease such as syphilis. Because of its potent connotation of sin and shame in middle-class America, most infected individuals do not seek medical aid at all. Other victims who can afford it go to discreet private physicians and are generally not officially recorded. Lower-class victims, disproportionately Negro, who receive medical assistance typically at public facilities, are recorded. Furthermore, the symptoms of the disease's initial stages clear spontaneously, leading some victims to think they have recovered. Consequently, Maxcy calculates "that more than one-half of the cases of syphilis go into the latent stage undiscovered and unreported."[39] And of those who are detected, lower-status persons are undoubtedly overrepresented.

Another difficulty in discussing racial rates of syphilis is that mass surveys utilizing blood screening tests are frequently employed. For instance, World War II induction blood tests are still widely quoted even though penicillin was not introduced into therapy until 1943, and this drug has vastly altered the modern dimensions of the disease. To complicate the statistical picture further, the blood screening tests can be falsely negative or falsely positive. Even an accurate positive blood test does not indicate infectivity, only that the person has or has had syphilis at some time in his life. Positive blood tests can remain after adequate treatment, and even without treatment an individual may suffer the ravages of the disease himself without being infectious to others.[39,48]

Moreover, reported mortality rates due to syphilis are notoriously unreliable.[39] Death develops from complications in the latent stage of the disease decades after the initial infection; and the shame surrounding the disease ensures that, particularly for high-status persons, syphilis as a direct or contributory cause of death frequently goes unlisted.

Within these severe restrictions, the available data suggest high rates of syphilis and its complications among Negroes. Public health data for 1960 to 1961, for instance, indicate an incidence rate for Negroes ten times greater than for whites and a death rate almost four times greater.[49] Research suggests these group differences are inflated through disproportionate underreporting of whites. Various autopsy investigations agree that from five to ten percent of the general population show evidence of syphilis, a figure far higher than other reported rates would indicate.[39] But if the Negro-white ratios usually quoted are too high, there is little doubt that Negroes do have elevated rates.

Greater susceptibility of Negroes to syphilis is not at issue. "There is no evidence," declares Dubos flatly, "that different races or different individuals differ in their susceptibility or resistance to [syphilitic] infection."[50] What, then, underlies the differential group rates? Maxcy declares: "The social and economic environment—including income, housing, education, medical care and availability, cost and use of medical services and provision of control measures—determine to a considerable extent the occurrence and distribution of the venereal diseases in a particular community."[39] It is therefore not surprising that American groups with the lowest incomes, poorest housing, least education, and most restricted medical facilities have the highest rates of venereal diseases and their sequelae. In addition, the prevalence of family disorganization among lower-class Negro Americans is an especially significant correlate.[51]

The other major venereal disease, gonorrhea, is subject to similar but even more serious recording errors. It is actually much more prevalent than syphilis, with reported rates for Negroes far exceeding those of whites.[39,43] Gonorrhea is related to the same social factors important in syphilis, and no group distinctions in susceptibility are known. The same general considerations apply to three other minor diseases regarded as venereal in their transfer: chancroid, granuloma inguinale, and lymphogranuloma venereum. The last of these was long thought to be limited to Negroes, but recent studies indicate that it is more wide-spread. One investigation found Southern Negro college students have a rate approximately that of whites, indicating that social factors are also paramount in this condition.[52]

Venereal diseases have been increasing disproportionately among the nation's youth.[48] These diseases present real problems for public education, although not the same problems as raised by segregationists. Southern white supremacists who infer immorality from reported venereal rates for Negroes might mollify their "logic" if they realized that the South has the highest white syphilis rates of any region in the United States.[43] Schools might well lead a massive informational campaign against venereal disease, since it is urgently needed by Americans of both races. Part of this informational campaign should be focused upon the many fear-ridden myths which surround venereal disease and become part of the desegregation controversy. Typical examples are the mistaken notions that venereal disease can be transferred via such objects as toilets (intimate physical contact is necessary) and that venereal disease contracted from a member of another race is especially potent.[48,50]

In addition to tuberculosis and the venereal diseases, communicable childhood diseases are important to Negro American health. Compared to mortality among whites, mortality rates among Negroes are particularly high during early life. This is in part due to diseases, such as whooping cough, meningitis, measles, diphtheria, and scarlet fever, for which there are no known racial susceptibilities. Though the fatal complications of these disorders can be drastically reduced by modern medicine, death rates from them for Negroes are at least twice those of whites.[22] Whooping cough, for example, is most fatal in the first two years of life, and it can be prevented during this critical period by immunization;[50] yet reported death rates for Negroes from this disease over the nation during 1949 to 1951 were six times more than for whites. Such data dramatize the continuing need for improved medical services for Negro children. The same need applies for adults so long as death rates for such treatable diseases as nephritis, influenza, and pneumonia remain high for Negroes.*

Two parasitic diseases, hookworm and malaria, offer significant racial comparisons.† Due to climate and poverty, the South has endured a wide variety of enteric infections. Hookworm, in particular, was once the scourge of the region, though in recent decades control measures have sharply decreased its incidence and confined it chiefly to the sandy coastal areas of the South. Most enteric infections, like typhoid and dysentery, are directly related to socioeconomic factors and reveal no racial differences in susceptibility; but hookworm is primarily a disease of rural white children.[43,53] Since it is concentrated among those who must live in deprived, unsanitary conditions, Negro Southerners would be expected to have an incidence above that of white Southerners. That this is not the case for hookworm suggests a relative immunity to the disease among Negroes.[43,54]

While malaria is not a public health threat in the United States today, it affords an instructive lesson in the evolution of racial differences. Malaria has for centuries been a mass killer in tropical Africa, setting the scene for the development among Africans of natural protections against the disease. Probably through mutation, an inherited ability to change red blood cells into sickle shapes under certain conditions sprang up that provided resistance to the severest forms of malaria.[55-58],‡ Over many generations, those tropical Africans

---

*National mortality rates for Negroes (1949–1951) for nephritis and influenza are nearly three times those of whites and for pneumonia nearly two-and-a-half times.[22]

† Yaws and pinta are nonvenereal, nonfatal, tropical parasitic diseases which are rare in the United States. They both affect the skin, but yaws also attacks bones and joints. Their infective agents are related to syphilis, and these diseases may be less severe, evolved forms of syphilis. Negroes were long thought to be the only victims; but when socioeconomic factors were controlled, no difference in the prevalence of yaws was noted between Negro and white Cubans.[50] Both diseases have been noted throughout the tropics in members of all major races.[53]

‡The sickle cell trait has been considered primarily a condition of people of African descent, but a high incidence of the sickling trait has been found in the Veddoids of southern India and southern Arabia, and in certain areas of Greece and Turkey. These peoples do not share other blood group characteristics common in Africa. Thus, the sickle cell trait actually may have been introduced into Africa from Asia.[59]

with this sickle cell trait were better able to survive and reproduce. Thus, through Darwin's "survival of the fittest" principle, tropical Africans evolved over time a special protection against one of the worst ravages in their midst.* Today those possessing the blood trait are especially resistant to the life-threatening forms of malaria. But since malaria is rare in the United States, the sickle cell trait is no longer an important protection for Negro Americans, and its gene frequency is declining.†

INHERITED DISEASES

Sickle cell anemia, primarily found in Negroes, is the favorite disease exhibit of white supremacists. Though it derives from an adaptive, evolutionary process, they feel the disease is ultimate proof of the innate inferiority of "Negro blood." The sickle cell trait is inherited as a Mendelian dominant from one parent (heterozygous state) and does not of itself produce ill-effects except under unusual conditions. By contrast, sickle cell anemia results only when the trait is inherited from both parents (homozygous state) and produces serious symptoms and anemia, usually causing death in the first decade of life.[56,58,59]

Inherited blood disease is by no means more common in Negroes. The white supremacist dotes on sickle cell anemia but conveniently overlooks other innate blood conditions —thalassemia, congenital hemolytic anemia, pernicious anemia, hemophilia, and Rh-negative erythroblastosis —which are more common among Caucasians.

Thalassemia resembles sickle cell anemia, for it, too, is an inherited trait involving a variation in hemoglobin production resulting in unusual red cell shapes (target cells). The

---

*The sickle cell trait is most frequent where malaria is most prevalent. Africans residing in areas of Africa where malaria is not common have a lower frequency of the trait (e.g. the Bantu of South Africa).[57,58]

†The gene frequencies determining the sickle cell trait change when the environmental stimulus, malaria, is removed. Thus, American Negroes have a lower incidence of the trait than Africans now living in those regions from which the Negro slaves were imported to America.[56-58]

heterozygous state (thalassemia minor) ranges considerably in its severity, but the homozygous state (thalassemia major) is severe, progressive, and usually fatal in early life. Though distributed widely throughout the world, the disease probably originated in the Mediterranean peoples and is found in the United States primarily among their descendants.[56,59] It is speculated that the thalassemia trait, like sickling, evolved as a defensive response against malaria and chronic parasitic anemias.[58]

Another closely related anemia, congenital hemolytic anemia, also results from a severe red cell defect. Inherited in a Mendelian dominant pattern, it strikes all ages, but symptoms usually appear in childhood. Though it has been reported for Negroes, congenital hemolytic anemia is best known as a disease affecting people of European origin.[56,58,59]

Excessive destruction of red blood cells occurs in a number of hereditary conditions. The Rh-negative factor in the blood becomes critical when an Rh-negative mother has several Rh-positive babies. Since there is a lower incidence of Rh-negatives among Negro Americans, this condition is less frequent among Negro babies.[60] In another condition, glucose-6-phosphate deficiency, otherwise healthy individuals are especially sensitive to certain drugs because they lack a particular enzyme. This condition is relatively common among Negroes and Caucasians of Mediterranean origins.[61]

Pernicious anemia "is a disease chiefly of the temperate zone and the white race."[59,62] It is a chronic anemia affecting older adults. Genetic factors predispose the individual to the disease, but accessory factors—climate, diet, age—are also involved. Another innate disorder involves excessive bleeding. Hemophilia, famous as the hereditary inability of the blood to clot among some of Europe's royal families, is quite rare among Negroes. Though not a common condition, it has been recognized for centuries among Europeans.[59,63]

Two additional blood diseases, for which the genetic factors have not been completely elucidated, also present Negro-white differences. Leukemia, considered a type of cancer, has prevalence rates among whites approximately twice that of rates among Negroes for all forms of the disease.[64] National death rates for 1949 to 1951 show a figure for whites 70 per cent more than that of Negroes.[22] These large discrepancies do not seem to be a function of reporting error, since statistics for many other cancers do not reveal comparable differences and the elevated mortality rates for leukemia existed for 1949 to 1951 in all 32 states reporting racial data. Finally, polycythemia vera (erythremia), an adult disorder involving an increase in red blood cell and blood volume ("thick blood"), is said to be rare among Negroes.[59]

Four metabolic abnormalities are significant among the genetically-linked diseases revealing racial distinctions: periodic paralysis, cystic fibrosis, diabetes mellitus, and phenylketonuria (phenylpyruvic oligophrenia). Periodic paralysis is a fairly rare innate disease which causes sudden episodes of muscular paralysis in otherwise healthy people. Most recorded cases are Caucasians from North America and Europe; no cases among Negroes have yet been described.[58]

Cystic fibrosis ranks high as a cause of death in childhood. This chronic disorder produces such serious glandular disturbances, especially in the respiratory and digestive systems, that death ensues for 94 per cent of the victims before the age of 15.[65,66] White children seem particularly vulnerable. For 1958 to 1959, the recorded death rate for cystic fibrosis in the United States was over twice as great for whites as Negroes, with an especially large racial differential for females.[66]

Diabetes mellitus, a common chronic abnormality of carbohydrate metabolism, results from a primary inherited predisposition made manifest by a variety of secondary factors. National death rates for 1958 to 1959 show a slightly higher rate among Negro males (29 percent) and a considerably higher rate for Negro females (88 percent).[67] The conspicuous overrepresentation of Negro females reflects the typically greater rate among women of all races who are obese and have borne large numbers of children.[68,69] Thus, it is unclear if racial origin is directly related to the condition.

Another hereditary metabolic disease is linked to skin pigmentation. Phenylketonuria is caused by an enzyme deficiency, which results in severe mental retardation and prevents the normal production of melanin pigments. Ninety per cent of phenylketonuric children are blue-eyed blondes with fair skins, and most cases are of northern European ancestry. Since the disease is estimated to be responsible for 1 percent of all of the nation's mental defectives and may be ameliorated by diet, it has been the focus of mass testing surveys. These surveys indicate the disease is rarely found among Negroes.[58, 70]

DISEASES OF VARIOUS AND UNDETERMINED ETIOLOGIES

Mention of skin pigmentation raises a special irony. Dark skin has long symbolized Negro "inferiority" to white supremacists.* Yet it seems to be an evolved adaptation still possessing survival value. While the near disappearance of malaria in America renders the sickling trait disfunctional, the sun and harmful radiation are still with us. And melanin pigmentation "protects the skin against injury by ultraviolet radiation and also enhances the skin's ability to resist other types of trauma. Deeply pigmented skin reacts less readily to chemical irritants, and it is also not so readily sensitized."[73] By contrast, albinos have a marked susceptibility to skin cancer, metastases, and resulting death.[58] Consequently, all three major types of skin cancer, together the most common of all cancers, occur far more often among Caucasians than Negroes. The most frequent of these, basal cell epithelioma, is concentrated among blonde and rufous individuals (85 per cent) and in body areas of greatest exposure to the sun (e.g. the face and neck).[73, 74, Δ]

---

*Racists base their symbol on a conspicuous but tenuous trait. Human skin does not differ by race in the number of pigment cells in particular body regions. Rather, an individual's skin color depends on the activity of a single enzyme system within the pigment cells. This system is influenced by many modifiable factors.[71, 72]

ΔAfter injury, some Negroes develop elevated scars called keloids. These arouse cosmetic attention, but are of no medical importance; they are neither cancerous nor contagious.

Another physical trait emphasized by white supremacists, the fuller lip of many Negroes, involves a similar irony. Negroes have a lower incidence of cancer of the lower lip.[65] Cancer of the gall bladder also offers a racial difference. It is more common in whites probably because Negroes have far fewer gallstones, a condition thought to be a precursor of gall bladder cancer.[65] Reporting errors are apparently not responsible for these racial differences, for most other cancers reveal comparable rates for both groups.[75,22] There is, however, a sex difference in total cancer mortality rates by race. While male rates are similar, Negro females tend to have slightly higher rates than white females.[22,76,77] This is true almost entirely because of cancer of the genital system, an area where cancer has been vastly reduced by advanced medical and surgical techniques more available to the prosperous segments of the population.[22] Cancer of the cervix offers an example. Grossly, it is twice as frequent among Negroes, but when white and Negro females from the same socioeconomic backgrounds are studied, the incidence is essentially the same.[78] In comparison, Negro males appear to have significantly lower rates of testicular tumors than white males.[79]

Two conditions with racial differentials are probably influenced by a variety of factors. Sarcoidosis is a relatively uncommon chronic disorder which resembles such infectious diseases as tuberculosis, leprosy, and syphilis. It is world-wide in distribution, although Scandinavia is the cradle of the disease. Nevertheless, in North America Negroes are more frequently afflicted than whites.[65,80] Multiple sclerosis is a fairly common neurological disease affecting the brain and spinal cord. Although it is more common in colder climates and among whites, further research is needed to determine the importance of race apart from climatic factors.[81,82]

Especially revealing are the group distinctions in cardiovascular diseases.* Total reported death rates among Negroes for these diseases remain over the years consistently above

*For a detailed description of racial distinctions in this area, including infectious, peripheral vascular, and collagen diseases, see reference 83.

those of whites, particularly for females.[22,76,77] But a break-down by type is necessary to see the significance of racial differentials. The most critical differential involves hypertension and hypertensive heart disease, with death rates for Negroes about three times those of whites.[22] Many factors contribute to the development of hypertension, including psychosocial influences. The anxious business executive is a familiar stereotype in this connection, but for Negroes the problem of dealing with antiwhite hostility may be an important contributing factor.

Arteriosclerosis, popularly known as "hardening of the arteries," and arteriosclerotic heart disease accompany the aging process and do not reveal striking racial differences. Yet white males appear especially vulnerable to arteriosclerotic heart disease.[22,85,86] A third group of cardiovascular diseases stems from infections and tends to have mortality rates for Negroes somewhat above rates for whites. This largely reflects differential infection rates (*e.g.*, tuberculosis). However, whites are felt to be more susceptible to the development of rheumatic fever and rheumatic heart disease, prominent examples of this group.[83]

There are also six orthopedic disorders which may be related to race. Two of these conditions—protrusion of the thigh bone through its hip socket and flexible flatfoot—are more frequently reported for Negroes; four—congenital dislocation of the hip, fracture of the hip, Dupuytren's contracture of the palm, and the "march fracture" of the foot—are more frequently reported for whites.[87,88] Some of these differences defy explanation. Others seem related to the diverse experiences of the two groups. Negro Americans may suffer from flatfeet simply because their jobs typically require standing for prolonged periods. Contrariwise, whites, less accustomed to strains of weight-bearing, often develop "march fractures" from sudden overuse of their feet, as in army basic training.

The birth processes create still further Negro-white disparities. Perinatal mortality rates in 1958 and 1959 were almost twice as high for Negroes and maternal mortality rates in 1959 four times as high for Negroes, though rapid improvements have been made in both over recent decades.[60,89,90] Moreover, premature births are roughly 50 percent more frequent among Negroes.[91,92] These three conditions are the consequences of the lack of prenatal care, faulty health education, inadequate diet, and inexpert delivery, and are found among the poor of all groups.

The importance of social class and life situation in so many of these medical problems requires a final look at a comprehensive health study which held economic and experimental factors relatively constant. In 1940, the Farm Security Administration studied unselected farm families in eleven rural counties throughout the South; in all, 1,714 low-income Negro and white Americans were examined at the same clinics.[93] Defective vision, impaired hearing, and deviated nasal septum were far more prominent, and diseased tonsils and dental caries somewhat more prominent, among the poor whites. But hypertension was the particular problem of the poor Negroes. For both sexes at virtually all ages, the Negroes evidenced higher systolic and diastolic blood pressure and somewhat greater incidence of heart disease. A last group distinction highlights the inferior medical care long accorded Negroes in such areas. Negro children were less often immunized against smallpox, diphtheria, and typhoid fever.

This cursory overview of Negro American health underscores the basic fact that serious illness—mental or physical, communicable or hereditary—is not an exclusive preserve of any one race or group of people. With inherited disease, black supremacists can make a case equal to that of white supremacists; both are wrong. Differences do exist between the groups, but they cannot be scientifically judged as signs of inferiority or superiority. Indeed, such innate conditions as sickle cell anemia and thalassemia are direct consequences of evolutionary adaptations various human subspecies have made to their diverse environments.

More crucial are the nongenetic threats to life, threats that can be substantially averted through higher living standards and better health care. Tuberculosis, syphilis, whooping cough, perinatal and maternal complications have all been reduced by advances in recent years and can all be reduced still further. The denial of personal diginity is also involved; mental illness and hypertension appear in part to be direct outgrowths of racial discrimination.

Longevity data tell the story.[94] At the turn of this century, the average Negro American at birth had a life expectancy between 30 and 35 years, 15 below that of the average white American. By 1957, this expectation had risen to between 60 and 65 years. The many improvements in their situation since 1900 rendered a dramatic increment in the health of Negroes, providing solid evidence that corrosive poverty and inadequate medical care were the reasons for their short life span of the past. Though over these 57 years the percentage gain in life expectancy for Negroes has been twice that of whites, there is still a discrepancy of seven to eight years. On the basis of the data reviewed here, this difference can be traced to the diseases which are preventable and unnecessary.

Thus, segregationists who employ health arguments in their last-ditch defense against racial change are on shaky ground. To be sure, considerations of health are irrelevant to the justice and constitutionality of desegregation. Indeed, the racial differences in health that do exist provide further evidence of the societal need for desegregation and improved living conditions for all Americans.

REFERENCES

1. *Southern School News*, 4:4, No. 11, May, 1958.

2. Glass, B.: On the unlikelihood of significant admixture of genes from the North American Indians in the present composition of the Negroes of the United States. *Am J Hum Genet*, 7:368-85, 1955.

3. Frumkin, R.M.: Race and major mental disorders: A research note. *J Negro Education*, 23:97-98, 1954.

4. Ivins, S.P.: Psychoses in the Negro: A preliminary study. *Del St Med J*, 22:212-13, 1950.

5. Malzberg, B.: Mental disease among Negroes in New York State, 1939–1941. *Ment Hyg*, 37:450-76, 1953.

6. ———: Mental disease among native and foreign-born Negroes in New York State. *J Negro Educ.* 25:175-81, 1956.

7. ———: Mental disease among Negroes: An analysis of first admissions in New York State, 1949–1951. *Ment Hyg. 43:*422–59, 1959.

8. Williams, E.Y., and Carmichael, C.P.: The incidence of mental diseases in the Negro. *J Negro Educ,18;*276–82, 1949.

9. Wilson, D.C., and Lantz, Edna M.: The effect of culture change on the Negro race in Virginia as indicated by a study of state hospital admissions. *Am J Psychiatry, 112:*25–32, 1957.

10. Schermerhorn, R.A., Psychiatric disorders among Negroes: A sociological note. *Am J Psychiatry, 112:*878–82, 1956.

11. Jaco, E.G.: *The Social Epidemiology of Mental Disorders.* New York, 1960.

12. Goldhamer, H. *Am J Sociol, 68:*279-80, 1962.

13. Kohn, M.: *Am Sociol Rev, 26:*493-94, 1961. A study of a nonhospitalized population in Baltimore reached a similar conclusion to that of Jaco and is likewise limited by methodological difficulties.

14. Pasamanick, B. (Ed.): *Epidemiology of Mental Disorder.* Washington, D.C., 1959, pp. 183-201.

15. Caldwell, M.G.: Personality trends in the youthful male offender. *J Crim Law Criminol Police Sci, 49:*405-16, 1959.

16. Hokanson, J.E., and Calden, G.: Negro-white differences on the MMPI. *J Clin Psychol, 16:*32-33, 1960.

17. Heyman, Dorothy: Manifestations of psychoneurosis in Negroes, *Ment Hyg, 29:*231-35, 1945.

18. Hunt, W.A.: The relative incidence of psychoneurosis among Negroes. *J Consult Psychol, 11:*133-34, 1947.

19. Gardner, G.E.: and Aaron, Sadie: The childhood and adolescent adjustment of Negro psychiatric casualties. *Am J Orthopsychiatry, 16:*481-512, 1946.

20. Ripley, H.S. and Wolf, S.: Mental illness among Negro troops overseas. *Am J Psychiatry, 103:*499-512, 1947.

21. Rowntree, L.G.: The unfit: How to exclude them. *Psychosom Med, 5:*324-30, 1943.

22. National Office of Vital Statistics: *Death Rates for Selected Causes by Age, Color, and Sex: United States and Each State, 1949-1951.* Washington, D.C., 1959, pp. 38, 110, 114, 117, 143, 146, 189, 192, 340, 420, 484, 724, 914.

23. Book, J.A.: A genetic and neuropsychiatric investigation of a north Swedish population. *Acta Genet Stat Med, 4:*1–100, 133–39, 345–414, 1953.

24. Kallman, F.J.: Twin samples in relation to adjustive problems of man. *Trans NY Acad Sci, 13:*270–75, 1951.

25. Hollingshead, A.B., and Redlich, F.C.: *Social Class and Mental Illness: A Community Study.* New York, 1958, Table 10, p. 202.

26. Faris, R.E.L., and Dunham, H.W.: *Mental Disorders in Urban Areas.* Chicago, 1939.

27. Evarts, Arrah B.: Dementia praecox in the colored race. *Psychoanal Rev, 1:*388–403, 1913.

28. Kardiner, A., and Ovesey, L.: *The Mark of Oppression*. New York, 1951.

29. Kleiner, R.J., and Parker, S.: Migration and mental illness: A new look. *Am Sociol Rev, 24*:687-90, 1959.

30. Malzberg, B., and Lee, E.S.: *Migration and Mental Disease*. New York, 1956.

31. Rotondo, U., Vigil, C.B., Pachecho, C.G., Mariategui, J., and Degaldo, Beatriz de: Personalidad basica: Dilemas y vida de familia de un grupo de mestizos. *Rev Psicologia*, Lima, Peru, 2:3–60, 1960.

32. Myers, J.K., and Roberts, B.H.: Some relationships between religion, ethnic origin and mental illness. In Sklare, M. (Eds.): *The Jews: Social Patterns of an American Group*. Glencoe, Ill., 1958.

33. Pavlov, I.P.: *Lectures on Conditioned Reflexes*. New York, 1928, ch. 36.

34. Liddell, H.S.: Conditioned reflex method and experimental neurosis. In Hunt, J.M. (Ed.): *Personality and the Behavior Disorders*. New York, 1946, vol. 1, ch. 12.

35. Myers, J.K., and Roberts, B.H.: *Family and Class Dynamics in Mental Illness*. New York, 1959.

36. Baumgartner, Leona: Urban reservoirs of tuberculosis. *Am Rev Tuberculosis*, 79:687–89, 1959.

37. Shaw, L.W., and Wyman, A.H.: *Reported Tuberculosis Data*, 1960 ed. Washington, D.C., 1960, pp. 27–8, 45.

38. Shaw, L.W., Glaser, S., and Wyman, A.H.: *Reported Tuberculosis Data, 1962 ed.* Atlanta, 1962, p. 8, 34.

39. Maxcy, K.F.: *Rosenau Preventive Medicine and Public Health*. New York, 1956, p. 8, 132, 264, 276-78, 285.

40. May, J.M.: *The Ecology of Human Disease*. New York, 1958, ch. 11., pp. 118-19, 132-33, 144.

41. Payne, H.M.: Leading causes of death among Negroes: Tuberculosis. *J Negro Educ, 18*:225-34, 1949.

42. Iskrant, A.P., and Rogot, E.: Trends in tuberculosis mortality in continental United States. *Public Health Rep*, 68:911-19, 1953.

43. Smillie, W.G.: *Preventive Medicine and Public Health*, 2nd ed. New York, 1957, pp. 247, 260, 270-71, 278-79, 289-90.

44. Karns, J.R.: Tuberculosis in medical students at the University of Maryland. *Am Rev Tuberculosis*, 79:746-55, 1959.

45. Smith, D.T., Johnston, W.W., Cain, I.M., and Schumacher, M.: Changes in the tuberculin pattern in students between 1930 and 1960. *Am Rev Respir Dis*, 83:213-34, 1961.

46. Furcolow, M.L.: Tests of immunity in histoplasmosis. *N Engl J Med*, 268:357-61, 1963.

47. Perkins, J.E.: The stage is set—a program for more effective control of tuberculosis in the United States. *Tuberculosis Abstracts, 27*, October, 1954, no. 10.

48. Fiumara, N.J., Appel, B., Hill, W., and Mescon, H.: Venereal diseases today. *N Engl J Med, 260*:863–68, 917–24, 1959.

49. *V.D. Fact Sheet, 1961*. Atlanta, 1962, pp. 7, 13.

50. Dubos, R.J.: *Bacterial and Mycotic Infections of Man*. Philadelphia, 1952, p. 569, 583.

51. Deschin, Celia S.: *Teen-Agers and Venereal Disease*. Atlanta, 1961, pp. 74-77.

52. Luger, N.M.: The incidence of lymphogranuloma venereum as determined by the quantitative complement-fixation test. *Am J Syphilis, 34*:351-55, 1950.

53. *Control of Communicable Diseases in Man*, 8th ed. New York, 1955, pp. 22, 125, 208.

54. Hilleboe, H.E., and Larimore, B.W. (Eds.): *Preventive Medicine*. Philadelphia, 1962, p. 416.

55. Crosby, W.H.: Diseases of the reticulo-endothelial system and hematology. *Ann Rev Med, 8*:151-76, 1957.

56. Dacie, J.V.: *The Haemolytic Anemias, Congenital and Acquired. Part I: The Congenital Anemias*. New York, 1960, pp. 85-86, 200-04, 246-50.

57. Dublin, T.D., and Blumberg, B.S.: An epidemiologic approach to inherited disease susceptibility. *Public Health Rep, 76*:499-505, 1961.

58. Stanbury, J.B., Wyngaarden, J.B., and Frederickson, D.S.: *The Metabolic Basis of Inherited Disease*. New York, 1960, pp. 323-34, 871-72, 1125, 1132-33, 1915-26.

59. Wintrobe, M.M.: *Clinical Hematology*, 5th ed. Philadelphia, 1961, pp. 468, 645, 670-71, 794, 862.

60. Eastman, N.J.: *Williams Obstetrics*, 11th ed. New York, 1956, p. 1048.

61. Marks, P.A., and Gross, Ruth T.: Erythrocyte glucose—6—phosphate dehydrogenase deficiency: Evidence of differences between Negroes and Caucasians with respect to this genetically determined trait. *J Clin Invest, 38*:2253-62, 1959.

62. Herring, B.D.: Pernicious anemia and the American Negro. *Am Pract, 13*:544-48, 1962.

63. Bass, L.N., and Yaghmai, H.B.: Report of a case of hemophilia in a Negroid infant. *J Natl Med Assoc, 54*:561-62, 1962.

64. Dameshek, W., and Gunz, F.: *Leukemia*. New York, 1958, p. 30.

65. Robbins, S.L.: *Textbook of Pathology with Clinical Application*, 2nd ed. Philadelphia, 1962, p. 216, 377, 636.

66. Metropolitan Life Insurance Co: Cystic fibrosis: A child health problem. *Stat Bull,43*:3-5, March, 1962.

67. Metropolitan Life Insurance Co.: Recent trends in diabetes mortality. *Stat Bull, 43*:1-3, August, 1962.

68. Forsham, P.H., Renold, A.E., and Thorn, G.W.: Diabetes mellitus. In Harrison, T.R. (Ed.): *Principles of Internal Medicine*. New York, 1958, pp. 605-06.

69. Anderson, R.S., and Gunter, Laurie M.: Sex and diabetes mellitus:

A comparative study of 26 Negro males and 26 Negro females matched for age. *Am J Med Sci, 242*:481-86, 1961.

70. Rapoport, M.: Inborn errors of metabolism. In Nelson, W.E. (Ed.): *Textbook of Pediatrics*, 7th ed. Philadelphia, 1959, pp. 259–260.

71. Lerner, A.B.: Hormonal control of pigmentation. *Ann Rev Med, 2*:187-94, 1960.

72. Lever, W.F.: *Histopathology of the Skin*, 3rd ed. Philadelphia, 1961, p. 15.

73. Pillsbury, D.M., Shelley, W.B., and Kligman, A.M.: *Dermatology*. Philadelphia, 1956, p. 15.

74. White, J.E., Strudwick, W.J., Ricketts, N., and Sampson, C.: Cancer of the skin in Negroes: A review of 31 cases. *JAMA, 178*:845–47, 1961.

75. Lew, E.A.: Cancer of the respiratory tract. *J Int Coll Surgeons, 24*:1227, 1955.

76. Metropolitan Life Insurance Co.: Improved mortality among colored policyholders. *Stat Bull, 43*:6-8, August, 1962.

77. Cancer mortality trends among urgan wage-earners. *Stat Bull, 43*:1-3, 1962.

78. Christopherson, W.M., and Parker, J.E.: A study of the relative frequency of carcinoma of the cervix in the Negro. *Cancer, 13*:711–13, 1960.

79. Koehler, P.R., Fabrikant, J.I., and Dickson, R.J.: Observations on the behavior of testicular tumors with comments on racial incidence. *J Urol, 87*:577-79, 1962.

80. Wintrobe, M.M.: Sarcoidosis. In Harrison, T.R. (Ed.): *Principles of Internal Medicine*. New York, 1958, pp. 1148–51.

81. Alter, M.: Multiple sclerosis in the Negro. *Arch Neurol, 7*:83–91, 1962.

82. Walton, J.N.: Multiple sclerosis. In Harrison, T.R. (Ed.): *Principles of Internal Medicine*. New York, 1958, pp. 1644-47.

83. Phillips, J.H., and Burch, G.E.: Cardiovascular diseases in the white and Negro races. *Am J Med Sci, 238*:97-124, 1959.

84. Metropolitan Life Insurance Co.: Recent trends in heart disease. *Stat Bull, 43*:1-4, June, 1962.

85. Lew, E.A.: Some implications of mortality statistics relating to coronary artery disease. *J Chronic Dis, 6*:192–309, 1957.

86. Stamler, J., Berkson, D.M., Lindberg, H.A., Miller, W., and Hall, Y.: Racial patterns of coronary heart disease. *Geriatrics, 16*:382–96, 1961.

87. Shands, A.R.: *Handbook of Orthopaedic Surgery*. St. Louis, 1957, pp. 67, 489, 524, 539, 602.

88. Gyepes, M., Mellins, H.Z., and Katz, I.: The low incidence of fracture of the hip in the Negro. *JAMA, 181*:1073-74, 1962.

89. Metropolitan Life Insurance Co.: Reduction in perinatal mortality. *Stat Bull, 43*:6-8, 1962.

90. Maternal mortality in recent years. *Stat Bull, 42*:6-8, 1961.

91. Pasamanick, B., and Knobloch, Hilda: The contribution of some organic factors to school retardation in Negro children. *J Negro Educ,* 27:4–9, 1958.

92. Rider, R.V., Taback, M., and Knobloch, Hilda: Associations between premature birth and socioeconomic status. *Am J Public Health, 45:*1022–28, 1955.

93. Gower, Mary: Physical defects of white and Negro families examined by the Farm Security Administration, 1940. *J Negro Educ, 18:*251–65, 1949.

94. Lew, E.A.: The trend of mortality in the United States. *Sixteenth International Congress of Actuaries,* 1960, pp. 44-67.

PART TWO
STRESS

There are a number of diseases, usually related to stress, which are markedly higher among American blacks than among other groups.

Shin Joong Oh shows in Chapter Four that the Negro rate for cerebrovascular disease is about twice as high as that for whites. He reviews the epidemiology of this disease in Negroes and discusses its clinical implications. He also mentions the lack of comparative clinical studies.

In discussing cardiovascular mortality, in Chapter Five, Geoffrey Rose finds a rate four times greater among black women aged 35 to 44 than among white women. Rose compares his data with those for hypertension mortality where the rates are extremely high for both sexes among blacks and ventures the hypothesis of a relationship between the two phenomena.

However, despite Negro men's high hypertension rates, J. Stamler, D.M. Berkson, H.A. Lindberg, W. Miller and Y. Hall do not find grossly higher rates for atherosclerotic coronary heart disease in this group. They offer some possible hypotheses to explain this based on lower rates of hypercholesteralemia, overweight, and heavy smoking among Negro men.

In a *New York Times Magazine* article (February 25, 1973) Frank A. Finnerty, Jr. described hypertension among Negroes as developing earlier and with greater severity. Among black males between the ages of 25 and 44, the mortality rate for hypertension-related heart disease is fifteen times greater than it is among white men. Among black women, it is seventeen times greater than it is among white women. Thus, as Finnerty concludes in Chapter Seven, "Hypertension is different in blacks."

Chapter 4

CEREBRO VASCULAR DISEASES IN NEGROES

SHIN JOONG OH

Cerebrovascular disease (CVD) has been the third leading cause of death in the United States comprising about 11 per cent of the total deaths.[1] This is true in whites as well as in Negroes. Excellent reviews of epidemiological problems of CVD have been published in recent years. [2-6]

Although CVD mortality rate in Negroes is one of the world's highest,[7] the epidemiological studies of CVD in Negroes have been scanty. Since the understanding of problems of a disease in the high risk group may often suggest etiological hypothesis and preventative avenues, it is doubly important to know the epidemiology of CVD in Negroes.

The present author attempts to review the epidemiology of CVD in Negroes and discuss its clinical implications.

MORTALITY

Although mortality data have their limitations,[3,6,8,9] valuable epidemiological information can be obtained from them.

When the mortality rates of CVD were compared among various nations,[4,10,11] the highest one was 208.6 in 100,000 in Japan and 164.6 in 100,000 in American Negroes followed next. In the same comparison, the mortality rate of CVD in American whites was 94.8 in 100,000.

Analysis of age-adjusted mortality rates of three leading causes in the United States[1] showed that the rates of all causes

Abridged and reprinted with permission from the *Journal of the National Medical Association*, March, 1971.

were higher in Negroes than in whites but the most remarkable difference was noted in CVD. The Negro rate was 125.5 in 100,000 and the white was 68.3 in 100,000. This trend was also confirmed by studies from various areas of the United States.[12-14]

Table 4-I describes the age-adjusted mortality rates of three main types of CVD. The rates of all three types of CVD are higher in Negroes. The marked difference is noted in cerebral hemorrhage (CH) and the least is noted in cerebral thrombosis (CT).

Analysis of age specific mortality rates by race and sex revealed that the highest peak was observed in the 40 to 60 year old group in subarachnoid hemorrhage (SH) and in the later age group in CH and CT. This discrepancy is due to the different pathogenic mechanism in SH. The congenital aneurysm is the major source of bleeding in spontaneous SH.

In either race, sex difference was not impressive. This is a good contrast to male predominance in arteriosclerotic heart diseases.[3,15]

The higher rates of all three types of CVD for Negroes of both sexes are striking. The "log" difference between two races is greatest for both sexes in the middle age and least in old age. This is to say that CVD is more common in younger Negroes, especially in CH. In the 85 year and over group, the higher rates of CH and CT are noted in whites.

Geographical variation of mortality rates of CVD within the United States[3] showed that the highest rates were found

TABLE 4–I
AGE-ADJUSTED DEATH RATES OF THE VARIOUS TYPES OF CVD,
BY RACE AND SEX; UNITED STATES, 1966*[1]

| | White | | | Negro | | |
	Both	Male	Female	Both	Male	Female
CVD	99.4	93.6	105.0	147.9	135.9	159.4
Subarachnoid hemorrhage (SH)	4.1	3.7	4.4	7.8	7.2	8.4
Cerebral hemorrhage (CH)	51.6	50.4	54.4	97.6	94.8	100.4
Cerebral thrombosis and embolism (CT)	28.7	30.3	27.1	41.8	42.9	40.7

* Age-adjustment was done using the age distribution of the 1966 estimated total resident population of the United States.

in southern states and the Applachian areas in both races. Similar mortality pattern for hypertension in both white and nonwhite populations was observed.[16] It suggests a strong association of hypertension with CVD and indicates that the predominant Negro residence in southern states does not explain the areal variation.[4]

The changing pattern of CVD mortality rates in both races was studied by Acheson,[3] Wylie,[17] Krueger et al,[12] and Kuller et al.[18] Along with the decreasing rates from all causes in both races over the past 40 years, there was substantial decline in the CVD rates. The more impressive change was noted in subtypes of CVD. The rates attributable to CT increased and on the other hand the rates due to CH fell. Similar pattern of changes was also noted in England and Wales[19,20] and Japan.[21,22]

When this trend was considered separately in both races, an important observation was made.[12,18] The rates due to CT were increasing steadily in both races. The rates due to CH, however, drastically decreased in recent years in whites while they were rather stationary in Negroes. This observation indicated that whatever factor was involved in the drastic decrease of the mortality rate of CH in whites was not working in Negroes and that CH is still a major problem in Negro CVD.

PREVALENCE AND INCIDENCE OF CVD

It is well known that the prevalence and incidence studies give a better understanding of the disease than the mortality studies.

TABLE 4–II
PREVALENCE AND INCIDENCE RATES OF CVD
IN WHITES AND NEGROES

	Total	Whites	Negroes
Prevalence: (Baltimore)	260/100,000	240/100,000 (200/100,000*)	320/100,000 (530/100,000*)
Incidence: (Mid-Missouri)	260/100,000	250/100,000	410/100,000

* Age-adjusted rates.

The Baltimore study[23] (Table 4-II) revealed the prevalence rate of CVD in whites, 240 in 100,000 and in Negroes, 320 in 100,000. When they were age-adjusted, the difference was highly statistically significant. This study did not provide any data in regard to the age specific rates. Thus crude prevalence rate of CVD in Negroes is one of the highest in the world and almost equivalent to that in Japan.[21,24]

The Mid-Missouri stroke survey[25] (Table 4-II) gave us the information on the incidence rate of CVD in Negroes; the rate in Negroes varies from 270 to 560 in 100,000 among the countries while the rates in whites from 200 to 380 in 100,000. The average rate in whites was 250 in 100,000 and that in Negroes 410 in 100,000. Statistical analysis showed a significantly higher rate of strokes among Negroes than among whites.

It is unfortunate that there was not any study which surveyed the prevalence and incidence rate of the subtypes of CVD in Negroes. Considering the higher mortality rate of CH in Negroes, it may be possible that CH occupies the higher percentage of the prevalence of CVD in Negroes.

FREQUENCY OF CVD IN AUTOPSY POPULATION

The recent study of autopsy population[26] provided some meaningful information. Frequency of CH was higher in

TABLE 4–III
RISK FACTORS IN THE PATHOGENESIS OF CVD AND THEIR
COMPARATIVE FREQUENCY BETWEEN TWO RACES

Cerebral Thrombosis	Cerebral Hemorrhage	Racial Difference in Prevalence
Hypertension	Hypertension	Higher in Negroes*
	Hypertensive heart dis.	Higher in Negroes*
Coronary heart disease		Higher in Whites*
Transient ischemic attack		Higher in Whites[30]
Hypercholesteremia		Higher in Whites*
Overweight		Higher in Whites*
Diabetes		Abnormal GTT higher in Negro female[39]

* 36, 37.

Negroes than in whites and this difference was statistically significant. It also showed that CH occurred at a younger age in the Negro than in the white. Unlike CH, myocardial infarction and coronary heart diseases were more common in whites. The same author concluded that equivalent states of hypertension led to more disastrous myocardial insults in whites than in Negroes and conversely that more disastrous hemorrhagic complications within the nervous system were found in Negroes than in whites. The frequency of cerebral thrombosis was not published.

Another survey of the pathological anatomy of 393 cases[27] in fatal hypertensive intracerebral hematomas from Baltimore was recently published. This study showed that the proportion of Negroes among the patients was high (48%) considering their percentage of Baltimore population (25–42%). Furthermore, Negro patients were on the average 12 years younger than white patients and in the younger group the number of Negroes was about six times higher than that of the white.

These autopsy studies have supported the trend seen in the mortality data: CH is more common and occurs in the younger age group in Negroes. In the Fraytag study,[27] pontine hematoma was reported to be more common in Negroes than in whites.

The comparative studies of the prevalence of cerebral atherosclerosis by the Minnesota scoring system were recently made between Negroes and whites.[28,29] No definite difference was found in the prevalence of cerebral atherosclerosis between Birmingham Negroes and whites.[28] On the other hand, a higher prevalence was observed in Maryland Negroes than in whites.[29] At least, the Maryland study is consistent with the higher frequency of CVD in Negroes.

It is interesting to note that in both studies, cerebral atherosclerosis was found to be less prevalent in Nigerian Negroes than in American Negroes. Since the West-African Negro and the American Negro are of the same ethnic origin, it is important to ascertain what factors are responsible for this difference.[29]

CLINICAL STUDY

Ostfeld[30] mentioned in passing that the prevalence of transient ischemic attacks (T.I.A.) was eight times higher in whites than in Negroes in old age assistance recipients in Chicago.

It is striking that there has not been any study which compares the clinical features of CVD between the two races. There is ample evidence that there are clinical and epidemiological differences of CVD between the two races. It is also unfortunate that there is not a comparative study of natural history of CVD between the two races; some differences of the mortality data may be explained by the different natural history of CVD between two races.

DISCUSSION

The present review has made it clear that there is a major deficit in the epidemiological and clinical study of CVD in the Negro. The reviewed evidence suggests that CVD is about 1.5 times more common in Negroes than in whites and CH remains to be the major problem in Negroes.

Kurtzke[6] was inclined to conclude that there is no major racial predilection for stroke in the United States Negro. The higher mortality rates of CVD in Negroes was attributed to the marked under-counting of Negro population in the decennial census. With correction of this bias, he recalculated the 1960 Negro CVD mortality rates and found that most age-specific rates are now considerably closer to those of the United States whites but there is still a clear excess.

In analysis of the incidence and prevalence data,[23,25] he states that numbers are too small for confidence. But, as noted in the present review, the racial discrepancy is statistically significant.

Three factors are contributory to the higher mortality rates of CVD in Negroes: 1) higher incidence and prevalence rates of CVD; 2) the lack of good medical care; 3) possibly higher prevalence of cerebral hemorrhage. Higher incidence and prevalence rates of CVD in Negroes are already presented in our review. It has been known that death rates of CVD are higher in the lower socioeconomic class[9] and this is partly due to lack of good medical care. As noted in the Memphis study,[12] cerebral hemorrhage is still a major problem in Negro CVD. It has been well known that cerebral hemorrhage has the higher mortality rate among three major types of CVD.

What are the reasons for the higher prevalence rate of CVD in Negroes? Is genetic factor significant? The higher mortality rate of CVD in South African Negroes was reported compared with South African whites.[31-33] The autopsy study [28,29] has found that there was a difference of prevalence of cerebral atherosclerosis between the Nigerian and American Negroes. This suggests that the epidemiological data is not comparable always between American and African Negroes.

Gordon,[33] Bennett and colleagues[34] have shown that the mortality rate from "stroke" among the Japanese living in Hawaii was lower than among those living in Japan and that the rate was lowest for Japanese residents in the continental United States. These observations strongly suggest that the cultural and/or environmental influence is more important in the pathogenesis of CVD.

Another aspect of understanding the higher prevalence rate of CVD is the comparison of the higher risk factors between the two races. Though all of the higher risk factors of CVD are not well delineated, at least some of them are known. [8,35] Table 4-III summarizes the known risk factors in CT and CH and the comparative frequency of these factors between two races. It becomes clear that the risk factors for CT are similar to those for coronary heart disease and hypertension is the only known risk factor for CH. Epidemiological studies in Evans County, Georgia [36,37] have clearly shown the higher prevalence of hypertension and hypertensive heart disease and a lower prevalence of coronary heart disease and a lower prevalence of coronary heart disease in Negroes. The significant difference was also observed between two races in regard to the serum cholesterol level and body weight. Diabetes death rate was a little higher in the Negro female than other race-sex groups[38] and they have higher levels of blood glucose following a 50 gram glucose challenge.[39] It is apparent that the high prevalence of hypertension in the Negro is a major contributor to the higher prevalence of CVD, especially that of the cerebral hemorrhage.

The higher mortality rate of CT in Negroes, though the risk factor in CT is more prevalent in whites, may suggest that hypertension is more important than any other factors in regard to the pathogenesis of CT in Negroes.

It has been reported that antihypertensive treatment has reduced the mortality and stroke among hypertensive patients [40,41] and introduction of antihypertension drugs has been suggested to be responsible for the drastic decline of the mortality rate of CH among American whites and British.[19,20] The present plateau line of mortality rates of CH in the Negro may well be due to the lack of adequate antihypertensive treatment. It may be very possible that with the gradual improvements of medical delivery to the Negro, the prevalence and mortality rates of CH would decline in the next few decades. Further study of all of these aspects will facilitate the prevention of CVD and the understanding of the pathogenesis in CVD.

SUMMARY

Epidemiology of cerebrovascular disease in Negroes is reviewed. The present review revealed that the mortality, prevalence and incidence rate of CVD have been about 1.5 times higher in Negroes than in whites. Cerebral hemorrhage remains to be the major problem in Negroes because of the higher mortality rate. All of the data suggests that the higher prevalence of hypertension in Negroes is responsible for the higher mortality, prevalence and incidence rates of CVD. Adequate antihypertensive treatment may change the pattern of CDV in Negroes.

Further need for the epidemiological studies in Negroes with CVD is also stressed.

REFERENCES

1. Vital Statistics of the United States, Mortality, 1966.

2. President's Commission on Heart Disease, Cancer, and Stroke: *Report*. Washington, D.C., U.S. Government Printing Office, 1965, vol. 2.

3. Acheson, R.M.: Mortality from cerebrovascular disease in the United States, *Public Health Monogr, 76*:23–40, 1966.

4. Stallones, R.A.: Epidemiology of cerebrovascular disease, a review. *J Chronic Dis, 18*:859–872, 1965.

5. Borhani, N.O.: Changes and geographic distribution of mortality from cerebrovascular disease. *Am J Public Health, 55*:673–681, 1965.

6. Kurtzke, J.F.: *Epidemiology of Cerebrovascular Disease*. New York, Springer-Verlag, 1969.

7. Berkson, D.M. and Stamler, J.: Epidemiological findings of cerebrovascular diseases and their implications. *J Atheros Research, 5*:189–202, 1965.

8. Ostfeld, A.M.: Are strokes preventable? *Med Clin North Am, 51*:105–111, 1967.

9. Kuller, L., Blanch, T., and Havlik, R.: Analysis of the validity of cerebrovascular disease mortality statistics in Maryland. *J Chronic Dis, 20*:841–851, 1967.

10. Goldberg, I.D. and Kurland, L.T.: Mortality in 33 countries from diseases of the nervous system. *World Neurol, 3*:444–465, 1962.

11. Joint Council Subcommittee on Cerebrovascular Diseases: B. Epidemiology of Cerebrovascular Disease. Survey Report. National Institute of Neurological Diseases and Blindness and the National Heart Institute, 1965, pp. 25–36.

12. Krueger, D.E., Williams, J.L., and Paffenbarger, R.S., Jr.: Trends in death rates from cerebrovascular disease in Memphis, Tennessee, 1920–1960. *J Chronic Dis, 20*:129–137, 1967.

13. Kuller, L. and Seltser, R.: Cerebrovascular disease mortality in Maryland. *Am J Epidemiol, 86*:442–450, 1967.

14. Nichaman, M.Z., Boyle, E. Jr., Lesesne, T.P., and Sauer, H.I: Cardiovascular disease mortality by race, based on a statistical study in Charleston, South Carolina. *Geriatrics, 17*:724–737, 1962.

15. Epstein, F.H.: The epidemiology of coronary heart disease: A review. *J Chronic Dis, 18*:735–774, 1965.

16. Rose, G.: The distribution of mortality from hypertension within the U.S. *J Chronic Dis, 15*:1017–1024, 1962.

17. Wylie, C.M.: Recent trends in mortality from cerebrovascular accidents in the United States. *J Chronic Dis, 14*:213–220, 1961.

18. Kuller, L.H., Selster, R., Paffenbarger, R.S., Jr., and Krueger, D.E.: Trends in cerebrovascular disease mortality based on multiple cause tabulation of death certificates, 1930–1960. *Am J Epidemiol, 88*:307–317, 1968.

19. Yates, P.O.: A change in the pattern of cerebrovascular disease. *Lancet, 1*:65–69, 1964.

20. Yates, P.O.: The changing pattern of cerebrovascular disease in the United Kingdom. In Siekert, R.G. and Whisnaut., J.P.: *Cerebrovascular Disease*. New York, Grune, 1966, pp. 67–82.

21. Katsuki, S.: Current concepts of the frequency of cerebral hemorrhage

and cerebral infarction in Japan. In Siekert, R.G. and Whisnaut, J.P.: *Cerebrovascular Disease*. New York, Grune, 1966, pp. 99–111.

22. Katsuki, S. and Hirota, Y.: Recent trends in incidence of cerebral hemorrhage and infarction in Japan. A report based on death rate, autopsy case and prospective study on cerebrovascular disease. *Jap Heart J*, 7:26–34, 1966.

23. Commission on Chronic Illness: Chronic Illness in the United States. Chronic Illness in a Large City. The Baltimore Study. Cambridge, Mass., Harvard U Pr, 1957, vol. 4.

24. Johnson, L.G., Yono, K., and Kato, H.L.: Cerebrovascular disease in Hiroshima. *Jap J Chron Dis*, 20:545–559, 1967.

25. Parrish, H.M., Payne, G.H., Allen, W.C., Goldner, J.C., and Sauer, H.I.: Mid-Missouri stroke survey: A preliminary report. *Mo Med*, 63:816–821, 1966.

26. Kane, W.C. and Aronson, S.M.: Cerebrovascular disease in an autopsy population. *Arch Neurol*, 20:514–526, 1969.

27. Freytag, E. Fatal hypertensive intracranial hematomas: A survey of pathological anatomy of 393 cases. *J Neurol Neurosurg Psychiatry*, 31:616–620, 1968.

28. Williams, A.O., Resch, J.A., and Loewenson, R.B.: A Cerebral Atherosclerosis. A Comparitive Autopsy Study Between Nigerian Negroes and American Negroes and Caucasians. *Neurol* (Minneapolis), 19:205–210, 1969.

29. Resch, J.A.: The epidemiology and geographic pathology of atherosclerotic cerebrovascular disease, current concepts of cerebrovascular disease. *Stroke*, 5:33–37, 1970.

30. Ostfeld, A.M.: In Siekert, R.G. and Whisnaut, J.P.: *Cerebrovascular Disease*. New York, Grune, 1966.

31. Walker, A.R.P. and Girusin, H.: Coronary heart disease and cerebral vascular disease in the South African Bantu: Examination and discussion of crude and age-specific death rates. *Am J Clin Nutr*, 7:204–270, 1959.

32. Walker, A.R.P.: Mortality from Coronary Heart Disease and from Cerebral Vascular Disease in the Different Racial Populations in South Africa. *S Afr Med J.*, 37:1155–1159, 1963.

33. Gordon, T.: Mortality experience among the Japanese in the U.S., Hawaii and Japan. *Public Health Rep* (Wash), 72:543–553, 1967.

34. Bennett, C.G., Tokuyama, G.H. and McBride, T.C.: Cardiovascular renal mortality in Hawaii. *Am J Public Health*, 52:1418–1431, 1962.

35. Kannel, W.B., Dawber, T.R., Cohen, M.E., and McNamara, P.M.: Vascular disease of the brain—epidemiologic aspects: The Framingham Study. *Am J Public Health*, 55:1355–1366, 1965.

36. McDonough, J.R., Hames, C.G., Stubb, S.C., and Garrison, G.W.: Coronary health disease among Negroes and whites in Evans County, Georgia. *J Chronic Dis*, 18:443–468, 1965.

37. McDonough, J.R., Garrison, G.E., and Hames, C.G.: Blood pressure and hypertensive disease among Negroes and whites: A study in Evans County, Georgia. *Ann Intern Med, 61:*408–428, 1964.

38. Newill, V.: Epidemiology of diabetes mellitus. *Med Services, 14:*31–39, 1963.

39. Vital and Health Statistics, Data from National Health Surveys, Blood Glucose Levels in Adults, United States, 1960–62. Series II, 1966.

40. Leishman, A.W.P.: Merits of reducing high blood pressure. *Lancet, 1:*1284–1288, 1963.

41. VA Cooperative Study Group on Antihypertensive Agents, Effects of Treatment on Morbidity in Hypertension. *JAMA, 202:*1028–1034, 1967.

Chapter 5

CARDIOVASCULAR MORTALITY AMONG AMERICAN NEGROES

GEOFFREY ROSE

Figure 5–1 shows the age-specific death rates for arterio-sclerotic heart disease (ASHD, category 420 in the International List, 6th revision) for white and nonwhite persons in the United States in 1958. Since Negroes form over 90 per cent of the nonwhite population, it may be said that these patterns reflect differences between white persons and Negroes. At ages 35 to 44 the male rates are almost identical in whites and nonwhites. By contrast the female rates are approximately four times greater for nonwhites. With advancing age the male and female rates for whites converge: evidently some selective factor (or factors) is acting differentially on the two sexes at different ages. For nonwhites this differential effect is not apparent, the lines for males and females remaining roughly parallel. As a result, by age 65 the difference between white and nonwhite females has disappeared.

The growth of mortality rates with age for nonwhites departs considerably from linearity; this is only slightly evident among whites. This declining rate of increase of age-specific death rates may have several possible explanations: (1) There may be relative under-diagnosis of ASHD among older Negroes. In order to account for all of the racial difference this would have to be on a very large scale. Prevalence surveys are needed to determine this issue. (2) There may be errors in the census population estimates for older Negroes. (3) There may be a cohort effect, with sharply increasing rates

Abridged and reprinted with permission from *Archives of Environmental Health*, November, 1962.

among younger Negro cohorts. Time-trends in diagnostic habits and changes in coding practice combine to impede cohort studies, but from such data as are available it seems unlikely that this could be an adequate explanation. (4) There may be a special predisposition to fatal ASHD among younger Negroes, this relative increase in risk bearing more or less equally upon both sexes.

International and interracial mortality comparisons are often rendered unreliable by variations in diagnostic standards. This is notably the case with cardiovascular disease,

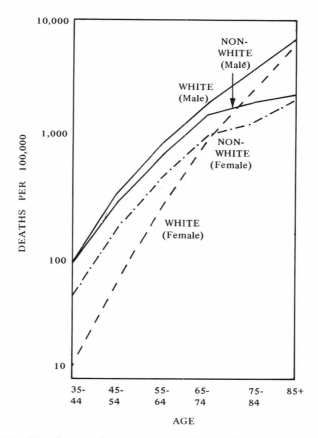

Figure 5–1.—Death rates by age, race, and sex for ASHD (420), United States, 1958.

where both terminology and diagnostic facilities are far from uniform. It may be more valid, however, to compare sex ratios of rates rather than the rates themselves, for here the only major assumption is that diagnostic variation bears equally on the two sexes.

Figure 5–2 shows the age-specific sex ratios for ASHD for the white and nonwhite populations of the United States in 1958. They follow quite different patterns. This may be said to support the reality of the racial differences which were indicated in Figure 5–1. It again indicates that the difference is greatest in the younger age-groups and thereafter diminishes progressively.

The sex ratios of mortality rates for ASHD in middle-age—though not in old age—also vary widely between other

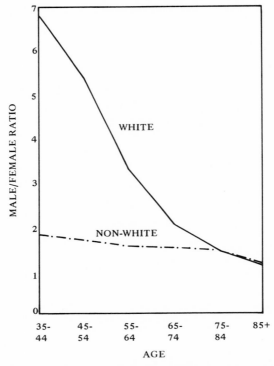

Figure 5–2.—Male:female ratios of age-specific death rates for ASHD (420) among the white and nonwhite populations of the United States (1958).

countries. In general however the male:female ratio is correlated with the male rate. That is to say, countries in which the male death rate in middle life is high do not tend to have equally high female rates.[1] The point of correlation for the United States white population fits into the general trend, but that for the nonwhite population is remote from it, being apparently subject to some special influence.

Figure 5–3 shows the age-specific death rates for hypertension (categories 440–447) for white and nonwhite persons in the United States in 1958. A tremendous excess is evident among the nonwhites, and this excess is common to both sexes. Up to the age of 65 the nonwhite females show a small

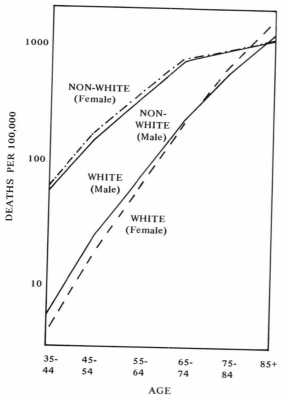

Figure 5–3.—Death rates by age, race, and sex for hypertension (440–447), United States, 1958.

but consistent excess, whereas for whites the reverse is the case. It may be seen, too, that whereas the rate of increase with age for whites is nearly linear, this is far from true for nonwhites. The same explanations must be considered as in the case of ASHD, but there is at least a strong suggestion of a special predisposition of Negroes of both sexes to fatal hypertension, this special predisposition diminishing with age.

There are then two problems of cardiovascular mortality among American Negroes: namely, for ASHD rates the problem of an unduly low male:female ratio, and for hypertension the problem of the high death rates for both sexes. The common age trend shared by these two phenomena suggests a possible link between them. This would not be unreasonable, since a raised blood pressure is associated with an increased risk of ischemic heart disease.[2] The hypothesis is therefore proposed that the primary cardiovascular problem for Negroes is the high prevalence of hypertension and that this leads to a secondary increase in ischemic heart disease. Since hypertension bears about equally on both sexes, one might also expect the hypertensive increment to ischemic heart disease to affect both sexes to about the same extent.

Such a situation is shown schematically in Figure 5–4. The

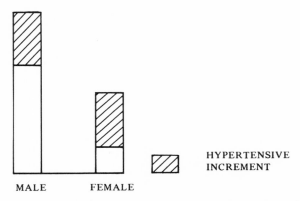

Figure 5–4.—Schematic representation of the possible effect of hypertension upon the sex ratio for ischemic heart disease rates among American Negroes.

clear parts of the columns represent the rates for ischemic heart disease that might obtain in the absence of hypertension, there being now a male:female ratio which is more in line with the experience of other populations. The shaded parts of the columns represent the increment, hypothetically equal in each sex, that might result from hypertension. Two conclusions would have to follow from this hypothesis: (1) The male:female ratio for ischemic heart disease would now be unduly low. This corresponds to what is observed. (2) The prevalence of hypertension would be greater among female Negroes with ischemic heart disease than among males. The truth of this inference could readily be put to observational test.

Summary

Cardiovascular mortality statistics for American Negroes under the age of 65 reveal two outstanding peculiarities: for arteriosclerotic heart disease the female rates are relatively very high, and for hypertension in both sexes the rates are extremely high. It is postulated that the primary phenomenon may be the excess of hypertension. Some implications of this hypothesis are considered.

REFERENCES

1. World Health Organization: *Annual Epidemiological and Vital Statistics, 1954.*

2. Society of Actuaries: *Body Build and Blood Pressure Study, 1959.* Chicago, Society of Actuaries, 1960.

Chapter 6

RACIAL PATTERNS OF
CORONARY HEART DISEASE

J. Stamler, D.M. Berkson, H.A. Lindberg,
W. Miller, and Y. Hall

Available data on occurrence rates of hypertensive and atherosclerotic diseases in middle-aged American whites and Negroes present a challenging paradox. Thus, middle-aged Negroes, both men and women, undoubtedly have considerably more hypertensive disease than do whites.[1-8] In the United States, hypertension is generally

Abridged and reprinted with permission from *Geriatrics*, August, 1961.

Presented at the thirty-third Scientific Sessions of the American Heart Association, October 23, 1960, St. Louis, Missouri. This research was supported by grants from the Chicago Heart Association and the National Heart Institute, United States Public Health Service (H-4197).

The authors are grateful to Samuel L. Andelman, M.D., M.P.H., commissioner of health, Chicago, for his valuable support; Arthur E. Rikli, M.D., formerly chief, Special Health Services, Regional Office, U.S. Public Health Service Chicago, for his help in initiating arrangements for cooperative work with the Public Health Service—Chicago Board of Health Venereal Disease Detection Program; Dr. Kathleen B. Muir, Dr. Seymour Weinstein, and Mr. Verne Fisher of this program and Dr. Robert MacFate, chief, Division of Laboratories, and the members of this division for their fine cooperation in collecting the specimens and field data in the communities and for processing the bloods; Messrs. Frank Bauer, Marvin Templeton, Carl Kolometz, Stanley Klis, Mrs. Juanita Ryan, and the other members of the Division of Vital Statistics and Informational Services, Chicago Board of Health, for their fine cooperation; and Mr. Guy Magnuson of the International Business Machines Corporation and Dr. Harry R. Rymer and Miss Louise Cowen of the Computer Center, Northwestern University, for their aid in the programming and computer analysis of the utility company data. It is also a pleasure to acknowledge the fine cooperative contribution of the utility company's executive leadership and medical department. Finally, this work could not have been accomplished without the fine contribution of the research staff of the Heart Disease Control Program, particularly Mr. Dana King, Mr. Jack Steinberg, and Miss Florence Modlinsky of the special research laboratory, who performed the cholesterol analyses.

associated with increased rates of clinical coronary heart disease (CHD) in middle age.[1-10] Therefore, it might be anticipated that Negroes would exhibit considerably higher coronary heart disease rates than whites. Unfortunately, reliable statistics on this point are scarce. By and large, the limited available data do not reveal this expected finding. Some published reports indicate that Negroes have less CHD in middle age than do whites; others estimate that rates for whites and Negroes are essentially similar.[1-4,11-41] Very few papers contain data suggestive of higher CHD rates for Negroes than whites, particularly insofar as men are concerned; limited evidence is available suggesting higher CHD mortality rates in middle-aged Negro women than in white women.*[1-4,26,34,35]

It was concluded that these contradictory and paradoxic findings merit further study, particularly since their investigation might yield data clarifying aspects of the etiology of atherosclerotic coronary heart disease. It was recognized that several abnormalities, in addition to hypertension, may influence the incidence of clinical coronary heart disease—for example, hypercholesterolemia, obesity, diabetes mellitus, heavy smoking, and so on.[1,2,4,5,7,9,10] It was therefore decided to approach the problem by collecting comparative data on these several parameters from middle-aged Negroes and whites.

Material and methods

Two population groups were surveyed, (1) white and Negro men employed by a Chicago utility company and (2) Negro men and women residing in low-income Chicago communities. The data on the utility company employees were obtained as part of long-term prospective epidemiologic studies of the total male labor force of this corporation, divided into two groups—ages 25 through 39 (approximately 1,500 men) and ages 40 through 59 (1,594 men).[5-8] Research on

* The interpretation of Negro-white differences in CHD mortality is complicated by the excess number of Negro deaths assigned to the category Degenerative Heart Disease (Code #422, International Statistical Classification of Diseases and Causes of Deaths, seventh revision).

the men aged 40 through 59 was initiated on January 2, 1958, and on the men aged 25 through 39, on January 2, 1959. A complete medical examination was available in the company medical department on an annual (persons 50 through 59), biennial (persons 40 through 49), or quadrennial (persons 25 through 39) basis for all employees. It consisted of a thorough history and physical examination, 12-lead electrocardiogram, 6-meter posteroanterior roentgenogram of the chest, urinalysis, serologic test for syphilis, and serum cholesterol analysis as routine procedures, as well as other determinations of a special nature for epidemiologic research purposes. The complete medical record of each participant, including the periodic examination, was individually reviewed by the research group's internist (D.M.B.). At the same time, the current and all previous electrocardiograms were reviewed. The chest roentgenograms had been previously interpreted by a radiologist; his reports were utilized in arriving at a final definitive diagnosis. The criteria and classification of disease (definite and suspect) have been described previously.[5-7, 42-46] Definite hypertension was defined as a diastolic blood pressure of 95 mm Hg or greater for most of the recorded readings in recent years. Borderline hypertension was diagnosed in individuals with diastolic levels of 90 to 94 mm Hg. A diagnosis of hypertensive heart disease was made if there was diastolic hypertension plus electrocardiographic evidence of left heart strain, roentgenographic evidence of cardiomegaly, or both. Socioeconomic data were obtained from the personnel records of the entire group.

Of the 1,594 utility company employees aged 40 through 59, complete data were available on 1,466, or 92 percent. Incomplete data were available on 128 men, some of whom were, by election, nonparticipants in the periodic examination program. Of the 1,466 examinees, 93 were Negro, all native-born; they were therefore compared with 1,065 native-born white men. Of the approximately 1,500 male utility company employees aged 25 through 39, data were available on a random sample of 38 Negroes and 492 whites aged 30 through 39; the white group included a few foreign-born.

The second source of data for this report was a survey of Negro residents of low-income Chicago communities. Through the cooperation of the Chicago Board of Health–United States Public Health Service Venereal Disease Detection Program, it was possible to obtain blood for serum cholesterol analysis on 1,430 men and women aged 25 through 64. Limited socioeconomic data were also collected, including place of birth, date of migration north if born in the south, employment status, occupation, and industry. Height and weight were also obtained by interview.

Serum cholesterol levels were determined in duplicate by the method of Abell and associates.[47] The ratio of measured or reported weight to desirable weight was calculated, using the life insurance tables for desirable weight for sex and height.[48]

Results

Occurrence rates of hypertensive disease and atherosclerotic coranary heart disease in the several age-sex-race groups. As already indicated, occurrence rates of hypertensive disease are considerably higher in middle-aged Chicago Negroes than in whites, irrespective of sex. These data also indicate that coronary heart disease occurrence rates are at least as high in Chicago Negroes as in whites. The data on the male employees of the Chicago utility company suggest that Negro men in the 40 to 59 age range may have slightly higher coronary heart disease prevalence rates than do age-matched whites. However, the differences are not great (1.3-fold) and are not statistically significant in view of the small size of the Negro male group. The comparison of CHD in middle-aged Negro and white women, limited here to mortality data, suggests at least a two-fold higher rate in the Negroes.

Serum cholesterol levels in the several age-sex-race groups. Data on the age trend of serum cholesterol for the four major sex-race groups show that for the utility company white men, mean serum cholesterol level rose with age from 213 mg percent at ages 30 through 34 to over 240 mg percent in the 40s and 50s. With respect to the Negro utility company employees, numbers are small and, therefore, the data must be interpreted with caution. At any given age, serum cholesterol levels appear to be slightly lower in these Negro men than in the white employees—for example, 203 mg percent compared with 214 at ages 30 through 39, and 229 compared with 242 at ages 50 through 59. Like the white men, these Negro men apparently exhibited a rise in serum cholesterol concentration with age. However, the plateau attained in the 40s and 50s seemed to be lower—less than 230 mg percent.

The Negro male residents of low-income Chicago communities had a somewhat different trend. They exhibited no rise in serum cholesterol levels beyond the 30 to 34 age period. Thereafter, serum cholesterol concentrations plateaued at values under 210 mg percent, sizably below those for both the Negro and, especially, the white male employees of the Chicago utility company. In contrast, Negro female residents of low-income Chicago communities exhibited a sizable rise in serum cholesterol levels with age. This increase was especially marked in the periods 40 to 44 and 45 to 49—that is, during the years of the menopause.

Age-specific data on the distribution of serum cholesterol levels for the four major sex-race groups of this study reveal that, at all ages, the prevalence rates of normal serum cholesterol levels (less than 200 mg %, or less than 225 mg %*) were lowest in the white male employees of the Chicago utility company. This rate was considerably higher in the Negro men, particularly those in the low-income communities, in whom it remained relatively high at all ages. This rate declined steadily with age among the Negro women.

With respect to prevalence rates of hypercholesterolemia (260 mg % or greater, 300 mg % or greater) among the males, these were greatest for the white employees of the utility company; they were only slightly less marked for the Negro employees of this company. In contrast, from age 40 on, rates of hypercholesterolemia were considerably lower—in the order of 50 to 65 percent less—in the Negro male resi-

---

* For discussion of the scientific basis for these cut-off levels for normal serum cholesterol see references 1 and 2.

dents of the low-income communities. For the Negro women, at age 40 and beyond, the prevalence rates for hypercholesterolemia were high, tending to approach or exceed those for the white men.

Of the 93 Negro men 40 to 59 years of age employed by the utility company, 62 were identified as having had only one to eight years of education and were employed almost exclusively as semiskilled, unskilled, or service workers. The mean serum cholesterol for this group was 219 ± 6* mg per cent.

Of the 672 Negro men aged 25 through 64 in the low-income communities, employment status was obtained on 655; 246, or 37.6 per cent, were unemployed at the time of the survey in 1958. The mean serum cholesterol levels were 199 ± 3 and 206 ± 2 mg percent for the unemployed and employed men, respectively.

Body weights in the several age-sex-race groups. Mean values for the ratio of weight to desirable weight were similar in the Negro and white employees of the Chicago utility company. The Negro men in the low-income communities tended to exhibit slightly lower mean values. From age 40 on, the Negro female groups from the low-income communities exhibited very high levels for this ratio, approaching or exceeding a mean level of 30 percent above desirable weight in the years from 45 through 59.

If a ratio of 0.95 to 1.04 is interpreted as indicative of desirable weight, then prevalence rates for this phenomenon were patently low for all groups.

Prevalence rates for moderate to marked overweight (ratio of weight to desirable weight of 1.15 or greater) and for marked overweight (ratio of weight to desirable weight of 1.25 or greater) were high for all sex-race groups. These prevalence rates were moderately lower for the Negro male groups from the low-income communities.

Prevalence rates of hypercholesterolemia and overweight in combination in the several age-sex-race groups. The white and Negro men employed by the utility company exhibited

* Standard error of the mean.

similar prevalence rates for various combinations of hypercholesterolemia and obesity. The Negro women demonstrated an even higher prevalence rate for this particular set of defects at ages 50 to 59. In general, the Negro women in the 40 to 49 and 50 to 59 age groups, particularly the latter, tended to have the highest prevalence rates for the several combinations of the two abnormalities. In contrast, the Negro male residents of low-income communities consistently exhibited rates for the various combinations of hypercholesterolemia and overweight that were considerably lower than those for the three other age-matched sex-race groups.

For the utility company employees only, data were available on one other factor possibly influencing risk of coronary heart disease—heavy smoking.* Prevalence rates for heavy smoking were $444 \pm 15^\Delta$ and 286 ± 48 per 1,000 for the white and Negro men, respectively; the difference was significant statistically.

Discussion

The findings of this study on serum cholesterol levels in middle-aged urban white American men are similar to those presented in other recent reports.[1,2,4,9,49,53] Before this investigation, virtually no representative data were available on serum cholesterol levels in sizable groups of adult American Negro men.† This study found significantly lower mean serum cholesterol levels and prevalence rates of hypercholesterolemia in low-income, middle-aged Negro men than in white men. The lowest values were observed in Negro men living in low-income communities, particularly those who were unemployed. The Negro men employed by a Chicago utility company had significantly higher values. However, their levels were not as high as those of the white men in

---

* Heavy smoking was defined as 20 or more cigarettes per day.

Δ Standard error of the prevalence rate per 1,000.

† One report of 63 Negro residents of Los Angeles, aged 40 to 59, gave a mean value of 249 mg percent, compared with a level for 503 age-matched whites of 265 mg percent. Socioeconomic data on the two groups were not included. This report also presented evidence on two small groups of Negro and white federal penitentiary prisoners.[51]

this company. The gradations of serum cholesterol in the groups of middle-aged Negro men stratified by socioeconomic criteria suggest that environmental and not racial factors are the main causes of the generally lower serum cholesterol levels in the Negro men compared with the white. International epidemiologic data, demonstrating considerably lower serum cholesterol levels in Negroes in Africa, are consistent with this concept.[1,2,4,54] (Here and elsewhere, reference is made to review sources with extensive bibliographies. The great research activity in this field has yielded a vast number of specific reports too numerous to include in any limited paper less than a review or a monograph in scope.) Further work is needed to test this hypothesis.

With respect to specific environmental factors possibly operating, only limited data are currently available. It has, of course, been extensively demonstrated that habitual diet is of key importance in accounting for different levels of serum cholesterol in different populations.[1,2,4,54] However, virtually no information is available on comparative patterns of diet in urban United States Negroes and whites of different socioeconomic levels. The few published reports in this area present data on diet among American Negroes in the South, chiefly in southern rural areas. These studies indicate that southern Negroes ingest significantly less saturated fats and cholesterol than do whites.[55-57] Here again, there is urgent need for further research, particularly comparative studies of northern urban, southern urban, and rural population groups at different socioeconomic levels. The authors are participating in cooperative studies along these lines.[58-59]

A second variable, habitual physical activity, may be important in influencing lipid metabolism and serum cholesterol levels. In view of the occupational classifications of the Negro men evaluated in this study, particularly those residing in low-income communities, it may be reasonable to infer that, as a group, they are generally more active than the white utility company employees, whose occupations are classifiable as sedentary, light, or medium in habitual physical activity. However, detailed data are lacking on this parameter for the Negro residents of low-income communities. In any case, evidence in the literature suggests that level of habitual physical activity is a minor factor, particularly compared with diet, in determining levels of serum cholesterol in middle-aged male population groups.[1,2,4,51,52]

The serum cholesterol levels of the Negro women reveal a marked rise with age, particularly during the years of the menopause. (A discussion of the hormonal factors contributing to this phenomenon is beyond the scope of this paper.[4,60,61]) The values for serum cholesterol at different ages for these women are generally similar to those reported for white women in the United States. These concentrations for the Negro women are perhaps slightly lower for each age than those for white women, depending upon which data in the literature are used for comparison.[49,51] It is, of course, recognized that limitations of interlaboratory comparability render such inferences tenuous. Nevertheless, the available data suggest that the race differential observed for men is not manifest for women. More studies are needed to evaluate this phenomenon further and to elucidate its mechanisms.

In this connection, the findings on body weight in the several age-sex-race groups may be relevant. The white men employed by the Chicago utility company manifest a high mean ratio of weight to desirable weight and high prevalence rates for both moderate and marked overweight. These findings are similar to those reported by other recent studies.[1,2,4,9,49,51] Previously reported data from the utility company epidemiologic study further demonstrate that a marked rise in weight occurs in these employees in the decades from young adulthood through middle age.[8] It is evident, therefore, that obesity is a highly prevalent phenomenon among middle-aged, employed, urban white American men. With respect to the small group of Negro men employed by the utility company, the data for this parameter are generally similar. However, in view of the possibility that the Negroes in this study were generally more active physically than the whites, it may be that their ratio of observed weight to desirable weight reflects greater muscle mass than in whites. In any case, the Negro men from low-income communities had lower mean values than the utility company employees for the ratio of observed weight to desirable weight and lower prevalence rates for both moderate and marked overweight. In view of the possibility that they, too, as a group have greater muscular development than the white men, this difference may assume greater significance.[52,62]

The data on the Negro women indicate a marked gain in weight from young adulthood to middle age, resulting in very high mean values for the ratio of observed weight to desirable weight and very high prevalence rates for both moderate and marked overweight. These findings are in accord with the available data in the literature.[63] With respect to this parameter, Negro women at present differ markedly from white women, who, among the four sex-race groups, manifest the lowest prevalence rates of overweight.

The findings on the prevalence rates for various combinations of hypercholesterolemia and overweight also reveal significant differences among the several age-sex-race groups. Thus, in middle age, the white male employees of the utility company and, particularly, the Negro women have high rates. In contrast, Negro male residents of low-income communities have significantly lower rates.

These data, together with the available information on the markedly greater prevalence rates for hypertension in Negroes, irrespective of sex, compared with whites, permit the formulation of a hypothesis concerning reported patterns of coronary heart disease occurrence in Negroes and whites. Thus, it has been demonstrated that risk of coronary disease in middle-aged men is related to such abnormalities as hypercholesterolemia, hypertension, overweight, diabetes mellitus, and heavy smoking. It has further been shown that various combinations of these factors—particularly hypercholesterolemia, hypertension, and overweight—are associated with markedly increased coronary susceptibility.[1,2,4,9] Based on this knowledge, it may be hypothesized that in Negro men, particularly low-income Negro men, the lower prevalence rates for hypercholesterolemia and obesity and the combinations of these abnormalities may result in their being protected against coronary disease and may operate to counter the greater susceptibility to coronary disease resulting from high prevalence rates of hypertension. The low prevalence rates of heavy smoking may also contribute to this presumed effect. The lower prevalence rates of hypercholesterolemia, overweight, and heavy smoking may account for the fact that Negro men, despite higher prevalence rates of hypertension, manifest middle-age coronary heart disease rates similar to those of white men.

Limited data from other sources are consistent with this hypothesis. Thus, coronary heart disease occurrence rates in middle-aged Japanese and South Africa Bantu men are considerably lower than in middle-aged white American men, despite apparently high prevalence rates of hypertension. This relative infrequency of coronary disease is associated with low prevalence rates of hypercholesterolemia and obesity.[1,2,4] The animal experimental laboratory has also yielded data consistent with this evidence on man. Thus, experimental hypertension by itself does not, under any circumstances, lead to the development of atherosclerosis. However, in animals with diet-induced hypercholesterolemia, hypertension accelerates and aggravates atherogenesis.[4,60] All these data support the conclusions that serum cholesterol levels play a key role in the pathogenesis of clinical atherosclerotic disease and that hypercholesterolemia and hypertension act synergistically in this process.

The data on Negro women are also consistent with the foregoing hypothesis. In comparison with white women, Negro women have greater prevalence rates for hypertension, obesity, and diabetes mellitus and similar prevalence rates for hypercholesterolemia.[64] They would therefore be anticipated to manifest greater atherosclerotic disease occurrence rate in middle age. The limited available data indicate this to be, in fact, the case.

Further studies are needed to verify the findings of this study, to extend them to whites and Negroes of different geographic and socioeconomic origins in the United States, to elucidate the mechanisms responsible for the observed differences, and to clarify the differential patterns of coronary heart disease incidence. To accomplish this last objective, there is a particular need for prospective epidemiologic investigations.

Summary

1. Negro men and women in the United States have markedly higher rates of hypertensive disease than do whites.

2. Despite their status with regard to the hypertensive risk factor, middle-aged Negro men have coronary heart disease occurrence rates not significantly higher than those of white men; Negro women apparently have higher rates than white women.

3. Negro men, particularly those residing in low-income communities, have significantly lower prevalence rates of hypercholesterolemia and obesity, singly and in combination, than do middle-aged white men.

4. Middle-aged Negro women have higher prevalence rates of hypertension, obesity, and diabetes and similar prevalence rates of hypercholesterolemia compared with white women.

5. It is hypothesized that the observed rates of occurrence of coronary disease in Negroes, compared with whites, can be accounted for by the observed patterns in the four sex-race groups of such risk factors as hypertension, hypercholesterolemia, overweight, diabetes, and heavy smoking, singly and in various combinations.

REFERENCES

1. Stamler, J.: Epidemiology of atherosclerotic coronary heart disease. *Postgrad Med, 25:*610, 685, 1959.

2. Stamler, J.: Epidemiology as investigative method for study of human atherosclerosis. *J Natl Med Assoc, 50:*161, 1958.

3. Stamler, J., Kjelsberg, M., and Hall, Y.: Epidemiologic studies on cardiovascular-renal diseases: I. Analysis of mortality by age-race sex-occupation. *J Chronic Dis, 12:*440, 1960.

4. Katz, L.N., Stamler, J., and Pick, R.: *Nutrition and Atherosclerosis.* Philadelphia, Lea & Febiger, 1958.

5. Stamler, J. et al.: Prevalence and incidence of coronary heart disease in strata of labor force of Chicago industrial corporation. *J Chronic Dis, 11:*405, 1960.

6. Stamler, J. et al.: Epidemiological analysis of hypertension and hypertensive disease in labor force of Chicago utility company. In Skelton, F.R. (Ed.): *Hypertension: Drug Action, Epidemiology and Hemodynamics.* New York, Proceedings of the Council for High Blood Pressure Research, American Heart Association, 1958, 1959, vol. VII.

7. Berkson, D.M. et al.: Socioeconomic correlates of atherosclerotic and hypertensive heart diseases. *Ann NY Acad Sci, 84:*835, 1960.

8. Stamler, J.: On epidemiology of hypertension and hypertensive disease. Proceedings of the World Health Organization International Symposium on Pathogenesis of Essential Hypertension, 1960. Prague, Czeckoslovakia, State Medical Publishing House, 1961, p. 107.

9. White, P.D.: Measuring risk of coronary heart disease in adult population groups: A symposium. *Am J Public Health, 47,* 1957, no. 4, pt. 2, p. 1.

10. Freis, E.D.: Role of hypertension. *Am J Public Health, 50,* 1960, no. 3, pt. 2, p. 11.

11. Stocks, P.: Race and climate as possible factors. In Cowdry, E.V. (Ed.): *Arteriosclerosis.* New York, Macmillan, 1933.

12. Rosenthal, S.R.: Atherosclerosis: Chemical, experimental and morphologic. *Arch Pathol, 18:*473, 660, 827, 1934.

13. Moriyama, I.M., and Gover, M.: Statistical studies of heart diseases: Heart diseases and allied causes of death in relation to age changes in population. *Public Health Rep, 63:*537, 1948.

14. Woolsey, T.D., and Moriyama, I.M.: Statistical studies of heart diseases: Important factors in heart disease mortality trends. *Public Health Rep, 63:*1247, 1948.

15. Gover, M.: Statistical studies of heart disease: Heart disease associated with other major causes of death as primary or contributory cause. *Public Health Rep, 64:*104, 1949.

16. Gover, M.: Statistical studies of heart disease: Mortality from heart disease (all forms) related to geographic section and size of city. *Public Health Rep, 64:*439, 1949.

17. Collins, S.D.: Statistical studies of heart disease: Illness from heart and other cardiovascular-renal diseases recorded in general morbidity surveys of families. *Public Health Rep, 64:*1439, 1949.

18. Woolsey, T.D.: Statistical studies of heart disease: Age at onset of heart and other cardiovascular-renal diseases. *Public Health Rep, 65:*555, 1950.

19. Gover, M., and Pennell, M.Y.: Statistical studies of heart disease: Mortality from 8 specific forms of heart disease among white persons. *Public Health Rep, 65:*819, 1950.

20. Pennell, M.Y., and Lehman, J.L.: Statistical studies of heart disease: Mortality from heart disease among Negroes as compared with white persons. *Public Health Rep, 66:*57, 1951.

21. Moriyama, I.M., and Woolsey, T.D.: Statistical studies of heart dis-

ease: Race and sex differences in trend of mortality from major cardiovascular-renal diseases. *Public Health Rep, 66:*355, 1951.

22. Moriyama, I.M., Woolsey, T.D., and Stamler, J.: Observations on possible causative factors responsible for sex and race trends in cardiovascular-renal disease mortality in United States. *J Chronic Dis, 7:*401, 1958.

23. Thomas, W.A.: Fatal acute myocardial infarction: Sex, race, diabetes and other factors. *Nutr Rev, 15:*97, 1957.

24. Hutcheson, J.M., Jr., Hejtmancik, M.R., and Herrmann, G.R.: Changes in incidence and types of heart disease: Quarter-century follow-up in southern clinic and hospital. *Am Heart J, 46:*565, 1953.

25. Roberts, D.W., Meek, P.G., and Krueger, D.E.: Prevalence of heart disease in population of Baltimore. *Circulation, 14:*988, 1956.

26. Lilienfeld, A.M.: Variation in mortality from heart disease—race, sex, and socioeconomic status. *Public Health Rep, 71:*545, 1956.

27. Lewis, J.H.: *The Biology of the Negro.* Chicago, U of Chicago Pr, 1942.

28. Smith, T.M.: Coronary atherosclerosis in the Negro: First annual oration in medicine: Analysis of 155 cases. *J Natl Med Assoc, 38:*193, 1946.

29. Blache, J.O., and Handler, F.P.: Coronary artery disease: Comparison of rates and patterns of development of coronary arteriosclerosis in Negro and white races with its relation to clinical coronary artery disease. *Arch Pathol, 50:*189, 1950.

30. Handler, F.P., Blache, J.O., and Blumenthal, H.T.: Comparison of aging processes in renal and splenic arteries in Negro and white races. *Arch Pathol, 53:*29, 1952.

31. Gray, S.H. et al.: Aging processes of aorta and pulmonary artery in Negro and white races: Comparative study of various segments. *Arch Pathol, 56:*238, 1953.

32. Weiss, M.M., and Gray, W.R.: Hypertension and myocardial infarction in the Negro. *Am J Med Sci, 227:*186, 1954.

33. Keil, P.G., and McVay, L.V., Jr.: Comparative study of myocardial infarction in white and Negro races. *Circulation, 13:*712, 1956.

34. McVay, L.V., and Keil, P.G.: Myocardial infarction with special reference to the Negro. *Arch Intern Med, 96:*762, 1955.

35. Thomas, W.A., Blache, J.O., and Lee, K.I.: Race and incidence of acute myocardial infarction. *Arch Intern Med, 100:*423, 1957.

36. Weissler, A.M., and Shapiro, O.W.: Alimentary lipemia and coronary artery disease in two racial groups. *Am J Med, 22:*976, 1957.

37. Strong, J.P. et al: Natural history of atherosclerosis: Comparison of early lesions in New Orleans, Guatemala, and Costa Rica. *Am J Pathol, 34:*731, 1958.

38. Holman, R.L. et al.: Observations on natural history of atherosclerosis. *J La Med Soc, 110:*361, 1958.

39. Groom, D. et al.: Coronary and aortic atherosclerosis in Negroes of Haiti and United States. *Ann Intern Med, 51:*270, 1959.

40. Spain, D.M., and Bradess, V.A.: Sudden death from coronary atherosclerosis: Age, race, sex, physical activity, and alcohol. *Arch Intern Med, 100:*228, 1957.

41. Kent, A.P. et al: Comparison of coronary artery disease (arteriosclerotic heart disease) deaths in health areas of Manhattan. New York City. *Am J Public Health, 48:*200, 1958.

42. New York Heart Association: *Nomenclature and Criteria for Diagnosis of Diseases of the Heart and Blood Vessels,* 5th ed., by Criteria Committee, Harold E.B. Pardee, chairman. New York, Am Heart, 1953.

43. Dawber, T.R. (Ed.): Report of Conference on Longitudinal Cardiovascular Studies, Brookline, Mass. June 17–18, 1957.

44. Expert Committee on Cardiovascular Disease and Hypertension: Hypertension and coronary heart disease: Classification and criteria for epidemiological studies, 1st report. *WHO Tech Rep Ser, 168,* 1959.

45. Pollack, H., and Krueger, D.E. (Eds.): Epidemiology of cardiovascular diseases—hypertension and arteriosclerosis. Report of Conference, Princeton, N.J., April 24–26, 1959. Supplement to *Am J Public Health, 50,* no. 10, 1960.

46. Stamler, J. et al.: Methodological evaluation of validity and reliability of special cardiovascular medical examination. Report submitted to National Health Survey, U.S. Public Health Service, August, 1959.

47. Abell, L.L. et al.: Simplified method for estimation of total cholesterol in serum and demonstration of its specificity. *J Biol Chem, 195:*357, 1952.

48. Report of the Food and Nutrition Board: Recommended Dietary Allowances, rev., 1958. Washington, D.C., Natl Acad Sci—National Research Council Publ. 589, 1958.

49. Lawry, E.Y. et al.: Cholesterol and *beta* lipoproteins in the serum of Americans: Well persons and those with coronary heart disease. *Am J Med, 22:*605, 1957.

50. Gofman, J.W. et al.: Evaluation of serum lipoprotein and cholesterol measurements as predictors of clinical complications of atherosclerosis. *Circulation, 14:*691, 1956.

51. Lewis, L.A. et al.: Serum lipid levels in normal persons: Findings of cooperative study of lipoproteins and atherosclerosis. *Circulation, 16:*227, 1957.

52. Keys, A.: Mode of life and prevalence of coronary heart disease. In Arteriosclerosis: A Symposium presented by the Minnesota Heart Association and the University of Minnesota, September 7–9, 1955. Reprinted from *Minn Med,* 1956. p. 28.

53. Keys, A.: Age trend of serum concentrations of cholesterol and of Sr 10–20, ("G") substances in adults. *J Gerontol, 7:*201, 1952.

54. Bronte-Stewart, B.: Lipids and atherosclerosis. *Fed Proc, 20:*127, 1961.

55. Adelson, S.F., and Blake, E.C.: *Diets of Families in the Open Country, a Georgia and Ohio County, Summer 1945.* Washington, D.C., US Department of Agriculture, 1950.

56. Clemson, S.C.: Family food consumption in three types of farming areas of the South. II. Analysis of weekly food records, late winter and early spring, 1958. *South Cooperative Ser Bull, 20,* 1951.

57. Grant, F.W., and Groom, D.: Dietary study among group of Southern Negroes. *J Am Diet Assoc, 35:*910, 1959.

58. Hames, D., and McDonough, J.: Personal communication. Claxton, Ga.

59. Boyle, E., and Nichaman, M.: Personal communication. Charleston, S.C.

60. Katz, L.N., and Stamler, J.: *Experimental Atherosclerosis.* Springfield, Ill., Thomas, 1953.

61. Pincus, G. (Ed.): *Hormones and Atherosclerosis.* New York, Acad Pr, 1959.

62. Brozek, J. (Ed.): *Body Measurements and Human Nutrition.* Detroit, Wayne U Pr, 1956.

63. Estimated prevalence of overweight in United States. *Public Health Rep, 69:*1084, 1954.

64. Joslin, E.P. et al.: *The Treatment of Diabetes Mellitus,* 10th ed. Philadelphia, Lea & Febiger, 1959.

Chapter 7

HYPERTENSION IS DIFFERENT IN BLACKS

FRANK A. FINNERTY, JR.

Hypertension *is* different in black people. It develops earlier in life, is frequently more severe, and results in a higher mortality at a younger age, more commonly from strokes than from coronary artery disease. Experience over the past 20 years with an inner city population readily attests to the high incidence of hypertension in blacks. Studies conducted in the Toxemia Clinic at D.C. General Hospital presented evidence that 70 percent of the patients originally diagnosed as toxemia of pregnancy by the obstetricians actually had hypertensive vascular disease as shown by a history of an elevated arterial pressure prior to pregnancy, and by arteriovenous nicking seen on opthalmoscopic examination.[1-3]

Studies during the past year conducted in the Birth Control Clinic at this hospital have reemphasized the high incidence of hypertension in young black women.[4] Forty-eight per cent of a random sample of black patients attending the Birth Control Clinic were found to have a documented history of elevated blood pressure above 135/85 mm Hg at some time in the past. One hundred of these patients, whose average age when attending the clinic was 23 years, were evaluated from the cardiovascular standpoint. In 76, the arterial pressure was found to be 140/90 mm Hg or above. In addition, ophthalmoscopic examination revealed increased arterial tortuosity and A-V nicking in 36 patients.

Reprinted with permission from the *Journal of the American Medical Association.* June 7, 1971.

The importance of slight rises in arterial pressure and their association with atherosclerotic cardiovascular and cerebral disease has been documented in many clinical studies in whites as well as in blacks.[5-7] Even a history of hypertension has been shown to be detrimental. Levy and others,[8] in a study of over 22,000 U.S. Army officers, found that men with transient elevations of blood pressure have as much as three to four times higher disability retirement rates and two to three times higher cardiovascular-renal death rates than the officers without this supposedly minor finding.

The Veterans Administration study has demonstrated that controlling the arterial pressure in middle-aged males has significantly reduced morbidity and mortality.[9] Even though good data are not yet available on patients with mild hypertension, it seems reasonable to apply these findings to patients with milder forms of hypertension, particularly to blacks, where such a high incidence of disease exists. Sound support for this plan can be found in the recent Framingham Report[10] which states that control of hypertension—labile or fixed, systolic or diastolic, at any age, in either sex—appears to be central in the prevention of atherothrombotic brain infarction.

Seventy-one percent of the District of Columbia population within the inner city is black. Seventy-five percent of the 645 deaths attributed to hypertension in 1965 were in black people. Even more striking was the fact that 88 percent of the hypertensive deaths below the age of 60 were in blacks.

To change these statistics, the first line of attack would be to initiate a mass education program not only for the inner-city resident, but also for the physician. Our studies during the past two years would indicate that the inner-city resident is concerned about his health and that with proper motivation, i.e. a health management plan which is concerned with his economic, emotional, and social needs, good cooperation can be expected (unpublished data).

A second line of attack therefore requires a plan to manage a large number of newly identified hypertensives in an environment which delivers medical care efficiently and is consonant with patient needs. Today's programs, even with limited numbers, fail because clinics operate on a mass rather than an individual base. (The usual clinic is organized for the convenience of the operating personnel; this must be changed if large numbers of patients are to be managed properly.)

A third line of attack involves reorientation of the physician to recognize the significance of mild rises in arterial pressure—even in systolic pressure—and to recognize that controlling the arterial pressure at any age might reduce morbidity and mortality. The Veterans Administration study has demonstrated that a long-acting thiazide diuretic administered alone or in combination with reserpine is effective in controlling moderately severe hypertension in many patients.[9] While more clinical studies are needed, it appears that this or similar therapy might well be effective in controlling a large majority of patients with milder forms of hypertension. Treatment therefore may be as simple as a pill a day.

Finally, the task of managing these newly identified hypertensives cannot be left entirely to the physician, although it must remain his responsibility. Innovative approaches must be developed to extend the physician's competence in the long-term management of this disease. Once a rigid prescriptive management plan has been instituted by the physician, a well-trained allied-medical person could visit the patient in the home, and thus reduce the number of clinic visits, improve compliance, and conserve valuable physician time. Furthermore, clinics separate and distinct from the hospital complex, i.e. neighborhood clinics, should be developed and utilized to provide a center for professional direction and support of the sizable hypertensive population. The expected influx of patients cannot be handled in the hospital clinics as they exist today.

The population of the United States is 20 per cent black. It is estimated that 240,000 of these people have hypertension as defined by an arterial pressure of 140/90 mm Hg or above. Only by making every effort to identify and treat them will the high incidence of stroke and early death in this population be decreased. The leadership must lie with us.

REFERENCES

1. Finnerty, F.A., Jr.: Does vascular damage follow toxemia of pregnancy?: An internist's appraisal of 303 patients in a toxemia clinic. *JAMA, 154:*1075–1079, 1954.

2. Finnerty, F.A., Jr.: Toxemia of pregnancy as seen by an internist: An analysis of 1,081 patients. *Ann Intern Med, 44:*358–375, 1956.

3. Finnerty, F.A., Jr, Buchholz, J.H.: Therapy of hypertensive states in pregnancy from the internist's standpoint. *GP, 16:*86–95, 1957.

4. Hypertension affects many young black women, Medical News. *JAMA, 215:*876, 1971.

5. Kannel, W.B., Dawber, T.R., Cohen, M.E., et al: Vascular disease of the brain—epidemiologic aspects: The Framingham Study. *Am J Public Health, 55:*1355–1366, 1965.

6. Chapman, J.M., Massey, E.J.: The interrelationship of serum cholesterol, hypertension, body weight, and risk of coronary disease. *J Chronic Dis, 17:*933–949, 1964.

7. Chapman, J.M., Reeder, L.G., Borun, E.R., et al: Epidemiology of vascular lesions affecting the central nervous system: The occurrence of strokes in a sample population under observation for cardiovascular disease. *Am J Public Health, 56:*191–201, 1966.

8. Levy, R.L., White, P.D., Stroud, W.D., et al: Transient hypertension: The relative prognostic importance of various systolic and diastolic levels. *JAMA, 128:*1059–1061, 1945.

9. Veterans Administration Cooperative Study on Antihypertensive Agents: Effects of treatment on morbidity in hypertension: II. Results in patients with diastolic blood pressure averaging 90 through 114 mm Hg. *JAMA, 213:*1143–1152, 1970.

10. Kannel, W.B., Wolf, P.A., Verter, J., et al: Epidemiologic assessment of the role of blood pressure in stroke: The Framingham Study. *JAMA, 214:*301–310, 1970.

PART THREE
THE GENETIC FACTOR

During the past few years, sickle cell anemia has been the subject of much discussion, even though the sickling phenomenon has been known for more than two decades.

As an introduction to the problem, Clement A. Finch describes the molecular changes involved in sickle cell anemia. He discusses the various stages of the disease and the crisis reached when oxygen saturation fails. He also discusses selected treatments and therapies.

In Chapter Nine, Robert M. Nalbandian suggests the therapeutic use of urea for chemical manipulation of the hemoglobin S molecule. He stresses, however, that the treatment must comply faithfully with the published protocols to avoid adverse consequences.

Robert B. Scott considers the many fund drives and federal grants for diseases less prevalent than sickle cell anemia and he calls for a reevaluation of priorities. He feels that with mass screening, sickle cell anemia "may be the first hereditary illness which could be controlled by genetic counselling."

In the final chapter of this section Dolores E. Jackson describes the day-to-day working of a large clinic geared to the detection and treatment of sickle cell disease. She surveys what is known about the various types of sickle cell disease, and their treatment. She stresses the human aspect—the need for counselling and support of parents and children, and the role of the nurse in the delivery of health care.

Chapter 8

PATHOPHYSIOLOGIC ASPECTS OF SICKLE CELL ANEMIA

CLEMENT A. FINCH

The single amino acid mutation of valine for glutamic acid in the beta polypeptide chain of hemoglobin has been shown to have serious consequences for over a quarter of a million people and to place the offspring of many millions of heterozygotes in genetic jeopardy. The abnormality permits stacking of hemoglobin molecules in a manner which converts the fluid contents of the erythrocyte into a rigid mass which has difficulty passing through the microvasculature.[1-3] This sickling process can occur only when the hemoglobin becomes deoxygenated. It may be produced *in vitro* under conditions which exist in the capillaries of the patient with sickle cell anemia.[4] It is influenced by the concentration of sickle hemoglobin within the erythrocyte[5], oxygen tension[6,7], pH[8] and osmolarity[9].

The consequences of the disease in involved subjects includes a constellation of thrombotic episodes which overshadow the manifestations of the hemolytic anemia which is also present[10,11]. Although there are favorite areas of involvement, virtually all body tissues are in jeopardy, and repeated bouts of local pain and inflammation occur as evidence of focal tissue destruction. What precipitates the thrombotic crisis is usually as unclear as the reasons for the lack of such complications over prolonged periods of time. Although the molecular abnormality and its gross anatomic

Abridged and reprinted with permission from the *American Journal of Medicine*, July, 1972.

This investigation was supported by U.S. Public Health Service research grant HE-06242.

consequences are well defined, the *in vivo* pathophysiology of the disease is less well understood than might be supposed.

Anemia

Sickle cell disease is usually associated with a hemoglobin value of about 8 gm percent (range 6 to 10 gm). There is a compensatory proliferation of the erythroid marrow into the enlarged medullary cavity of the entire skeleton; despite repeated infarcts of the marrow, basal production rates calculate to over four times normal. A corresponding increase in reticulocytes is seen in the circulating blood, indicating that erythropoiesis is effective. Within a few days of its appearance in circulation the red cell may become permanently misshapen and is referred to as the irreversible sickle cell[12]; the amount of cell destruction appears related to the number of these cells present[13]. Destruction is most likely the result of cumulative mechanical damage which occurs during repeated intravascular sickling. It might be suggested that stasis also contributes to hemolysis, since a considerable improvement in hemoglobin concentration has resulted from the removal of enlarged spleens[14]. Survival measurements also suggest a considerable difference before and after splenectomy[15-18] However there is more than one possible explanation for these effects. In one patient studied carefully before and after splenectomy, although the hematocrit increased there was no significant change in the red cell turnover rate as a result of the removal of sequestered splenic cells which constituted over 40 percent of the entire red cell mass[19]. If sequestration has a tissue holding time of several days, red cell survival measurements would reflect not only destruction but also sequestration. A corollary of this is that the true red cell mass may not be measured by the early dilution of injected red cells. It seems possible that in sickle cell anemia the red cell mass is in excess of that suggested by the hematocrit.

In addition to an occasional aplastic crisis and the development of folate deficiency as occurs in all types of hemolytic anemia[20], there are two types of anemia unique to sickle cell disease. The first is sudden massive trapping of red cells in the spleen which may occur with infection in childhood and may result in a marked increase in the severity of the anemia within a few hours.[20] The second is the occurrence of what is believed to be a mechanical type of ineffective erythropoiesis. Past studies have indicated that a more complete shutoff of erythropoiesis following transfusion or the inhalation of a high concentration of oxygen occurs in sickle-cell anemia than is seen with other hemolytic anemias.[21,22] Reticulocytes fall to extremely low levels despite a continued proliferation of nucleated red cells within the marrow and a normal or increased erythroid iron turnover. This disparity appears to be the result of a difficulty of sickle cells in leaving the marrow except under the influence of a high erythropoietin level.

Oxygen Transport

The anemia in sickle cell disease is probably less important for its direct effect on oxygen transport than for its possible effect on the sickling process. Oxygen extraction is determined by supply (oxygen flow and hemoglobin affinity for oxygen content is reduced to 50 percent of normal by the anemia present (10 volumes percent as compared to a normal of 21 volumes percent). In contrast to other anemias in which increased red cell diphosphoglycerate and through an increased cardiac output. In sickle cell disease under basal conditions, tissue requirements are normal whereas blood oxygen content is reduced to 50 percent of normal by the anemia present (10 volumes percent as compared to a normal of 21 volumes percent). In contrast to other anemias in which compensation is achieved by several mechanisms, in both children and adults with sickle cell anemia there is a marked increase in cardiac output which by itself corrects the oxygen flow deficit.[25,26] A study of cerebral circulation also showed a greater flow response in sickle cell anemia than in other anemias,[27] indicating that this compensation pertains to the blood flow in at least one of the vital organs. Thus deoxygenation of venous blood, which is so critical in determining the amount of sickling, is nearly normal. The reason for this increased cardiac output is not hypoxia, since with the increased P_{50} reported in this disorder,[24] one can calculate a mean venous oxygen tension (PO_2) of about 44 mm Hg as compared to the normal of 39 mm Hg. Indeed cardiac· output would not be expected to be sensitive to oxygen tension since it depends more on venous return, viscosity of blood and the regulation of peripheral resistance.[23] A possible cause of the increased output is an expanded blood volume. Published reports indicate a total blood volume of about 95 ml/kg in contrast to the normal of 65 ml/kg.[28] It has recently been suggested that this apparent difference may be artifactual due to the difference in body composition of the patient with sickle-cell anemia.[29] This should probably be examined further, since an explanation for the increased cardiac output is needed, and since a disturbance of water exchange and extracellular osmolarity has been recorded in sickle-cell anemia.[30]

Erythrocyte Stasis

Within the microvasculature of the patient with sickle cell disease, red cell stasis occurs as a forerunner of thrombosis. In certain tissues sequestration is particularly evident. In younger subjects the spleen is congested with sickle cells. The kidneys are frequently enlarged when studied roentgenographically[31] and at necropsy show engorgement with sickled red cells.[32] Conjunctival examination shows comma-shaped vessels packed with red cells; these vessels are said to retain their distended appearance for several days[33,34]. Erythrocyte sequestration in the erythroid marrow, although not directly demonstrated, is implied by repeated episodes of bone pain and embolization of infarcted marrow to the lungs.[35] Stasis may impose a functional abnormality which is reversible. Loss of phagocytic function by the spleen is illustrated by the negative technetium scan,[36] and loss of function of medullary nephrons is reflected in the inability of the kidney to concentrate urine beyond 400 mOsm.[37] With replacement of sickle cells by normal cells, the function of both of these organs may be regained.[38,39] With time, however, the congested vasculature in both organs is gradually obliterated by a thrombotic process.[40]

The reason for involvement of some tissues more than others seems explainable on the basis of those factors shown *in vitro* to affect sickling. Thus the spleen has a high degree of deoxygenation and an acid pH; blood in the kidney medulla is highly unsaturated[41] and has a high osmolarity[42]; bone marrow involvement probably relates to the high degree of oxygen desaturation in the medullary cavity resulting from the oxygen requirements of the hyperplastic erythroid marrow. More than the degree of local oxygen extraction must be involved, however, for the heart, in which the tissue oxygen tension is the lowest, is rarely involved in the thrombotic process. Although increased viscosity may be demonstrated within a second of deoxygenation of the sickle cell, cell deformity takes considerably longer.[43] The high flow rate occurring in the heart and striate muscle with exercise may flush through the deoxygenated cell into general circulation before obstructive sickling occurs.

Crisis

Tissue infarction, responsible for most of the "crisis" of sickle cell anemia, might be expected to occur when local or general oxygen saturation falls. Although certain local areas are obviously predisposed to infarction, the multi-episodic nature of many crises suggests a general state rather than a local lesion. Symptoms are not produced by a half-hour period of hypoxia,[28] but there is good evidence that several hours of hypoxia may produce the infarction even in the patient with heterozygous sickle cell disease.[44] It remains to be demonstrated whether a consistent decrease in oxygen saturation of central venous blood occurs as a major precipitating factor in crisis. If this be so, it must be due to either a decrease in cardiac output or to an increase in tissue metabolism. The malignant course of sickle cell disease in the presence of cardiac failure and the deleterious effect of alcohol, a known cardiotoxin, are consistent with the former[45];

the association of crisis with infection and its hypermetabolic state are consistent with the latter.[46]

Treatment

The record of treatment in sickle cell disease is not impressive. The only dependable measure has been the replacement of sickle cells by normal red cells. Exchange transfusion normalizes the patient except for residual vascular lesions and is particularly useful as an emergency procedure during delivery of the pregnant woman[47] or with life-threatening crises.[48] The maintenance of the hematocrit above 35 gm per cent virtually ends endogenous production of sickle cells for reasons previously discussed. It has proved possible to couple a donor on continuous oral iron therapy with a patient for the support of two blood volumes from one erythroid marrow as long as blood type incompatibility does not arise. It has been suggested that smaller amounts of transfused blood sufficient to maintain a proportion of 30 percent hemoglobin A-containing cells to 70 percent sickle hemoglobin cells may reduce the number of sickle cells in circulation and the viscosity, and prevent thrombotic manifestations.[49] Hyperbaric oxygen has been suggested to be of therapeutic value[50,51], but further evidence is required.

Fluid and electrolyte balances have been of concern. Saline depletion could depress cardiac output by its effect on plasma volume, whereas volume expansion with colloidal substances might increase it. Although beneficial effects have been reported from the administration of fluids and electrolytes,[52] there is no general agreement of its effectiveness. Acidosis has been shown to provoke crisis, although its role as a causative factor in spontaneous crisis is unclear[53-55].

The most promising line of therapy is the alteration of the hemoglobin molecule so as to prevent sickling at the molecular level.[56] Methemoglobin and carboxyhemoglobin have been produced in an attempt to reduce the amount of hemoglobin capable of sickling within the cell,[57,58] but these substances in themselves interfere with oxygen transport and have not appeared useful. Recently favorable effects have been reported with urea.[59,60] It appears that the active substance in the urea solution may be a transformation product, cyanate.[61] This substance by its specific binding to the hemoglobin molecule reduces sickling. Oxygen transport is maintained, although the oxygen dissociation curve is shifted to the left of normal. The usefulness of this substance in the treatment of sickle-cell anemia and its safety in man remains to be explored, but the possibility is promising.

The prevention of crisis is the ultimate objective of therapy, but there is a need to develop quantitative measurements of physiologic parameters of the amount of red cell stasis, of oxygen transport and of red cell kinetics in order to evaluate therapeutic efforts. It is possible that new forms of therapy will impose problems of their own, and these are best dealt with on the basis of a sound understanding of the pathophysiology of the disease.

REFERENCES

1. Murayama, M.: Molecular mechanism of red cell "sickling." *Science,* *153:*145, 1966.

2. Perutz, M.F.: Stereochemistry of cooperative effects in hemoglobin. *Nature* (Lond), *228:*726, 1970.

3. Bertles, J.F., Rabinowitz, R., Döbler, J.: Hemoglobin interaction: modification of solid phase composition in the sickling phenomenon. *Science, 169:*375, 1970.

4. Jensen, W.N., Rucknagel, D.L., Taylor, W.J.: *In vivo* study of the sickle cell phenomenon. *J Lab Clin Med,* 56:854, 1960.

5. Greenberg, M.S., Kass, E.H., Castle, W.B.: Studies on the destruction of red blood cells. XII. Factors influencing the role of S hemoglobin in the pathologic physiology of sickle cell anemia and related disorders. *J Clin Invest, 36:*833, 1957.

6. Harris, J.W., Brewster, H.H., Ham, T.H., Castle, W.B.: Studies on the destruction of red blood cells. X. The biophysics and biology of sickle-cell disease. *Arch Intern Med, 97:*145, 1956.

7. Griggs, R.C., Harris, J.W.: The biophysics of the variants of sickle-cell disease. *Arch Intern Med, 97:*315, 1956.

8. Lange, R.D., Minnich, V., Moore, C.V.: Effect of oxygen tension and of pH on the sickling and mechanical fragility of erythrocytes from patients with sickle cell anemia and the sickle cell trait. *J Lab Clin Med,* 37:789, 1951.

9. Perillie, P.E., Epstein, F.H.: Sickling phenomenon produced by hypertonic solutions: a possible explanation for the hyposthenuria of sicklemia. *J Clin Invest, 42:*570, 1963.

10. Diggs, L.W.: Sickle cell crises. *Am J Clin Pathol, 44:*1, 1965.

11. Walters, J.H.: Vascular occlusion in sickle cell disease. *Proc R Soc Med, 51:*646, 1958.

12. Bertles, J.F., Milner, P.F.A.: Irreversibly sickled erythrocytes: a consequence of the heterogeneous distribution of hemoglobin types in sickle-cell anemia. *J Clin Invest, 47:*1731, 1968.

13. Sergeant, G.R., Sergeant, B.E., Milner, P.F.: The irreversibly sickled cell; a determinant of haemolysis in sickle cell anemia. *Br J Haematol 17:*527, 1969.

14. Shotton, D., Crockett, C.L., Jr., Leavell, B.S.: Splenectomy in sickle cell anemia: Report of a case and review of the literature. *Blood, 6:*365, 1951.

15. Erlandson, M.E., Schulman, I., Smith, C.H.: Studies on congenital hemolytic syndromes. III. Rates of destruction and production of erythrocytes in sickle cell anemia. *Pediatrics, 25:*629, 1960.

16. Hathorn, M.: Patterns of red cell destruction in sickle cell anemia. *Br J Haematol, 13:*746, 1967.

17. Sprague, C.C., Paterson, J.C.S.: Role of the spleen and effect of splenectomy in sickle cell disease. *Blood, 13:*569, 1958.

18. McCurdy, P.R.: Erythrokinetics in abnormal hemoglobin syndromes. *Blood, 20:*686, 1962.

19. Motulsky, A.G., Casserd, F., Giblett, E.R., Broun, G.O., Jr., Finch, C.A.: Anemia and the spleen. *N Engl J Med, 259:*1164, 1215, 1958.

20. Charney, E., Miller, G.: Reticulocytopenia in sickle cell disease. Aplastic episodes in the course of sickle cell disease in children. *Am J Dis Child, 107:*450, 1964.

21. Tinsley, J.C., Jr., Moore, C.V., Dubach, R., Minnich, V., Grinstein, M.: The role of oxygen in the regulation of erythropoiesis. Depression of the rate of delivery of new red cells to the blood by high concentrations of inspired oxygen. *J Clin Invest, 28:*1544, 1949.

22. Donegan, C.C., Jr., MacIlwaine, W.A., Leavell, B.S.: Hematologic studies on patients with sickle cell anemia following multiple transfusions. *Am J Med, 17:*29, 1954.

23. Finch, C.A., Lenfant, C.: Oxygen transport in man. *N Engl J Med, 286:*407, 1972.

24. Charache, S., Grisolia, S., Fiedler, A.J., Hellegers, A.E.: Effect of 2,3-diphosphoglycerate on oxygen affinity of blood in sickle cell anemia. *J Clin Invest, 49:*806, 1970.

25. Leight, L., Snider, T.H., Clifford, G.L., Hellems, H.K.: Hemodynamic studies in sickle cell anemia. *Circulation, 10:*653, 1954.

26. Etteldorf, J.N., Tharp, C.P., Turner, M.D.: Studies on the cardiovascular dynamics in children with sickle cell anemia (abstract). *Am J Dis Child, 90:*571, 1955.

27. Heyman, A., Patterson, J.L., Jr., Duke, T.W.: Cerebral circulation and metabolism in sickle cell and other chronic anemias, with observations on the effects of oxygen inhalation. *J Clin Invest, 31:*824, 1952.

28. Sproule, B.J., Halden, E.R., Miller, W.F.: A study of cardiopulmonary alterations in patients with sickle cell disease and its variants. *J Clin Invest, 37:*486, 1958.

29. Gross, S., Godel, J.C.: Comparative studies of height and weight as a blood volume reference standard in normal children and children with sickle cell anemia. *Am J Clin Pathol, 55:*662, 1971.

30. Saxena, U.H., Scott, R.B., Ferguson, A.D.: Studies in sickle cell anemia. XXV. Observations on fluid intake and output. *J Pediatr, 69:*220, 1966.

31. Plunket, D.C., Leiken, S.L., LoPresti, J.M.: Renal radiologic changes in sickle cell anemia. *Pediatrics, 35:*955, 1965.

32. Berstein, J., Whitten, C.F.: A histologic appraisal of the kidney in sickle cell anemia. *Arch Pathol, 70:*407, 1960.

33. Paton, D.: The conjunctival sign of sickle cell disease. *Arch Ophthalmol, 68:*627, 1962.

34. Funahashi, T., Fink, A., Robinson, M., Watson, R.J.: Pathology of conjunctival vessels in sickle cell disease. A preliminary report. *Am J. Ophthalmol, 57:*713, 1964.

35. Charache, S., Page, D.L.: Infarction of bone marrow in the sickle cell disorders. *Ann Intern Med, 67:*1195, 1967.

36. Pearson, H.A., Spencer, R.P., Cornelius, E.A.: Functional asplenia in sickle-cell anemia. *N Engl J Med, 281:*923, 1969.

37. Statius van Eps, L.W., Schouten, H., la Porte-Wijsman, L.W., Struyker Boudier, A.M.: The influence of red blood cell transfusions on the hyposthenuria and renal hemodynamics of sickle-cell anemia. *Clin Chim Acta, 17:*449, 1967.

38. Pearson, H.A., Cornelius, E.A., Schwartz, A.D., Zelson, J.H., Wolfson, S.L., Spencer, R.P.: Transfusion-reversible functional asplenia in young children with sickle cell anemia. *N Engl J Med, 283:*334, 1970.

39. Keitel, H.G., Thompson, D., Itano, H.A.: Hyposthenuria in sickle cell anemia: a reversible renal defect. *J Clin Invest, 35:*998, 1956.

40. Statius van Eps, L.W., Pinedo-Veels, C., de Vries, G.H., de Koning, J.: Nature of concentrating defect in sickle cell nephropathy. Microradioangiographic studies. *Lancet, 1:*450, 1970.

41. Aperia, A.C.: The influence of arterial PO_2 on renal tissue PO_2. *Acta Physiol Scand, 75:*353, 1969.

42. Perillie, P.E., Epstein, F.H.: Sickling phenomenon produced by hypertonic solutions: a possible explanation for the hyposthenuria of sicklemia. *J Clin Invest, 42:*570, 1963.

43. Messer, M.J., Harris, J.W.: Filtration characteristics of sickle cells: rate of alteration of filterability after deoxygenation and reoxygenation, and correlations with sickling and unsickling. *J Lab Clin Med, 76:*537, 1970.

44. Smith, E.W., Conley, C.L.: Sicklemia and infarction of the spleen during aerial flight. Electrophoresis of the hemoglobin in 15 cases. *Bull Johns Hopkins Hosp, 96:*35, 1955.

45. Rubler, S., Fleischer, R.A.: Sickle cell states and cardiomyopathy. Sudden death due to pulmonary thrombosis and infarction. *Am J Cardiol, 19:*867, 1967.

46. Wright, C.-S., Gardner, E., Jr.: A study of the role of acute infections in precipitating crises in chronic hemolytic states. *Ann Intern Med, 52:*530, 1960.

47. Ricks, P., Jr.: Further experience with exchange transfusion in sickle cell anemia and pregnancy. *Am J Obstet Gynecol, 100:*1087, 1968.

48. Brody, J.I., Goldsmith, M.H., Park, S.K., Soltys, S.D.: Symptomatic crises of sickle cell anemia treated by limited exchange transfusion. *Ann Intern Med, 72:*327, 1970.

49. Anderson, R., Cassell, M., Mullinax, G. L., Chaplin, H., Jr.: Effect of normal cells in viscosity of sickle cell blood. *In vitro* studies and report of six years' experience with a prophylactic program of "partial exchange transfusion." *Arch Intern Med, 111:*286, 1963.

50. Laszlo, J., Obenour, W., Jr., Saltzman, H.A.: Effects of hyperbaric oxygenation on sickle syndromes. *South Med J, 62:*453, 1969.

51. Reynolds, J.D.H.: Painful sickle-cell crisis. Successful treatment with hyperbaric oxygen therapy. *JAMA, 216:*1977, 1971.

52. Barreras, L., Diggs, L.W.: Sodium citrate orally for painful sickle cell crises. *JAMA, 215:*762, 1971.

53. Greenberg, M.S., Kass, E.H.: Studies on the destruction of red blood cells. XIII. Observations on the role of pH in the pathogenesis and treatment of painful crisis in sickle cell disease. *Arch Intern Med, 101:*355, 1958.

54. Barreras, L., Diggs, L.W.: Bicarbonates, pH and percentage of sickled cells in venous blood of patients in sickle cell crisis. *Am J Med Sci, 247:*710, 1964.

55. Ho Ping Kong, H., Alleyne, G.A.O.: Acid-base status of adults with sickle cell anemia. *Br Med J, 3:*271, 1969.

56. Kosower, E.M., Kosower, N.S., LaCourse, P.C.: The solubilization of deoxyhemoglobin S. *Proc Natl Acad Sci USA, 57:*39, 1967.

57. Purugganan, H.B., McElfresh, A.E.: Failure of carbonmonoxy sickle cell haemoglobin to alter the sickle state. *Lancet, 1:*79, 1964.

58. Beutler, E.: The effect of methemoglobin formation in sickle cell disease. *J Clin Invest, 40:*1856, 1961.

59. Nalbandian, R.M., Shultz, G., Lusher, J.M., Anderson, J.W., Henry, R.L.: Sickle cell crisis terminated by intravenous urea in sugar solutions—a preliminary report. *Am J Med Sci, 261:*309, 1971.

60. McCurdy, P.R., Mahmood, L.: Urea therapy for sickle cell disease (abstract). *Blood, 36:*841, 1970.

61. Cerami, A., Manning, J.M.: Potassium cyanate as an inhibitor of the sickling of erythrocytes *in vitro. Proc Natl Acad Sci USA, 68:*1180, 1971.

Chapter 9

SICKLE CELL ANEMIA
Conquest of a Molecular Disease

ROBERT M. NALBANDIAN

Sickle cell anemia is a cruel, crippling, episodic disease. Although it lingers, it is lethal for its victims, 99 per cent of whom are black. The epochal paper of Pauling and associates[1] formulated and supported by experimental evidence the penetrating concept that sickle cell anemia was caused by genetically controlled structural features of an abnormal hemoglobin molecule. According to Pauling this disease now has "a known molecular basis for pathogenesis, a molecular basis for diagnosis, and a molecular basis for treatment."[2] His statement is supported by a series of brilliant investigations since 1949 on hemoglobin at the molecular level. Murayama of the National Institutes of Health achieved a major, significant advance when, based upon his construction of a precision scale model of the hemoglobin molecule, he elucidated his hypothesis[3,4] for the molecular mechanism of sickling, recently only slightly modified by him.[2] Our inferences and deductions, made from the assumption that the modified Murayama hypothesis was correct, have produced an astonishing number of important discoveries, strengthening thereby the validity of his hypothesis very substantially. As a consequence, for the first time in medicine, we have a uniquely comprehensive view of a lethal disease extending as a continuous spectrum from the aberrant hemoglobin molecule to the clinical level of diagnosis and treatment in the afflicted patient.

Reprinted with permission from the *Journal of the National Medical Association,* January, 1972.

These recent advances, all derived from the Murayama hypothesis, are discussed in detail elsewhere.[2,5,8]

1. The Murayama test is the first specific test with a molecular basis for the detection of S hemoglobin.[2,5,8]

2. A therapeutic molecular strategy directed at the sickling event was developed.[2,5-7] This consisted of mounting a chemical attack on the implicated hydrophobic bonds between interacting tetramers of S hemoglobin.

3. In the search for a chemical desickling agent the specifications of molecular properties were first derived from molecular theory and *preceded* the selection of urea.[2,5]

4. An automated dithionite test[10] and a tube version,[9] each with a molecular basis for the detection of hemoglobin S, have been developed, appropriate for mass screening of large human populations. The automated method processes 120 specimens per hour at a reagent cost of two cents each. The testing techniques have been shown to be entirely accurate in two extended field trials: 1) more than 23,000 soldiers examined at the U. S. Army Medical Research Laboratory at Fort Knox, Kentucky and 2) over 5000 black school children and indicated blood relatives in Grand Rapids, Michigan.

5. Experimental work has led directly to the design of successful clinical protocols for the use of intravenous urea in the treatment of sickle cell crisis[2,6] and the use of oral urea in the prophylactic treatment of sickle cell disease.[2,7]

The therapeutic decision *deduced* from molecular information to use urea in the treatment of sickle cell disease moved Pauling to write:[2] "Most methods of therapy have been empirical in origin. We might consider that medicine is now entering a new stage in which detailed molecular understanding of the nature of disease will be used effectively in the search for therapeutic methods." The protocols[2,5-7] which we have published for the intravenous and oral modes of urea therapy in the treatment of sickle cell disease were evolved with great care over the past two years, drawing upon the collected experience of several clinicians at several medical centers. The treatment is safe and effective IF the protocols are faithfully followed in all particulars. Urea, even though produced in the liver and endogenous to the body, when used as a pharmaceutical agent may, like any other agent, be mishandled with adverse consequences for the patient. Hence, faithful compliance with the provisions of the published protocols is essential if therapeutic failures and medical misadventures are to be avoided.

These investigations of the therapeutic use of urea for sickle cell disease, shown to be safe and effective, are now in the final stage of evaluation, namely, controlled randomized studies. Substantial funding will be required to expedite the last phase of this research. Our clinical protocols are published[2,5-7] for the attention of serious students of this disease so that evaluation of this chemotherapeutic modality may proceed at an accelerated pace by the use of identical, reliable protocols simultaneously at independent medical centers. Until such studies have been completed and reported, these protocols are not intended for general medical use. Pauling states[2] that the urea modality of treatment "offers a great promise for the future. The suffering of the sickle cell homozygotes can be and should be decreased by the use of methods of therapy" as described.

While the conquest of this disease is of vital concern to 500,000 American blacks and to millions of Africans and non-blacks elsewhere in the world there are even more profound aspects to this body of research. Lethal effects of a genetic disease have ostensibly been conquered by chemical methods deduced from a fund of specific, highly sophisticated molecular information. Our attention was directed toward the incorrect structure of the genetic product, S hemoglobin, rather than toward the incorrect code in the gene. By chemical manipulation of the hemoglobin S molecule with urea, the deadly property of sickling was inhibited without interference with the critically essential function of oxygen transport. Certainly, this is exquisitely delicate molecular remodeling. The methods culminating in the chemotherapeutic use of urea in sickle cell disease now become a model for the conquest of other genetic disease, well before the era of genetic engineering.

Investigators are invited to turn their attention to these recent innovative diagnostic and therapeutic advances in sickle cell anemia at the molecular level of reference. There are no final answers in medicine. Imminent discoveries beckon us all onward.

REFERENCES

1. Pauling, L., Itano, H.A., Singer, S.J., and Wells, I.C.: Sickle cell anemia, a molecular disease. *Science, 110:*543, 1949.

2. Nalbandian, R.M. (Ed.): *Molecular Aspects of Sickle-Cell Hemoglobin: Clinical Applications.* Springfield, Ill., Thomas, 1971.

3. Listing of U. S. Army Medical Research Laboratory Reports No. 893 through 898. *N Engl J Med, 284:*165, 1971.

4. Murayama, M.: Molecular mechanism of red cell "sickling." *Science, 153:*145, 1966.

5. Murayama, M.: Structure of sickle-cell hemoglobin and molecular mechanism of the sickling phenomenon. *Clin Chem, 14:*578, 1967.

6. Nalbandian, R.M., Shultz, G., Lusher, J.M., Anderson, J.W., and Henry, R.L.: Oral urea and the prophylactic treatment of sickle cell disease—a preliminary report. *Am J Med Sci, 261:*325, 1971.

7. Nalbandian, R.M., Anderson, J.W., Lusher, J.M., Agustsson, A., and Henry, R.L.: Oral urea and the prophylactic treatment of sickle cell disease—a preliminary report. *Am J Med Sci, 261:*325, 1971.

8. Nichols, B.M., Nalbandian, R.M., Henry, R.L., Wolff, P.L., and Camp, F.R., Jr.: Murayama test for hemoglobin S: Simplification in technique. *Clin Chem, 17:*1057, 1971.

9. Nalbandian, R.M., Nichols, B.M., Camp, F.R., Jr., Lusher, J.M., Conte, N.F., and Henry, R.L.: Dithionite tube test—a rapid, inexpensive technique for the detection of hemoglobin S and non-S sickling hemoglobin. *Clin Chem, 17:*1028, 1971.

10. Nalbandian, R.M., Nichols, B.M., Camp, F.R., Jr., Lusher, J.M., Conte, N.F., and Henry, R.L.: Automated dithionite test for the rapid, inexpensive detection of hemoglobin S and non-S sickling hemoglobinopathies. *Clin Chem, 17:*1033, 1971.

Chapter 10

HEALTH CARE PRIORITY
AND SICKLE CELL ANEMIA

ROBERT B. SCOTT

Since its clinical description 60 years ago[1] sickle cell anemia has become a well-known clinical entity. The molecular alteration in the hemoglobin molecule which results in the disease was discovered 20 years ago[2] and has stimulated many biochemists toward productive study of the structure and function of the molecule. Likewise, study of the genetics of sickle cell trait, and particularly its protection against malaria, has elucidated an important genetic principle, and explains why a hereditary trait could become so common among a population. What has been little appreciated, despite all this study and interest, is the real importance of the disease as a community health problem.

Sickle cell anemia is actually one of the most common long-term illnesses of Negro children. It occurs in about one in 500 Negro births. In Table 10-I, its incidence is compared

TABLE 10-I

INCIDENCE OF SOME IMPORTANT CHILDHOOD DISEASES

Sickle cell anemia	1 : 500	Negro births
Diabetes mellitus	1 : 2,500	Births[13] (2 : 1 White: Negro)[5]
Acute leukemia	1 : 2,880	Children under 15[14] (majority white)[6]
Cystic fibrosis	1 : 2,940	Births[15] (98% white)[3]
Muscular dystrophy	1 : 5,000	Births[7]
Phenylketonuria	1 : 10,000	White births[4]

Abridged and reprinted with permission from the *Journal of the American Medical Association*, October 26, 1970.

Mortality data were obtained from the National Center for Health Statistics, Washington, D.C.

with that of some other well-known serious childhood disorders. All except acute leukemia are hereditary. In the United States, sickle cell anemia occurs almost entirely among Negroes, although it may occur in white families of Mediterranean origin. Conversely, 98 per cent of patients with cystic fibrosis are white[3] and phenylketonuria (PKU) is virtually unknown among Negroes.[4] Childhood diabetes[5] and leukemia[6] occur more often among white persons, and muscular dystrophy is believed to occur with equal frequency in both races.[7] Health professionals have generally failed to recognize sickle cell anemia as a major community health concern, and consequently the public has been poorly informed. A recent survey revealed that only three out of ten adult Negros had ever heard of the illness.[8]

The treatment of patients with sickle cell anemia remains a difficult clinical problem, since there is no cure and no truly effective management.

Although longevity has no doubt improved for these patients, still only half with homozygous sickle cell anemia survive to adulthood. The nationwide data for 1967 also include mortality related to sickle cell trait, but the great majority of deaths no doubt result from sickle cell anemia. Sickle cell trait is associated with serious complications only under unusual circumstances and individuals with sickle cell trait have a normal life expectancy.[9]

Given the fact that sickle cell anemia is a serious, incurable disease which occurs frequently, one then may ask what efforts are being made to remedy the problem? Specifically, what is being done in basic research to seek a cure of the disease, what is being done in clinical investigation to find a more effective management for the illness, and what steps are being taken to prevent the illness?

An even more pertinent question would be, what priority does this problem deserve and what priority does it presently receive in the distribution of health care resources? Priority must be determined by the prevalence and severity of an illness. It also can be gauged by existing standards of support given to similar diseases whose importance is better understood.

There are other hereditary illnesses which are similar in incidence and severity but for which there are effective nationwide campaigns to support patient care and research. Good examples include muscular dystrophy, cystic fibrosis, and PKU. That these illnesses are of incidence similar to sickle cell anemia is shown in Table 10-II. These figures are derived from the incidence at birth of these conditions related to the total number of white and Negro births in the year 1967 in the United States. Estimated new cases of sickle cell anemia, cystic fibrosis, and muscular dystrophy are of similar order of magnitude, and there are somewhat fewer patients with phenylketonuria.

The number of white births in the United States with sickle cell anemia is small and presently undetermined with accuracy. National mortality statistics for patients with sickle cell anemia or with sickle cell trait show that 1.1 percent of deaths due to these causes are listed as white during the years 1962 to 1967.

Since sickle cell anemia occurs in numbers comparable to some diseases which have been widely publicized in recent years, how much public and professional support does sickle cell anemia receive compared to the support for these other categories? First, there is no nationwide volunteer organization devoted to sickle cell anemia. There are groups in cities throughout the country which are active and no doubt increasing in effectiveness but not coordinated nationwide. In Los Angeles, there is the Sickle Cell Disease Research Foundation; in New York, the Foundation for Research and Education in Sickle Cell Disease; in Washington, D.C., the Association for Research and Sickle Cell Anemia; in Memphis, Tenn. the National Sickle Cell Anemia Foundation; in Richmond,

TABLE 10-II
ESTIMATED NEW CASES IN U.S. 1967*

	Sickle Cell Anemia	Cystic Fibrosis	Muscular Dystrophy	Phenylketonuria
Negro	1,142	17	114	0
White	13	1,189	699	350
Total	1,155	1,206	813	350

* US births, 1967: 3.496 × 10⁶ white; 0.571 × 10⁶ Negro.

Va. the Virginia Sickle Cell Anemia Awareness Program (VaSCAP), and similar groups in other cities throughout the country. Nationwide volunteer organizations involved in cystic fibrosis and muscular dystrophy are quite prominent and effective. The revenues of these volunteer groups in 1968 were as follows: muscular dystrophy, $7,203,000; cystic fibrosis, $1,998,716; sickle cell anemia, an estimated $50,000. The sickle cell anemia estimate is based on data supplied by several of the larger local groups. It is obvious that the volunteer revenues for this cause lag far behind those for other similarly important illnesses.

Another measure of support is that of research grant support by the National Institutes of Health. Grants relating to a specific disease category depend on the interest of individual investigators in a given subject, by the priority policies of the advisory councils in the National Institutes of Health, and in some cases by funds earmarked for certain disease categories. From the listings of the Research Grants Index[10] for fiscal year 1968, a selected group of important childhood diseases were listed in Table 10-III. Sickle cell anemia finds a low position in the grant support and is exceeded by such exceedingly rare conditions as glycogen storage diseases.

These data argue for the need for support for sickle cell anemia and the need for increased priority and attention by both the public and the health professions. Where to place emphasis for the most effective use of funds and effort is another important question. Since the majority of Negroes now live in metropolitan areas, sickle cell anemia becomes

TABLE 10-III
NIH GRANT SUPPORT FOR
SELECTED CHILDHOOD DISEASES, 1968

Diseases	No. of Grants
Acute leukemia	92
Muscular dystrophy	66
Cystic fibrosis	65
Phenylketonuria	41
Thalassemia	32
Glycogenoses	23
Sickle cell anemia	22

TABLE 10-IV
PREVALENCE ESTIMATES: SELECTED LONG-TERM ILLNESSES
(WHITE AND NEGRO CASES/100,000 CHILDREN)

Diagnosis	Philadelphia 32% Negro	Richmond, Va 44% Negro	Detroit 47% Negro	Washington, DC 68% Negro
Sickle cell anemia[5]	61	84	89	129
Diabetes mellitus[5]	50	47	46	39
Nephrosis[5]	15	16	16	16
Cystic fibrosis[3,5]	10	8	8	5

a major health consideration for those involved in urban community health. In cities with sizeable Negro populations, sickle cell anemia is not just another significant health problem but one of the more prevalent health problems. The data in Table 10-IV show prevalence estimates based on both white and black children combined. Sickle cell anemia is compared to several other important childhood conditions for which there are good prevalence data. The estimates are based on data obtained in the Erie County, New York, study of long-term childhood illness.[5] In the Negro population, sickle cell anemia has a prevalence of 190 cases per 100,000 children under the age of 16 years. Diabetes mellitus occurs somewhat more frequently in white than black children and childhood nephrosis occurs with about equal frequency in the two races. In Philadelphia, with its 32 per cent Negro population, sickle cell anemia is at least as prominent as childhood diabetes. With a proportionate increase in Negro population, sickle cell anemia becomes vastly more important in that community's health consideration. In Washington, D.C., where Negroes comprise 68 per cent of the population, sickle cell anemia far exceeds childhood diabetes, nephrosis, or cystic fibrosis as a cause of illness. At present, seven of the ten largest cities in the nation have more than 30 per cent Negro population.[11]

Having shown evidence that sickle cell anemia is an important but inadequately supported health concern, the next consideration would be to determine which approaches might be most feasible and most likely to produce tangible results. Obviously no single course of action or emphasis would provide a remedy to all the aspects of the problem. Patient care, early diagnosis of patients, and rehabilitation can be given special attention through special clinics. But without available cure or improved therapy, these benefits will necessarily be somewhat limited.

Research is under way and can be stimulated further to learn the mechanisms of the sickling process and how it might be prevented. More study needs to be done to elucidate the mechanisms involved in switching from fetal to adult hemoglobin so that this mechanism might be reversed in the adult and to overcome the difficult problems of rejection involved in attempts to transplant normal bone marrow into patients.

Another alternative to consider is prevention through genetic counseling. In the past, genetic counseling has not been successfully applied in sickle cell disease or in other major hereditary illnesses except sporadically. There have been a number of reasons for this lack of success. The fact that both parents are heterozygotes for a recessive trait is usually determined only when they produce a child with the illness. Only rarely have such parents had the opportunity of knowing in advance of marriage or in advance of childbearing that they were trait carriers. Such information can only be made available if there is a suitable test to determine the carrier state. The test for sickle cell trait has been available for many years[12] but never widely applied in conjunction with genetic counselling. Only in recent years have the concepts of heredity and heritable diseases been widely taught below the college level, thus, not widely disseminated. Previous generations of parents had little understanding of these illnesses. Family planning has until very recently been either unacceptable to large segments of the public or ineffective.

Today young people are learning principles of heredity in high school, and family planning has become acceptable and more effective. Lack of awareness of the illness is a lesser problem to solve today because of the effectiveness of educational and communication media. The most important factor which would make a preventive program effective would be the early knowledge of trait-carrying. If screening were offered prior to marriageable age, those who were found to carry an abnormal hemoglobin gene could be counselled to be sure that their mates were tested at the time of marriage. Only in this way, can heterozygote pairs (pairs of parents each carrying an abnormal hemoglobin gene) be detected and only in this way can informed decisions be made about childbearing among parents at risk.

Approximately one in 12 carries the sickle trait, so the chance of a pair of parents both carrying the trait is one in 144. This small number of parent pairs (approximately 0.7% of all Negro families) are at risk of having children with this tragic disease. Whether a young couple will decide to have no children or plan a limited family size or disregard the knowledge of the risk would be entirely their own decision, one which no one could make for them. However, the *opportunity* to protect their families from the tragedy of sickle cell anemia has not been offered.

The data presented here attempt to define a major public health consideration, to suggest its neglect in the past, and to suggest avenues of approach which can be given better emphasis. It is not only because of its neglect that sickle cell anemia deserves higher priority. With the availability of a simple test for sickle trait carriers which makes mass screening possible, this may be the first hereditary illness which could be controlled by genetic counselling. As suitable screening tests are developed for other conditions such as cystic fibrosis or muscular dystrophy, they too can be approached with similar preventive methods. Success in ameliorating one hereditary illness will mean that control of any hereditary illness will be limited only by the development of suitable tests for accurate mass screening of trait carriers.

REFERENCES

1. Herrick, J.B.: Peculiar elongated and sickle-shaped red blood corpuscles in a case of severe anemia. *Arch Intern Med, 6:*517–521, 1910.

2. Pauling, L., Itano, H.A., Singer, S.J., et al: Sickle-cell anemia: A molecular disease. *Science, 110:*543–548, 1949.

3. diSant' Agnese, P.A., Talamo, R.C.: Pathogenesis and physiopathology of cystic fibrosis of the pancreas (mucoviscidosis). *N Engl J Med,* 277:1287–1294, 1967.

4. Hsia, D.Y.: *Inborn Errors of Metabolism,* 2nd ed. Chicago, Year Bk Med, 1966, Part 1, p. 136.

5. Sultz, H.A., Schlesinger, E.R., and Mosher, W.E.: The Erie County survey of long-term childhood illness: II. Incidence and prevalence. *Am J Public Health,* 58:491–498, 1968.

6. Ederer, F., Miller, R.W., Scotto, J.: US childhood cancer mortality patterns, 1950–1959: Etiologic implications. *JAMA, 192:*593–596, 1965.

7. Morton, N.E., Chung, C.S., Peters, H.A.: Genetics of muscular dystrophy. In Bourne, G.H., Golarz, N. (Eds.): *Muscular Dystrophy in Man and Animals.* New York, Hafner, 1963, pp. 323–365.

8. Lane, J.C., Scott, R.B.: Awareness of sickle-cell anemia among Negroes in Richmond, Va. *Public Health Rep,* 84:949–953, 1969.

9. McCormick, W.F., Kashgarian, M.: Abnormal hemoglobins: V. Age at death of patients with sickle cell trait. *Am J Hum Genet,* 17:101–103, 1965.

10. Public Health Service: *Research Grants Index,* fiscal year 1968, No. 925. U.S. Government Printing Office, 1968.

11. *Congressional Quarterly Weekly Reports,* 27:1683, 1969.

12. Daland, G.A., Castle, W.B.: A simple and rapid method for demonstrating sickling of the red blood cells: The use of reducing agents. *J Lab Clin Med,* 33:1082–1088, 1948.

13. White, P.: Juvenile diabetes. In Williams, R.H. (Ed.): *Diabetes.* New York, Paul B. Hoeber, 1960, pp. 381–388.

14. Miller, R.W.: Persons with exceptionally high risk of leukemia. *Cancer Res,* 27:2420–2423, 1967.

15. Sultz, H.A., Schlesinger, E.R., and Mosher, W.E.: The Erie County survey of long-term childhood illness: I. Methodology. *Am J Public Health,* 56:1461–1469, 1966.

Chapter 11

SICKLE CELL DISEASE:
MEETING A NEED

DOLORES E. JACKSON

Sickle cell disease is the most common inherited disorder in the United States.[6]

Ms. Jackson, why don't they do for sickle cell anemia what they're doing for muscular dystrophy and cerebral palsy? You never even hear about sickle cell.

THE NEED

If the Borough of Brooklyn were a separate entity it would be the fourth largest city in the United States, with a population of 2.6 million people. Blacks make up about one quarter of that population—656,000. Forty percent of New York City's black people now live in Brooklyn.

The majority of Brooklyn's black people live in a concentrated area that has been designated as "central Brooklyn." The Kings County Hospital—Downstate Medical Center is the major supplier of health care to this centralized population. Many of the original observations on various clinical manifestations of sickle cell disease originated at Kings County Hospital under the leadership of the late Janet Watson, M.D. The Pediatric Outpatient Service is one of the largest in the country, serving predominantly blacks and Puerto Ricans—the "at risk" population for sickle cell disease. In 1970 patient visits to the area exceeded 180,000; more than two to three patients per day were seen with acute sickle-cell crises.

Prior to 1970, about 225 children with sickle cell disease

Abridged and reprinted with permission from *Nursing Clinics of North America*, December, 1972.

were treated at the Hematology Clinic. I noted, through reviewing charts and laboratory slips, about another 65 to 75 patients who were just receiving "crisis" care (emergency room visit for an acute problem).

The anguish of the parents of children with sickle cell disease impressed me deeply. I heard tales of what I considered "poor practice" perpetrated upon them by the providers of health care. Alienation appeared to be the prevailing attitude of these parents. A lack of understanding of the condition, combined with frequent abuse or apathy by those from whom they sought help, compounded the awesome burden of the families with these chronically ill children.

I, too, began to feel helpless. I tried to correct their misconceptions and allay their fears, but that was not enough. I recalled how much support parents of other children with "more popular"[1] chronic illnesses received when I referred them to the appropriate organizations. I needed somewhere to refer these parents. I tried to locate a sickle cell parents' club; I called other hospitals, I searched agencies' directories, and could not find one. Someone said, "Do it yourself."

General health care for many of this group had been fragmented, partly because the health problems of children with sickle-cell disease are complex. Their dental care is often a problem because some dentists do not understand the hemic murmur and/or the necessary caution regarding anesthesia. Immunization status often lapses because of frequent upper respiratory infections; school adjustment suffers because of frequent absences and lack of understanding of the disease entity by school personnel; family relationships are strained by the emotional and financial stress of the unpredictable, frequent crises of this inherited disorder. The need for care by others besides the hematologist was apparent and an interdisciplinary approach was required.

Therefore, the services and facilities of the Pediatric Comprehensive Care Clinic were made available to children with sickle cell disease about two years ago. There are now over 400 children with sickle cell disease receiving continuous care at this facility. The pediatric sickle cell clinic stimulated the establishment of an adult sickle cell anemia clinic which has a registration of over 250 patients. The clinics' sessions meet simultaneously. The parents, and therefore the patients, report that they feel better knowing that there are now special facilities to deal with their special needs.

THE PROBLEM

Sickle cell disease is a comprehensive term used to include all those hereditary disorders whose clinical, hematologic, and pathologic features are related to the presence of sickle hemoglobin (hemoglobin S) in the red cells. In this country the most common conditions are: homozygous sickle cell anemia (S-S); sickle cell thalassemia; and sickle cell hemoglobin C disease.[16]

It is a hereditary disorder with highest incidence in the United States among blacks. Puerto Ricans, and persons of Greek, Italian, Spanish, French, Turkish, North African, Middle Eastern, and Indian ancestry also may be affected.

The clinical syndrome was first described to the American medical community in 1910 by J.B. Herrick, when upon examining the blood smear of a black student from the West Indies with chronic anemia, he noticed elongated and sickle-shaped red blood corpuscles.[4]

Sickling

The sickling phenomenon is attributed to a mutant gene which is responsible for the synthesis of hemoglobin that is different from normal hemoglobin. Until sickling occurs, the affected red cells are indistinguishable from the normal biconcave erythrocytes. The basic abnormality of the sickle red cell resides in the hemoglobin.[9]

Hemoglobin, the coloring matter of red corpuscles, is composed of a pigment (heme), which accounts for the characteristic red color, and a protein, globin. Abnormalities in the globin fraction, which is comprised of two beta chains and two alpha chains, has been shown by investigators, to be responsible for the characteristics of sickle-cell disease. [5,7] That is, each hemoglobin molecule consists of 574 amino acids. Hemoglobin S, the hemoglobin present in sickle cell defect, differs from hemoglobin A, the normal type of hemoglobin, only in the substitution of one amino acid for another. Valine instead of glutamic acid resides in the sixth position of the beta chains. This is the sole abnormality of hemoglobin S. All clinical manifestations of sickle cell disease are presumably attributable to this single alteration in the molecular structure of hemoglobin.[4]

This change of amino acids causes a change in the electric charge of the hemoglobin molecule and permits separation and identification by electrophoresis (thereby establishing a method of differential diagnosis). The electric charge of the hemoglobin molecule determines its rate of mobility under the influence of an electric current (electrophoresis). For example, hemoglobin S moves more slowly than hemoglobin A but more rapidly than hemoglobin C, another abnormal type of hemoglobin. [9,15]

The intrinsic features of the sickling mechanism become visible when hemoglobin is reduced, following exposure to low oxygen tensions or pH. The sickling of red cells with defective hemoglobin is rapid and the hemoglobin assumes a filamentous form. When reduced, hemoglobin S tends to come out of solution in the form of spindle-shaped microcrystals, forming a gel. Investigators believe that this distortion of the cell is caused by the formation of "intermolecular hydrophobic bonds."[7]

The Sickle Hemoglobinopathies

SICKLE TRAIT. The sickle cell trait is present in those individuals who are heterozygous for the gene for sickling and represents a combination of sickle hemoglobin and normal hemoglobin. The prevalence of the trait is reported in the literature as anywhere from 8 to 12 percent in the black population.

HOMOZYGOUS S. In persons with sickle cell anemia the character for sickling is present in the homozygous state and therefore sickling genes have been inherited from both parents. The frequency of this type of disease is reported as 1 in 400 or 1 in 500 in black Americans.

SICKLE-HEMOGLOBIN C. Sickle cell hemoglobin C disease is caused by simultaneous presence of the gene for sickle hemoglobin and the gene for hemoglobin C. This variant of sickle cell disease is second in frequency to classic sickle cell anemia (S-S) among Afro-Americans.

SICKLE CELL-THALASSEMIA. Sickle cell thalassemia disease is a combination of sickle cell trait and beta thalassemia trait. Thalassemia, or Mediterranean anemia, is still another hereditary condition in which the hemoglobin is defective, and the principal type is that in which the defect is in the beta chain of the globin. Sickle cell thalassemia accounts for most of the cases of sickle cell disease in nonblacks, usually those of Greek or Italian origin, but it is present in blacks also.

Pathogenesis

The varied manifestations of sickle cell disease result from the insolubility of reduced sickle hemoglobin (this is also the rationale for some screening test solutions) and the formation of sickle shaped cells, which follows exposure to lowered oxygen tension in the tissues.

The entanglement and enmeshing of these rigid and inflexible sickle cells with one another result in an increased viscosity of the whole blood. The sickling and increased blood viscosity combine to produce capillary stasis, the formation of masses and plugs of impacted red cells, thrombi, vascular occlusion, infarction, and ischemic necrosis. Infection presumably increases plasma viscosity and causes an extreme degree of stasis of the red cells.[16]

In sickle hemoglobin C disease, the presence of a normal or near normal hemoglobin level instead of an anemia causes these patients to be more susceptible to thrombosis and infarction.

Sickle cells are extremely fragile. The shortened life span of the cells, during movement in the circulation and passage through the organs, leads to a hemolytic anemia. The accelerated rate of destruction of RBC's together with an increased rate of production establishes an equilibrium at a hemoglobin level lower than that of normal subjects. In sickle hemoglobin C disease the half life of the RBC is not so greatly shortened, hence the normal or almost normal hemoglobin level.

The spleen removes red cells with abnormal hemoglobin from the circulation. Therefore, enlargement of the spleen may be associated with an increased rate of red cell destruction and a stagnation or pooling of the blood in this organ.

Clinical Manifestations

Sickle Cell Trait

Sickle cell trait is not a disease (in the usual meaning of the word) because it is almost impossible to distinguish clinically, under normal circumstances, between a person with normal hemoglobin (AA) and one with sickle cell trait (SA). The red cells of individuals with sickle trait are almost normal, unless and until the blood is partially deoxygenated. The hemoglobin and the hematocrit are also within normal limits.

Sickling can be produced in the laboratory by mixing a drop of fresh blood with a reducing agent such as sodium metabisulfite (sickle cell preparation). Sickling is slower in persons with the trait than those persons with the disease, and the cells form a holly leaf appearance rather than the typical crescent shape.

Persons with the trait are not anemic, show no physical abnormalities, and are usually asymptomatic. Occasionally they may experience an incapability of concentrating urine, gross hematuria, acute pyelonephritis, priapism, and retinal hemorrhage. Splenic infarction has also been reported in sickle trait individuals resulting from vascular occlusion at moderate and high altitudes during flight.

The black community became alarmed when the sudden deaths of four black recruits were attributed to the combination of their having the trait for sickling and the strenuous exercises of basic training at a high altitude camp.[1] This caused many to move to establish sickle cell trait as a cause for draft deferment.

Homozygous Sickle Cell Disease

Sickle cell anemia (SS) is by far the most common form of sickle cell disease.

INFANCY. Although sickle cell anemia develops at conception, the infant is generally symptom-free because of the temporary presence of elevated levels of fetal hemoglobin (hemoglobin F), which tends to prevent the symptoms. The diagnosis is generally made (depending upon the astuteness of the medical facility) during the preschool period. The average age of onset, according to some authors, is about two years; however, there are several infants under six months receiving care at our medical center. Some signs and symptoms of infants with the disease are: concurrent infection, failure to thrive, irritability and colic, fever, swelling of hands and/or feet, abdominal distention, jaundice, pallor, nausea and vomiting.

Physical examination may reveal cardiac murmur, hepatomegaly, splenomegaly, and cardiac enlargement on X-ray. The hemoglobin level is generally low, under 9 grams per cu. ml.

The serious and sometimes fatal complications of SCA during this period are infections and hemolytic crises. To illustrate the susceptibility to infections, one of the clinic's patients had had pneumonia thirteen times and meningitis three times before he entered kindergarten.

Parents are taught to observe for signs of a drop in hemoglobin in their already anemic infant: conjunctival and palmar pallor, listlessness, and/or refusal to eat or drink. Observation of these symptoms could possibly indicate the life-threatening "sequestration crisis," in which an accelerated rate of splenic function results in a sudden, severe drop in hemoglobin level and little time to get to the hospital. It is essential that these parents be able to participate intelligently in their child's care.

CHILDREN. In children over two years, the most common complaints are joint, back, and abdominal pain. The child generally immobilizes the affected area. Children also commonly suffer vomiting, fever, frequent upper respiratory infections, fatigability, and anorexia.

Physical findings vary and may include: marked pallor of mucous membranes; greenish yellow discoloration of the sclera; lymphadenopathy; cardiac enlargement; blindness (retinal hemorrhage); aseptic necrosis of femoral head; ulcers of inner aspect of ankle; ascites; joint swelling; cholelithiasis; hemiplegia; quadriplegia; nocturia; enuresis; epistaxis. The spleen, which is often enlarged in young children, atrophies with advancing age.

The painful or thrombotic crisis, which is caused by the intertwining of sickle cells resulting in a clogging of the small capillaries of the body, and the aplastic crisis, where a fall in the rate of production of RBC's leads to an aggravation of the anemia, are more common in childhood than in infancy or later life.

Physical appearance. Some children with SCA have a characteristic appearance. They are asthenic, with increased arm span, disproportion between the length of the trunk and the legs, and long tapering fingers. They generally appear younger than their chronologic age, and some show retardation in secondary sexual characteristics with late onset of menarche and puberty. They may also exhibit frontal bossing, prominent upper central incisor teeth, and unusual facial appearance.[16]

Sickle Cell Hemoglobin C Disease

The next most common type of sickle cell disease among blacks is hemoglobin S-C disease. The symptoms and the clinical picture are less severe than those of sickle cell anemia (SS) but can be extremely variable, ranging from asymptomatic to severe. Crises are of lesser severity and are less frequent. The liver is usually enlarged and splenomegaly is moderate or marked.

Symptoms which may be present are: fatigue, dyspnea, jaundice, migratory arthralgia, recurrent abdominal pain, and hematuria.

Aseptic necrosis of the head of the femur, vitreous hemorrhages, complications of pregnancy, and hematuria occur more frequently in sickle C disease than in classic sickle cell anemia. The anemia is mild, hemoglobin levels range from 9 to 10 grams on the average, and may even rise to normal levels.

Splenic infarction has been reported during aerial flights.

Sickle Cell Thalassemia Disease

A more unusual variant of sickle cell disease is sickle cell-thalassemia. A hemolytic anemia is manifested but of a lesser degree than sickle cell anemia. It is generally moderate.

The clinical course of this variant is less severe than in either sickle cell anemia or thalassemia major. Crises are rare but pain in the abdomen, bones, or joints may occur. Unexplained fever, too, may be observed. Jaundice is very mild and splenomegaly, which ranges from mild to moderate, is more common in these patients than in those with Hb-SS and persists longer. The liver also may be enlarged. Severe crises of sickle thalassemia have occasionally been observed.

Treatment

There is no cure for sickle cell disease. Treatment is supportive and symptomatic.

The painful or thrombotic crisis is generally treated with bed rest, analgesics, and hydration to increase blood volume and encourage the mobilization of stagnant sickle cells. Antibiotics are used when infection is present. Transfusion therapy is employed generally in cases of severe anemia, such as that accompanying an infection, in sequestration and aplastic crises, or prior to surgery. In patients who have very large spleens and who require excessive transfusions, a splenectomy may be performed. These children are then placed on prophylactic antibiotics for an extended period.

For those children who may suffer frequent attacks of acute tonsillitis, a T. and A. may be advised. If so, a preoperative transfusion is given to prevent anoxia.

The pH is also carefully monitored, as acidity promotes sickling. Alkaline fluids are given at times, especially in priapism. Children are encouraged to force fluids, particularly orange juice, which is alkaline in the body, and to avoid substances like aspirin.

Two new chemotherapeutic substances are currently being investigated that are said to impair the sickling process: urea and potassium cyanate. They both have been heralded by the lay press as "cures" but the researchers make no such claim. Their use is still highly experimental.[3,8]

A RESPONSE TO THE NEED

The Pediatric Comprehensive Care Sickle Cell Anemia Clinic

Intake

The Sickle Cell Anemia Clinic meets every Tuesday morning. Only patients with sickle cell disease are registered. Patients with S trait are not seen here, nor is it a general sickle-cell screening clinic. Patients are referred from: The Pediatric Hematology Clinic, where the diagnostic workup generally takes place; Inpatient Service (all hospitalized patients receive appointments upon discharge); the Pediatric Emergency Area when physical findings and laboratory data are diagnostic for sickle cell disease; other hospitals and community agencies and private physicians.

Staff

The health team consists of: two pediatricians, one hematology fellow, one hematology consultant, one laboratory technician, one social worker, one paraprofessional, one public health nurse, two clinical nurses, and one clerk.

Audiovisual and dental screening are immediately available in the area. Students of various health disciplines are continually being rotated through the clinic. Twenty to thirty patients are generally seen each session.

Clinic Procedure

RECORDS. Each patient who is registered in the clinic has a general pediatric record which includes growth and development charts, immunization history, etc. This is the same record that is used when the patient comes to the emergency area with an acute problem. He also has a special sickle-cell disease history check list and a hematology chart which includes only pertinent hematologic data.

The employees of the medical center launched a fund-raising drive to enroll all sickle cell anemia patients in the Medic Alert Foundation, which provides a Medic Alert emblem on a pendant or bracelet with diagnosis engraved on the reverse side, and a central registration service.

LABORATORY SERVICE. The technician obtains specimens for hematocrit and hemoglobin and whatever other tests are indicated. Urine specimens for routine and microscopic examinations are collected every three months, by using midstream voided specimens. Specimens for liver profile and other blood work are drawn by physicians during the examination.

SCREENING. Height and weight are measured on each visit. All new children receive audiovisual and dental screening. This is repeated annually or as required. Macular hemorrhage of the retina was first detected in a patient when she failed the vision screening.

Several of the patients, who have what some authors refer to as "characteristic protrusion of the central incisors,"[15] are receiving orthodontia therapy.

MEDICAL EVALUATION. Each patient is assigned to a specific physician. He or she receives a complete medical evaluation, management of his medical problem, and immunizations. Patients are generally given a prescription for Darvon to relieve their pain and any other medications their condition requires.

PUBLIC HEALTH NURSE. After the examination each family is referred to the PHN where:

1. The doctor's pertinent findings and recommendations are discussed with parents and child (when possible).

2. School problems are discussed and the school is contacted when necessary, i.e. to permit patients to leave the classroom to force fluids or void during morning and afternoon sessions; to arrange for appropriate class placement, i.e. health

class to regular class; to report present status and recommendations to the school's health service.

3. The disease entity is discussed with the parent, who is then advised when to bring the child for care. The sickle cell program at KC/DMC is explained. Siblings are referred to the clinic for testing.

SOCIAL SERVICE. A social history is taken on each family and is included in the general pediatric record. Pertinent factors such as financial status, housing conditions, school programs, family relationships, and health coverage are covered and appropriate action is taken. Parents are also referred to parent education sessions.

APPOINTMENTS. The clerk gives each child a return appointment to the clinic. Appointments are spaced according to the needs of the patient, the greatest length of time being three months. Whenever an appointment lapses, the parent is sent another one. Attendance at the clinic is good, with a better than 80 percent rate for keeping appointments. Generally, parents call, when they miss appointments, to arrange for another.

Parent Education Sessions

Following the clinical session every Tuesday, parents, particularly new ones, are encouraged to stay for the education session. These sessions are conducted by the social worker, an examining pediatrician, and related health workers. The disease entity and the problems that might be encountered are discussed by the physician. Parents share their various methods of handling their problems. This sharing of experiences is beneficial, even therapeutic. A short course in sickle cell genetics is offered, explaining the method of transmission of the disease according to the mendelian law. If both parents are carriers of the trait, for each pregnancy the chances are one in four that the offspring will have the disease, two in four that the offspring will be a carrier, and one in four that he will be normal.

The very first question that was asked by a parent in that historic first parents' session was, "Is it true that I gave this to my child?" She (the mother) then burst into tears. This feeling of guilt is expressed and dealt with each week. One father said, "When you see your child in that bed, laying there, dying, and you realize what your love created, love goes out of the window." According to another mother, "We blamed each other until we blamed ourselves right out of the marriage." In the sessions we help the parents realize that there is no fault or blame.

The fear of death is most prevalent. If the parents have heard anything at all about sickle cell, it is that their child will die . . . soon. The presence of parents of older affected children or adult patients in the session is most supportive to the young parents. The fear of death is not totally unwarranted, particularly for the young child under five. The mortality rate for children at KC/DMC is about 6 percent and 70 percent of those deaths are due to infections.[17] Parents are therefore taught to observe for signs of infection, and to bring the child for care upon such findings. The mere existence, however, of an adult sickle cell clinic helps to allay fear and lends hope. The parents are told that 94 percent of our patients "graduate" to the adult services.

Enuresis is another frequently discussed problem. Efforts are made to convert the "socially unacceptable" bed-wetting to "socially acceptable" nocturia. One parent revealed that she had been physically punishing her child nightly, until she learned this symptom was caused by his inability to concentrate his urine because of his condition and was not due to laziness.

The crises of the young sickler are generally unpredictable and result in having to undergo frequent hospitalizations. This situation causes some parents to overprotect and overindulge the sickler at the expense of the other children. At the time of hospitalization, it is usually the parent who cries and not the patient. Parents generally state that the siblings understand the "sick" child's needs for "extra love" and "extra time." A parent of a teen-ager disclosed that she had believed this until she discovered that the reason that her other children allowed the sickler to have the room alone was not extra love for her, but that they thought that she was a vampire because of her periodic need for blood.

The parents report that since the advent of the parent education sessions they are better able to cope with their child's illness and they feel that the children seem better.

Social Action and the Community

An outgrowth of the parents' sessions was the establishment of the Association for Sickle Cell Anemia, Inc., Brooklyn Branch. This organization has provided an opportunity for the parents to "do something" about their problem. All officers are either parents or sicklers themselves. The general membership consists of parents, patients, and interested lay and professional community members. The clinic staff are consultants.

The objectives of the organization are to:
1. Disseminate information about SCA.
2. Raise funds to assist affected Brooklyn families.
3. Raise funds to support and stimulate screening programs.
4. Raise funds to support SCA clinics and research.
5. Render support to parents of newly diagnosed patients.
6. Support and stimulate legislation regarding SCA.

General membership meetings which are open to the public, are held monthly at the KC/D Medical Center. Prominent speakers from the health, welfare, and political arena are invited to address the groups. Sickle cell screening is performed at these meetings. Fathers and other working members of the family are generally invited to these sessions.

In the two years of existence, the Association has purchased a hospital bed, wheel chair, and eyeglasses, and has financed sicklers' camp attendance, sponsored community seminars, and rendered emotional support where needed. The chairman or president of the group is the mother of four children with sickle cell disease. Membership is now around 400.

In the community there is an enormous demand for information and testing and it far exceeds the supply of existing facilities and available funds. My phone rings constantly with requests from schools, churches, social clubs, professional and lay community organizations to come and "talk to us about SCA." Requests for testing come in by the thousands. I receive letters from all over the country requesting pamphlets. Students from most colleges in the metropolitan area have observed the clinic sessions and interviewed the staff, to gather data for their papers. Everyone wants to test: teachers, club presidents, Boy Scout leaders. Literature on the subject is written and disseminated by people from all walks of life.

This is certainly a much different picture from the one Dr. Scott found in Richmond in 1967.[12] Many more than three out of ten blacks have heard about SCA, but much of the information that has been disseminated is misinformation. Much of the mass screening that has been performed has not had sufficient back-up services, such as adequate education or counselling. Privacy of the patient has often been sacrificed. Anyone can buy and use SICKLEDEX.[18] As an article in Medical World News stated, there has been "progress amidst chaos."[13] There is certainly a need to "do something" about sickle cell. But the response to the need must be responsible, not merely visible.

Sickle cell screening is rampant in the community, but "back-up" facilities are not being expanded. Clinic staffs are being decreased because hospital budgets are cut while clinic attendance and demand for service accelerates. What is accomplished by telling a parent that her child is "positive" and offering nothing else? Or what undue stress does a parent have to bear when she must wait two or three months to know whether her child had trait or disease? What service is rendered by puncturing fingers without adequate counselling? What progress is made by passing legislation without appropriating funds to render the law operant? Who is helped by resolutions being issued to increase sickle cell screening while cutting the funds to hire the necessary personnel to enact them?

Much controversy surrounds the questions of screening and genetic counselling. Who should do it? Who should be screened? Is simply screening for Hb-S enough? What about those with Hb-C trait and B-thalassemia trait? Can we really tell a couple that they don't have to worry about having children with sickle cell disease because only one parent is positive for Hb-S? Should the literature still say both parents must have S-trait in order for the child to have the disease?

I recently attended a community symposium where an eminent hematologist recommended that all persons with sickle cell trait should be sterilized. Conversely, another noted researcher stated that he "steers clear" of the question of reproduction when he counsels positive reactors. Then there are those who say test, record, but don't tell. We at KCH/DMC are in agreement with those who present individuals the facts of transmission of the disease and allow them to make whatever decision they wish. No one has the right to make these decisions for them.

Pamphlets that state "most sicklers die before age five" do not disseminate information but merely spread ignorance. Newspaper articles that declare "cure found for sickle cell" do not inform but raise hope falsely. The need is great; the community is pregnant with interest and awareness; the response, therefore, must be responsible!

CONCLUSIONS

Sickle-cell disease is a complex problem. Its many ramifications require the resources of all members of the health team to aid its victims. A coordinated effort is essential if it no longer is to be considered "the most neglected major health problem in the nation today."[13] The belated recognition of its importance has led to an "energetic mobilization of resources to combat sickle cell disease."[10] It is therefore mandatory that the energies of the nurse be utilized: to care, to teach, to treat, to observe, to interpret, to support, to refer, to intervene, and to coordinate efforts of all those who are working together to make life more meaningful and less painful for sicklers and their families.

REFERENCES

1. Brody, J.: Test for sickle cell trait urged for Negro recruits. *New York Times*, February 7, 1970.
2. Campbell, D.: Sickle cell anemia and its effect on black people. *Crises*, January-February, 1971.

3. Cerami, A., and Manning, J.M.: Potassium cyanate as an inhibitor of sickling of erythrocytes *in vitro. Proc Natl Acad Sci, 68:* 1183. 1971.

4. Herrick, J.B.: Peculiar elongated and sickle-shaped red blood corpuscles in a case of severe anemia. *Arch Intern Med, 6:*517-521, 1910.

5. Ingram, V.M.: Gene mutations in human hemoglobin: The chemical difference between normal and sickle cell hemoglobin. *Nature, 180:*326-328, August 17, 1957.

6. Miner, E.: Department of Health, Education and Welfare, Public Health Service, National Institute of Health, News Release, November 9, 1971.

7. Murayama, M.: Molecular mechanism of sickled erythrocyte formation. *Nature, 202:*258-260, April 18, 1964.

8. McCurdy, P., and Mohmood, L.: Intravenous urea treatment of the painful crises of sickle cell disease: A preliminary report. *N Engl J Med, 285:*992, 1971.

9. Pauling, L., Itano, H.A. et al.: Sickle cell anemia—a molecular disease. *Science, 110:*543, 1949.

10. Ranney, H.M.: Sickle-cell disease. *Blood, 39:*433, March, 1972.

11. Scott, R.: Sickle-cell anemia—high prevalence and low priority. *N Engl J Med, 282:*164, January 15, 1970.

12. Scott, R.: Health care priority and sickle cell anemia. *JAMA, 214:*731, Oct. 26, 1970.

13. Sickle cell disease—progress amidst chaos: *Med World News,* May 28, 1971.

14. Sickle cell anemia, advances continue amidst medical, political controversies. *Med World News,* December 3, 1971.

15. Lewis, R.: *Sickle States: Clinical Features in West Africans.* Accra, Ghana, Ghana U Pr, 1970.

16. Smith, C.: *Blood Diseases of Infancy and Childhood,* 2nd ed. St. Louis, Mosby, 1966.

17. Sickle cell anemia gets increasing attention from public health workers. *Downstate Reporter,* vol. 3, no. 1, Winter, 1972.

18. Ballard, M.S., et al.: A new diagnostic test for hemoglobin S. *J Pediatr,* 76:117-119, January, 1970.

PART FOUR
CANCER

There have been very few studies of the epidemiology of cancer according to race. The landmark research by Ernest L. Wynder, Irwin J. Bross, and Takeshi Hirayama, "A Study of the Epidemiology of Cancer of the Breast," (*Cancer*, 13:559–601, 1960) mentions a higher incidence among whites in the United States. There is also the impression that cancer of the breast occurs less frequently among the poor.

In "Epidemiology of Cancers of Uterine Cervix and Corpus, Breast, and Ovary in Israel and New York City," (*Journal of the National Cancer Institute*, vol. 37, no. 1, July, 1966) Harold L. Steward, Lucia J. Dunham, Julian Casper, Harold F. Dorn, Louis B. Thomas, John H. Edgcomb, and Alexander Symeonidis used Negro and Puerto Rican women as control groups.

Thus, although the report concentrated on Jewish women, there are some data available for other groups. Cancer of the cervix among Negro women in New York was 49.6 per 100,000 compared to 15.0 among non-Jewish whites.

In Chapter Twelve, Fred Burbank and Joseph F. Fraumeni, Jr. analyze all deaths from cancer in the United States, 1950–1967. Their analysis reveals an increasing nonwhite-to-white ratio of age-adjusted death rates. Each cancer site is analyzed with respect to race differential and change in nonwhite mortality. Burbank and Fraumeni suggest that a possible causal factor for the shift to nonwhite predominance in cancer mortality may be the greater exposure of nonwhites to carcinogenetic factors.

William M. Christopherson and James E. Parker focus on the problem of higher rates of carcinoma of the cervix in Negro women. Their field study, conducted in Kentucky, suggests that these rates may be correlated to socioeconomic factors.

Chapter 12

U.S. CANCER MORTALITY: NONWHITE PREDOMINANCE

FRED BURBANK, AND JOSEPH F. FRAUMENI, JR.

Analysis of recent cancer mortality patterns in the United States revealed a trend toward higher age-adjusted rates for nonwhites than for whites.[1] This trend is described more fully in the present report.

MATERIALS AND METHODS

All death certificates in the United States listing cancer as the cause of death, 1950–67, were analyzed from a series of magnetic tapes provided by the National Center for Health Statistics.[1] During this period over 4.5 million deaths were attributed to cancer and were represented by list numbers 140 to 205 of the International Classification of Diseases (ICD)[2,3]. Tallied from each certificate were the cause of death according to the sixth revision of the ICD code, sex, race, calendar year, and age at death. Compensation was made in all calculations for changes to the seventh revision of the ICD code in 1958, particularly with respect to the major reclassification of the four-digit categories within the leukemias (International List Nos. 204.0–204.4). The racial categories for this study were "white" (persons reported as white, Mexican, Puerto Rican, or Cuban) and "nonwhite" (all other races). Population estimates were obtained from Bureau of Census publications as previously described[1].

For 1962 to 1967, a comparison between whites and nonwhites was made as follows for each site of cancer: a)

Abridged and reprinted with permission from the *Journal of the National Cancer Institute*, September, 1972.

149

The number of persons dead and the number at risk were summarized; b) sex and age-specific death rates for whites were applied to the nonwhite population to derive expected numbers of deaths among nonwhites; and c) the expected deaths were compared to the number observed as Poisson variables[4] and the significance levels computed[5] (Table 12-I).

For each site of cancer among nonwhites, 1962 to 1967, the age-adjusted death rates (direct method, by use of the U.S. population of 1960 as a standard) were calculated and ranked by order of magnitude.

For the overall period, 1950 to 1967, the trends in age-adjusted death rates for each cancer site were measured by linear regression[1]. (Major shifts in classification occurred in 1958 for the four-digit categories within the leukemias, so data for the interval 1959–67 were used to calculate these regression coefficients.) Significance levels (Table 12-I) for the trends were calculated by the Mantel-Haenszel procedure[6]. To compare changes in death rates for cancers of exceedingly different frequency, the regression coefficient for each site was divided by its intercept and multiplied by 100, producing a percentage change per year. The percentage change for each site of cancer was ordered and graphed with the significance code.

RESULTS

The nonwhite predominance in cancer mortality began for females in 1950 and for males in 1956, and has increased

TABLE 12-I

SIGNIFICANCE CODES AND CALENDAR YEARS ANALYZED FOR STUDIES ON RACIAL DIFFERENCES AND TIME TRENDS

Analysis	*Years analyzed*	*Statistical distribution*	*Significance codes (2-tailed)*
Race comparison	1962–67	Poisson	$1 = P \leq 0.001$ $2 = P \leq 0.01$ $3 = P > 0.01$
Time trend	1950–67	Chi-square	$1 = P \leq 0.001$ $2 = P \leq 0.01$ $3 = P > 0.01$

steadily with time (Table 12-II). (Annual mortality statistics published for calendar years before 1950 consistently showed excesses of cancer in the white population.) Since 1950, males in both races experienced upward trends in mortality, but the increase has been much more rapid among nonwhites than whites. For females, the increasing percentage of nonwhites reflects the declining mortality among whites, compared with stable death rates for nonwhites.

Nonwhite-White Comparisons (1962–67)

For each site of cancer, 1962 to 1967, the observed number (O) of deaths among nonwhites is compared to the expected number (E) based on the mortality experience of whites. Table 12-III shows the race differentials for males, and Table 12-IV for females. Nonwhite-predominant tumors have an O/E ratio greater than 1.00, and white-predominant tumors have an E/O ratio greater than 1.00. The total cancer mortality reported for nonwhites was higher than for whites; the O/E ratio was 1.14 for males and 1.08 for females.

TABLE 12-II
RATIO OF NONWHITE TO WHITE AGE-ADJUSTED DEATH RATES FOR
ALL SITES OF CANCER (INTERNATIONAL LIST NOS. 140–205),
BY CALENDAR YEAR AND SEX, UNITED STATES, 1950–67

Year	Male	Female
1950	0.92	1.03
1951	0.92	1.02
1952	0.94	1.02
1953	0.94	1.02
1954	0.99	1.04
1955	0.97	1.04
1956	1.01	1.07
1957	1.03	1.06
1958	1.03	1.08
1959	1.06	1.06
1960	1.07	1.10
1961	1.08	1.11
1962	1.09	1.12
1963	1.14	1.11
1964	1.13	1.12
1965	1.14	1.12
1966	1.19	1.14
1967	1.20	1.14

TABLE 12-III

RACE DIFFERENTIALS IN CANCER MORTALITY BY PRIMARY SITE AMONG MALES, UNITED STATES, 1962–67*

	Nonwhite predominance			White predominance	
Site†	O/E	Significance code‡	Site†	E/O	Significance code‡
Esophagus (150)	2.87	1	Melanoma (190)	4.63	1
Male genital organs NOS (179)	2.75	1	Lip (140)	4.24	1
Digestive organs NOS (159)	2.46	1	Giant follicular lymphoma (202.0)	2.95	1
Stomach (151)	1.90	1	Testis (178)	2.87	1
Nasopharynx (146)	1.70	1	Nervous system (193)	1.65	1
Multiple myeloma (203)	1.69	1	Eye (192)	1.64	1
Prostate (177)	1.69	1	Monocytic leukemia (204.2)	1.62	1
Biliary passages and liver (155)	1.52	1	Acute leukemia (204.3)	1.62	1
Nose (160)	1.51	1	Lymphosarcoma (200.1)	1.54	1
Mycosis fungoides (205)	1.50	3	Skin (191)	1.47	1
Mesopharynx (145)	1.40	1	Reticulum cell sarcoma (200.0)	1.39	1
Floor of mouth (143)	1.35	1	Lymphatic leukemia (204.0)	1.34	1
Breast (170)	1.33	1	Hodgkin's disease (201)	1.33	1
Tongue (141)	1.28	1	Kidney (180)	1.31	1
Larynx (161)	1.23	1	Other reticuloses (202.1)	1.25	1
Pharynx NOS (148)	1.23	1	Rectum (154)	1.23	1
Mouth NOS (144)	1.21	1	Other lymphoid neoplasms (200.2)	1.22	1
Hypopharynx (147)	1.18	2	Myeloic leukemia (204.1)	1.22	1
Pancreas (157)	1.14	1	Large intestine (153)	1.22	1
Lung (162,163)	1.07	1	Bladder (181)	1.20	1
Mediastinum (164)	1.03	3	Salivary gland (142)	1.14	3
			Peritoneum (158)	1.13	3
			Leukemia NOS (204.4)	1.12	3
			Thyroid (194)	1.11	3
			Bone (196)	1.03	3
			Small intestine (152)	1.03	3
			Connective tissue (197)	1.03	3

*Based on observed (O) and expected (E) numbers of deaths among nonwhites. O/E ratios greater than 1.00 indicate sites with nonwhite predominance, and E/O ratios greater than 1.00 indicate sites with white predominance.
† Parentheses show International List Nos., sixth revision (seventh revision for the leukemias).
‡ *See* Table 12-I for definitions.

TABLE 12-IV

RACE DIFFERENTIALS IN CANCER MORTALITY BY PRIMARY SITE AMONG FEMALES, UNITED STATES, 1962-67*

Nonwhite predominance			*White predominance*		
Site†	O/E	Significance code‡	Site†	E/O	Significance code‡
Chorioepithelioma (173)	2.65	1	Melanoma (190)	4.05	1
Cervix (171)	2.58	1	Giant follicular lymphoma (202.0)	3.88	1
Esophagus (150)	2.55	1	Eye (192)	2.31	1
Mycosis fungoides (205)	2.37	1	Lymphosarcoma (200.1)	1.88	1
Digestive organs NOS (159)	2.16	1	Nervous system (193)	1.76	1
Lip (140)	2.01	2	Hodgkin's disease (201)	1.70	1
Floor of mouth (143)	1.68	1	Acute leukemia (204.3)	1.69	1
Stomach (151)	1.62	1	Reticulum cell sarcoma (200.0)	1.66	1
Multiple myeloma (203)	1.60	1	Other lymphoid neoplasms (200.2)	1.56	1
Larynx (161)	1.57	1	Monocytic leukemia (204.2)	1.56	1
Body of uterus (172)	1.54	1	Kidney (180)	1.45	1
Pharynx NOS (148)	1.54	1	Ovary (175)	1.28	1
Nasopharynx (146)	1.49	1	Lymphatic leukemia (204.0)	1.25	2
Bladder (181)	1.45	1	Other reticuloses (202.1)	1.24	1
Female genital organs NOS (176)	1.36	1	Biliary passages and liver (155)	1.23	1
Nose (160)	1.35	1	Large intestine (153)	1.16	1
Mesopharynx (145)	1.34	2	Myeloid leukemia (204.1)	1.14	2
Mouth NOS (144)	1.31	1	Small intestine (152)	1.10	3
Pancreas (157)	1.19	3	Breast (170)	1.09	1
Hypopharynx (147)	1.19	3	Salivary gland (142)	1.08	3
Mediastinum (164)	1.16	3	Rectum (154)	1.03	3
Thyroid (194)	1.14	2			
Connective tissue (197)	1.13	2			
Bone (196)	1.10	3			
Peritoneum (158)	1.10	3			
Leukemia NOS (204.4)	1.07	3			
Lung (162, 163)	1.04	2			
Tongue (141)	1.03	2			
Skin (191)	1.03	3			

* Based on observed (O) and expected (E) numbers of deaths among nonwhites. O/E ratios greater than 1.00 indicate sites with nonwhite predominance, and E/O ratios greater than 1.00 indicate sites with white predominance. Parentheses show International List Nos.

† Parentheses show International List Nos., sixth revision (seventh revision for the leukemias).

‡ See Table 12-I for definitions.

Nonwhite predominance in mortality is statistically significant at $P < 0.001$ for: *a*) both sexes with cancers of the nose, most parts of the mouth and pharynx, esophagus, stomach, pancreas, larynx, and multiple myeloma; *b*) males with cancers of the biliary passages and liver, lung, breast, and prostrate; *c*) females with cancers of the cervix, body of uterus, chorioepithelioma, bladder, and mycosis fungoides.

At the same significance level ($P<0.001$) is the white predominance for: *a*) both sexes with cancers of the large intestine, kidney, melanoma, eye, nervous system, leukemia, Hodgkin's disease, and other lymphomas; *b*) males with cancers of the lip, rectum, testis, bladder, and skin; *c*) females with cancers of the biliary passages and liver, breast, and ovary.

Compared to whites, the age-specific death rates for nonwhites were higher and rose more rapidly with age through middle life. After 65 to 69 years of age, the nonwhite mortality began to plateau and was surpassed by steadily climbing rates for whites.

Nonwhite Rates (1962 to 1967)

The age-adjusted death rates for cancer sites among nonwhites, 1962 to 1967, are ranked in Tables 12-V and 12-VI. Cancers of the lung, prostate, stomach, large intestine, pancreas, and esophagus comprise the bulk (70%) of the malignant neoplasms among nonwhite males. For females, cancers of the breast, cervix, large intestine, stomach, lung, pancreas, and ovary account for 70 percent of the malignant tumors.

Nonwhite Trends (1950 to 1967)

For each cancer site among nonwhites, the change in mortality since 1950 is quantitated and ranked in Table 12-VII (males) and Table 12-VIII (females). The increase in total cancer mortality in nonwhite males reflects rising trends for a variety of cancers, whereas the relatively stable pattern for females represents a balance of neoplasms increasing and decreasing over time.

TABLE 12-V
AVERAGE ANNUAL AGE-ADJUSTED DEATH RATES FOR
SPECIFIC SITES OF CANCER AMONG NONWHITE MALES,
UNITED STATES, 1962–67*

Position	Site†	Death rate per 100,000	Percent of all sites	Cumulative percent
1	Lung (162, 163)	46.32	24.93	24.93
2	Prostate (177)	28.89	15.55	40.48
3	Stomach (151)	22.03	11.86	52.34
4	Large intestine (153)	13.39	7.21	59.54
5	Pancreas (157)	11.44	6.16	65.70
6	Esophagus (150)	10.93	5.88	71.58
7	Rectum (154)	5.43	2.92	74.50
8	Bladder (181)	5.27	2.84	77.34
9	Biliary passages and liver (155)	4.56	2.45	79.79
10	Multiple myeloma (203)	3.20	1.72	81.51
11	Larynx (161)	3.00	1.61	83.12
12	Kidney (180)	2.96	1.59	84.72
13	Nervous system (193)	2.66	1.43	86.14
14	Acute leukemia (204.3)	2.29	1.24	87.38
15	Hodgkin's disease (201)	1.70	0.92	88.29
16	Lymphatic leukemia (204.0)	1.66	0.90	89.19
17	Tongue (141)	1.60	0.86	90.05
18	Lymphosarcoma (200.1)	1.60	0.86	90.91
19	Pharynx NOS (148)	1.29	0.70	91.61
20	Bone (196)	1.11	0.60	92.20
21	Myeloid leukemia (204.1)	1.09	0.59	92.79
22	Digestive organs NOS (159)	1.06	0.57	93.36
23	Mouth NOS (144)	0.92	0.49	93.85
24	Skin (191)	0.90	0.49	94.34
25	Reticulum cell sarcoma (200.0)	0.88	0.47	94.81
26	Leukemia NOS (204.4)	0.77	0.42	95.22
27	Male genital organs NOS (179)	0.75	0.40	95.62
28	Connective tissue (197)	0.72	0.39	96.01
29	Other lymphoid neoplasms (200.2)	0.66	0.36	96.37
30	Mesopharynx (145)	0.65	0.35	96.71
31	Nasopharynx (146)	0.63	0.34	97.05
32	Nose (160)	0.55	0.29	97.35
33	Floor of mouth (143)	0.52	0.28	97.63
34	Other reticuloses (202.1)	0.51	0.28	97.90
35	Monocytic leukemia (204.2)	0.43	0.23	98.13
36	Hypopharynx (147)	0.42	0.23	98.36
37	Small intestine (152)	0.41	0.22	98.58
38	Melanoma (190)	0.41	0.22	98.80
39	Peritoneum (158)	0.39	0.21	99.00
40	Salivary gland (142)	0.36	0.20	99.20
41	Thyroid (194)	0.35	0.19	99.39
42	Breast (170)	0.34	0.18	99.57
43	Testis (178)	0.30	0.16	99.73
44	Mediastinum (164)	0.25	0.13	99.86
45	Eye (192)	0.10	0.05	99.92
46	Mycosis fungoides (205)	0.08	0.04	99.96
47	Lip (140)	0.05	0.02	99.98
48	Giant follicular lymphoma (202.0)	0.03	0.02	100.00

* Rates are ranked in order of decreasing magnitude and expressed in terms of percentage of all sites and cumulative percentage.
† Parentheses show International List Nos., sixth revision (seventh revision for the leukemias).

TABLE 12-VI
AVERAGE ANNUAL AGE-ADJUSTED DEATH RATES FOR
SPECIFIC SITES OF CANCER AMONG NONWHITE FEMALES,
UNITED STATES, 1962–67*

Position	Site†	Death rate per 100,000	Percent of all sites	Cumulative percent
1	Breast (170)	23.14	19.11	19.11
2	Cervix (171)	17.68	14.60	33.71
3	Large intestine (153)	13.66	11.28	44.99
4	Stomach (151)	9.82	8.11	53.10
5	Lung (162, 163)	7.34	6.06	59.16
6	Pancreas (157)	7.18	5.93	65.10
7	Ovary (175)	6.77	5.60	70.69
8	Rectum (154)	4.08	3.37	74.06
9	Bladder (181)	3.21	2.65	76.71
10	Biliary passages and liver (155)	2.71	2.24	78.95
11	Esophagus (150)	2.49	2.06	81.00
12	Body of uterus (172)	2.25	1.86	82.87
13	Multiple myeloma (203)	2.14	1.76	84.63
14	Nervous system (193)	1.63	1.35	85.98
15	Acute leukemia (204.3)	1.57	1.30	87.27
16	Kidney (180)	1.51	1.24	88.52
17	Female genital organs NOS (176)	0.99	0.82	89.33
18	Lymphatic leukemia (204.0)	0.92	0.76	90.09
19	Lymphosarcoma (200.1)	0.86	0.71	90.80
20	Digestive organs NOS (159)	0.83	0.69	91.48
21	Bone (196)	0.81	0.67	92.15
22	Myeloid leukemia (204.1)	0.80	0.66	92.81
23	Hodgkin's disease (201)	0.80	0.66	93.47
24	Thyroid (194)	0.70	0.58	94.05
25	Skin (191)	0.63	0.52	94.56
26	Connective tissue (197)	0.61	0.50	95.07
27	Leukemia NOS (204.4)	0.57	0.47	95.53
28	Reticulum cell sarcoma (200.0)	0.50	0.41	95.94
29	Peritoneum (158)	0.41	0.33	96.28
30	Larynx (161)	0.39	0.33	96.60
31	Mouth NOS (144)	0.38	0.32	96.92
32	Other lymphoid neoplasms (200.2)	0.36	0.30	97.22
33	Tongue (141)	0.36	0.30	97.51
34	Pharynx NOS (148)	0.35	0.29	97.80
35	Other reticuloses (202.1)	0.32	0.27	98.07
36	Monocytic leukemia (204.2)	0.32	0.26	98.33
37	Melanoma (190)	0.32	0.26	98.59
38	Small intestine (152)	0.30	0.25	98.84
39	Nose (160)	0.27	0.22	99.06
40	Salivary gland (142)	0.20	0.17	99.23
41	Nasopharynx (146)	0.18	0.15	99.37
42	Floor of mouth (143)	0.15	0.12	99.49
43	Mesopharynx (145)	0.14	0.11	99.61
44	Chorioepithelioma (173)	0.13	0.11	99.72
45	Mediastinum (164)	0.09	0.08	99.79
46	Hypopharynx (147)	0.07	0.06	99.85
47	Eye (192)	0.06	0.05	99.90
48	Mycosis fungoides (205)	0.06	0.05	99.95
49	Lip (140)	0.04	0.03	99.98
50	Giant follicular lymphoma (202.0)	0.02	0.01	100.00

* Rates are ranked in order of decreasing magnitude and expressed in terms of percentage of all sites and cumulative percentage.
† Parentheses show International List Nos., sixth revision (seventh revision for the leukemias).

TABLE 12-VII

PERCENTAGE CHANGE PER YEAR (1950 BASE YEAR) IN AGE-ADJUSTED CANCER MORTALITY
BY PRIMARY SITE AMONG NONWHITE MALES, UNITED STATES, 1950-67*

Falling trends			Rising trends		
Site†	Percent change per year	Significance code‡	Site†	Percent change per year	Significance code‡
Lip (140)	-3.50		Hypopharynx (147)	67.74	1
Eye (192)	-2.04	2	Floor of mouth (143)	18.77	1
Stomach (151)	-1.67	3	Lung (162, 163)	18.38	1
Bone (196)	-1.62	1	Giant follicular lymphoma (202.0)	15.67	3
Nose (160)	-1.57	2	Reticulum cell sarcoma (200.0)	14.08	1
Male genital organs NOS (179)	-1.46	1	Multiple myeloma (203)	11.57	1
Breast (170)	-1.40	3	Acute leukemia (204.3)	9.76	1
Peritoneum (158)	-1.36	3	Connective tissue (197)	8.59	1
Mediastinum (164)	-1.11	3	Mesopharynx (145)	8.42	
Digestive organs NOS (159)	-0.93	3	Myeloid leukemia (204.1)	7.86	2
Rectum (154)	-0.86	1	Biliary passages and liver (155)	7.25	1
Thyroid (194)	-0.38	3	Melanoma (190)	6.00	1
Leukemia NOS (204.4)	-0.28	3	Other lymphoid neoplasms (200.2)	5.41	1
Skin (191)	-0.04	3	Pancreas (157)	5.31	1
			Larynx (161)	4.95	1
			Esophagus (150)	4.69	1
			Kidney (180)	4.18	1
			Nervous system (193)	4.14	1
			Mouth NOS (144)	3.77	1
			Nasopharynx (146)	3.60	1
			Large intestine (153)	3.29	1
			Salivary gland (142)	2.70	2
			Lymphosarcoma (200.1)	2.52	1
			Mycosis fungoides (205)	2.36	3
			Other reticuloses (202.1)	2.27	2
			Tongue (141)	2.14	1
			Prostate (177)	2.03	1
			Monocytic leukemia (204.2)	1.64	3
			Bladder (181)	1.07	1
			Lymphatic leukemia (204.0)	0.96	3
			Hodgkin's disease (201)	0.64	3
			Pharynx NOS (148)	0.44	3
			Testis (178)	0.19	3
			Small intestine (152)	0.17	3

* Trends for leukemia categories confined to 1959-67 interval to avoid classification changes. *See* text for methods.
† Parentheses show International List Nos., sixth revision (seventh revision for the leukemias).
‡ *See* Table 12-I for definitions.

TABLE 12-VIII

PERCENTAGE CHANGE PER YEAR (1950 BASE YEAR) IN AGE-ADJUSTED CANCER MORTALITY BY PRIMARY SITE AMONG NONWHITE FEMALES, UNITED STATES, 1950-67*

Falling trends			Rising trends		
Site†	*Percent change per year*	*Significance code‡*	*Site†*	*Percent change per year*	*Significance code‡*
Lip (140)	−3.59	3	Hypopharynx (147)	118.49	1
Chorioepithelioma (173)	−2.63	2	Reticulum cell sarcoma (200.0)	32.61	1
Bone (196)	−2.52	1	Mesopharynx (145)	23.97	1
Mediastinum (164)	−2.51	3	Connective tissue (197)	11.69	1
Eye (192)	−2.39	3	Multiple myeloma (203)	11.54	1
Small intestine (152)	−2.16	1	Lung (162, 163)	8.07	1
Stomach (151)	−2.10	1	Nasopharynx (146)	7.95	1
Monocytic leukemia (204.2)	−2.02	3	Floor of mouth (143)	6.25	2
Digestive organs NOS (159)	−2.01	1	Pancreas (157)	5.57	1
Rectum (154)	−1.67	3	Body of uterus (172)	5.49	1
Pharynx NOS (148)	−1.53	1	Other lymphoid neoplasms (200.2)	5.22	2
Cervix (171)	−1.42	3	Esophagus (150)	4.29	2
Skin (191)	−0.74	3	Other reticuloses (202.1)	3.66	3
Female genital organs NOS (176)	−0.68	3	Mycosis fungoides (205)	3.49	1
Leukemia NOS (204.4)	−0.44	3	Larynx (161)	3.42	3
Hodgkin's disease (201)	−0.41	3	Nervous system (193)	2.56	3
Tongue (141)	−0.38	3	Melanoma (190)	2.46	3
Thyroid (194)	−0.01	3	Mouth NOS (144)	2.09	3
			Large intestine (153)	2.08	1
			Ovary (175)	2.05	1
			Myeloid leukemia (204.1)	1.79	3
			Biliary passages and liver (155)	1.74	1
			Kidney (180)	1.49	1
			Nose (160)	1.36	3
			Acute leukemia (204.3)	1.12	3
			Breast (170)	0.93	1
			Lymphosarcoma (200.1)	0.74	3
			Lymphatic leukemia (204.0)	0.67	3
			Bladder (181)	0.64	3
			Giant follicular lymphoma (202.0)	0.41	3
			Salivary gland (142)	0.24	3
			Peritoneum (158)	0.23	3

*Trends for leukemia categories confined to 1959-67 interval to avoid classification changes. *See* text for methods.

° Parentheses show International List Nos., sixth revision (seventh revision for the leukemias).

/ *See* Table 12-1 for definitions.

The upward trend in mortality among nonwhites is statistically significant at $P<0.001$ for: *a*) both sexes with cancers of the mesopharynx, hypopharynx, nasopharynx, esophagus, large intestine, biliary passages and liver, pancreas, larynx, lung, kidney, nervous system, connective tissue, reticulum cell sarcoma, and multiple myeloma; *b*) males with cancers of the tongue, floor of mouth, prostate, bladder, melanoma, lymphosarcoma, and acute leukemia; *c*) females with cancers of the breast, body of uterus, and ovary.

Significant downward trends ($P<0.001$) are seen for: *a*) both sexes with cancers of the stomach, rectum, and bone; *b*) females with cancers of the cervix and small intestine.

DISCUSSION

Trends in cancer mortality statistics in the United States since 1950 have featured a diminishing white-to-nonwhite ratio of age-adjusted death rates. This shift resulted in a nonwhite predominance in cancer mortality starting in 1950 for females and 1956 for males. Recent mortality statistics should not be considered definitive, however, until reanalyzed with updated population estimates based on the 1970 census. The patterns will be clarified also by breakdown of nonwhite mortality into specific racial or ethnic groups. Although blacks account for most of the U.S. nonwhites, the percentage of blacks is estimated by the Bureau of Census to have declined from 95.5 percent in 1950 to 88.7 percent in 1970. Nevertheless, the changing white-nonwhite differentials in cancer mortality are consistent with and probably reflect the relative shifts in cancer incidence among whites and blacks in the United States. A recent preliminary report of the Third National Cancer Survey showed that in 1969 blacks were at a greater risk of developing cancer than were whites[7], as contrasted with the white predominance in cancer incidence at the last survey in 1947[8].

Racial variation in the reported frequency of cancer in the United States may be useful in providing leads to etiologic influences, either environmental or genetic. However, it is difficult at times to determine whether racial differences in cancer are real or artifactual, e.g. based on socio-economic variability in the diagnosis and reporting of disease, in census ascertainment, or in case fatality. Nonetheless, the artifacts seem insufficient to account for the substantial white or non-white predominance reported for many cancer sites. In evaluation of the cancer experience of nonwhites in the United States, it is useful to make comparisons with similar racial groups in other countries. Most common cancers among U.S. nonwhites (or blacks) are prevalent also in U.S. whites (Tables 12-V, 12-VI), but relatively uncommon in black populations of Africa [9,10]. However, blacks in Africa have higher rates than do U.S. blacks for some cancers (e.g. hepatoma, Kaposi's sarcoma, and esophageal cancer in certain areas). Clear-cut differentials in cancer risk among widely separated black populations indicate the activity of environmental carcinogens in both continents. On the other hand, genetic factors may be responsible for racial variation in some cancers (e.g. skin, testis, brain, and hematopoietic system), since the rates among U.S. whites are much higher than among blacks in either the United States or Africa[9,10].

Substantial increases in mortality were reported during 1950 to 1967 for a variety of cancers, with upward trends more pronounced in nonwhites than in whites[1]. The climb in mortality may be ascribed in part to improvements in diagnostic accuracy and reporting or to refinements in death certificate classification. For some cancer sites, however, the rising rates probably reflect to some extent an increase in exposure to environmental carcinogens. Such may be the situation for the smoking-associated sites of cancer[11] (lung, larynx, mouth and pharynx, esophagus, pancreas, bladder), all of which have increased much more rapidly in the nonwhite population. Analysis of racial *trends* in tobacco usage should help to evaluate the increasing predominance of nonwhites with an array of cancers linked to smoking.

The age distribution of cancer mortality also showed significant racial differences in this study. Nonwhites in the United States had higher death rates for cancer than did whites at young and middle ages, but substantially lower rates later in life. The deficiency in cancer mortality among elderly nonwhites stands in contrast to the continual rise with age among whites. This pattern is seen for many specific types of cancer[1] and is attributable in part to discrepancies in the reporting of age on the death certificates and census records of nonwhites[12]. Another factor may be that the reporting of cancer in nonwhites is especially incomplete at older ages. For example, the low leukemia rate among elderly blacks seems to reflect a diminished access to medical care[13]. In addition, the crossing of age curves by race may result from heterogeneity of environmental influences. Consistent with this possibility is a recent study of prostatic cancer that related early occurrence with low social class and late occurrence with high social class[14]. Genetic mechanisms are believed to account for some racial peculiarities in age distribution (e.g. peaks in young white people for leukemia and testicular tumors are absent in blacks[1]), but there is no evidence that the racial configuration of age patterns for a wide variety of cancers is genetically programmed.

For some sites of cancer in this study, racial differences in mortality were masked by categories which are too broad or heterogeneous. Cancer of the "biliary passages and liver" had no consistent racial differential, but application of the more detailed seventh revision of the ICD code (available for mortality data after 1957) showed that liver-cancer mortality predominated among nonwhites and biliary-tract cancer among whites.[15]

In addition, mortality from all bone cancers did not differ significantly by race in this study; however, hand-sorting of death certificates for childhood cancer uncovered a marked deficiency of Ewing's sarcoma in nonwhites.[16] A similar survey of retinoblastoma showed excess mortality among blacks,[17] though, in the present study, mortality from all eye cancers predominated among whites. These findings illustrate the limitations of diagnostic categories that are conventionally used in cancer surveys, and the advantages of obtaining demographic and epidemiologic information on cancers that are anatomically and histologically distinct.

REFERENCES

1. Burbank, F.: Patterns in cancer mortality in the United States, 1950–1967. *Natl Cancer Inst Monogr, 33:*1–594, 1971.

2. *Manual of the International Statistical Classification of Diseases, Injuries, and Causes of Death,* 6th rev., adopted 1948. Geneva, WHO, 1948, vol. 1, pp. 79–89.

3. *Manual of the International Statistical Classification of Diseases, Injuries, and Causes of Death;* 7th rev., adopted 1955. Geneva, WHO, 1955, vol. 1, pp. 78–98.

4. Pearson,E.S.,Hartley,H.O.: *Biometrika Tables for Statisticians,* vol. 1. England, Cambridge U Pr, 1954, Table 40, vol. 1, p. 203.

5. Goldstein, A.: *Biostatistics.* New York, MacMillan, 1964, p. 120.

6. Mantel, N.: Chi-square tests with one degree of freedom: Extensions of the Mantel-Haenszel procedure. *J Am Stat Assoc, 58:*690–700, 1963.

7. Biometry Branch, National Cancer Institute: Preliminary Report, Third National Cancer Survey, 1969 Incidence.

8. Dorn, H.F., Cutler, S.J.: Morbidity from cancer in the United States. *Public Health Monogr,* 56, Public Health Service Publ. No. 590. Washington, D.C., U.S. Govt Print Off, 1959.

9. Oettle, A.G.: Cancer in Africa, especially in regions south of the Sahara. *J Natl Cancer Inst, 33:*383–439, 1964.

10. Davies, J.N.P., Knowelden, J., Wilson, B.A.: Incidence rates of cancer in Kyadondo County, Uganda, 1954–1960. *J Natl Cancer Inst, 35:*789–821, 1965.

11. *The Health Consequences of Smoking. A Report to the Surgeon General:* 1971. DHEW Publ. No. (HSM) 71–7513: Washington, D.C., U.S. Govt Print Off, 1971.

12. National Center for Health Statistics: *Comparability of Age on the Death Certificate and Matching Census Record,* United States, May-August, 1960. Vital and Health Statistics. Public Health Service Publ. No. 1000, Series 2, No. 29. Washington, D.C., U.S. Govt Print Off, June, 1968.

13. McPhedran, P., Heath, C.W., Garcia, J.S.: Racial variations in leukemia incidence among the elderly. *J Natl Cancer Inst, 45:*25–28, 1970.

14. Winkelstein, W., Jr., Gay, M.L., Sacks, S.: Race, economic status, and prostatic cancer in Buffalo. Abstract of contributed papers (No. 208–0), 99th annual meeting of the American Public Health Association. Minneapolis, October 10–15, 1971.

15. Mason, T.J., Fraumeni, J.F., Jr.: Unpublished data.

16. Fraumeni, J.F., Jr., Glass, A.G.: Rarity of Ewing's sarcoma among U.S. Negro children. *Lancet, 1:*366–367, 1970.

17. Jensen, R.D., Miller, R.W.: Retinoblastoma: Epidemiologic characteristics. *N Engl J Med, 285:*307–311, 1971.

Chapter 13

A STUDY OF THE RELATIVE FREQUENCY OF CARCINOMA OF THE CERVIX IN THE NEGRO

WILLIAM M. CHRISTOPHERSON, AND JAMES E. PARKER

Racial selectivity for squamous carcinoma of the cervix has often been implied by relative frequency data obtained from many parts of the world.[4] From our own available data, based on the screening of more than 60,000 women, it would seem that squamous carcinoma of the cervix is more than twice as common in the Negro race as in the Caucasian race. The higher prevalence rate among Negroes in various regions of the United States has been amply demonstrated by several studies.[2,3,6,7] Many workers have doubted that the obviously higher rate among Negroes is a matter of racial susceptibility. Rather they have felt it is the result of other factors that could be grouped as socioeconomic.[1,5,9] Stocks[8] studied mortality data from Great Britian and concluded that there was a relationship between incidence and overcrowded housing, social class distribution, and predominant industry 20 years before.

In order to determine the factors that might account for the apparent impressive racial difference in the prevalence of squamous carcinoma of the cervix among our own patients,

Reprinted with permission from *Cancer*, July-August, 1960.

This work was supported by grants from the Field Investigations and Demonstrations Branch, National Cancer Institute, of the National Institutes of Health, Public Health Service, the Kentucky Division of the American Cancer Society, Inc., and the Department of Health of the Commonwealth of Kentucky.

We are grateful for the assistance of Anne Baranovsky, Field Investigations and Demonstrations Branch, National Cancer Institute, and Mr. Thomas Miller, University of Louisville School of Medicine.

we attempted to match them according to economic conditions.

Method and Material

Since April, 1956, an attempt has been made to screen the women of Jefferson County, Ky., for cervical cancer by means of cervical and vaginal cell studies.

In a group of 32,590 women for whom statistical data were available, 10,045 were women with sufficiently low incomes (not more than $30.00 a week) to qualify for admission to the clinics of the Louisville General Hospital, Louisville, Ky., a charity institution. The 32,590 women represent consecutive women who have had cell studies. The abnormal cell studies were documented by tissue examination. The group with which we will concern ourselves during the remainder of this study consists of the charity patients. Among the 10,045 women in this latter group, there were 5,882 Negroes and 4,163 Caucasians.

Results

Among the 10,045 women, 151 had cell studies that were sufficiently abnormal as to require a cervical biopsy. Of the 151 biopsies requested, 141 were performed. We have thus far been unable to obtain biopsies on the remaining ten. Of the 141 biopsies performed, 26 showed no significant change in the cervix other than inflammation. This group of 26 included biopsy material that we considered insufficient for diagnosis. In the group of the 115 abnormal biopsies, there were 30 invasive squamous cell carcinomas, 25 intraepithelial carcinomas and 60 cases of cervical dysplasia. The comparative prevalence of the various findings according to race is given in Table 13-I.

Comment

From the data it would seem that in this comparative study of patients of similar socioeconomic status, the relative fre-

TABLE 13-I
COMPARATIVE STUDY OF RATES UN-
CORRECTED FOR AGE DIFFERENCE

Results smear or biopsy	Group			
	Negro		Caucasian	
	No. cases	Rate/1,000 cases	No. cases	Rate/1,000 cases
Abnorm. smears	79	13.43	72	17.29
Invas. squam. ca.	13	2.21	17	4.08
Intraepith. ca.	12	2.04	12	3.12
Dysplasia	30	5.10	30	7.21
Neg. biopsy	16	2.71	10	2.40

quency of squamous carcinoma of the cervix is indeed no greater in the Negro than in the Caucasian. As a matter of fact the frequency of invasive carcinoma, intraepithelial carcinoma, and dysplasia was greater in Caucasian women in this series. We hasten to point out that perhaps the reason for this latter observation is that there were eight biopsies not done in the Negro group and only two not performed in the Caucasian group. Furthermore, the age groups were not exactly comparable. Fourteen percent of the Negroes were under 20 years of age and 10.5 percent of the Caucasians were in this age range. The average age was 34.6 years for the Negroes and 41.6 years for the Caucasians. It should be noted that no significant cervical lesion occurred before the age of 20 years in either group. Using the age distribution of the Caucasians and Negroes combined as the standard age distribution to "correct" the various rates for the differences in age between the groups, we obtained the rates in Table 13-II. The magnitude of the new rates themselves is unimportant, being affected by the choice of the standard. However, the standard used has little effect on the difference in rates obtained, which is what we are interested in. In testing the differences in *crude* rates for invasive squamous carcinoma between Caucasians and Negroes, the difference is not statistically significant. The probability of getting such a difference, or a greater one, by chance is 9 percent.

TABLE 13-II
COMPARATIVE RATES CORRECTED FOR
AGE DIFFERENCE*

| Results | Rates in: | |
biopsy	Caucasian gp.	Negro gp.
Invas. squam. ca.	3.33	2.65
Intraepith. ca.	3.26	2.29
Dysplasia	7.48	4.88

*Per 1,000 women screened.

In order to compare the racial groups with respect to factors that might play a part in the prevalence of cervical cancer, and to test the homogeneity of the group, data were compiled on several items. Eighty-four percent of the Caucasians had at one time been married as compared to 76 percent of the Negroes. Three per cent of the records of both groups did not record marital status. The average age at first marriage was 19.3 years for the Caucasian group and 19.8 years for the Negro group. The average age at first pregnancy was 19.8 years for the Caucasian group and 18.8 years for the Negro group. It should be noted that whereas the Negro group did not marry until an average age of 19.8 years, the age of first pregnancy was a full year earlier. It is also important to note that there were 672 Negro women who claimed to be single and had borne children, some as many as ten. This information tends to make one question the importance of marital status data.

The average number of pregnancies was four for the Caucasian group and 3.5 for the Negro group among those tabulated as ever married. It averaged 0.4 pregnancies for the single Caucasian group and 1.4 for the single Negro group.

It should be emphasized that only squamous cell carcinoma of the cervix and related atypias of squamous mucosa were considered in this study. Adenocarcinomas of the cervix and endometrium probably involve a different set of factors and thus were purposely excluded.

The extremely high prevalence rate of carcinoma and dysplasia in this group of patients is noteworthy and does not reflect the findings in the private patient group. It does, however, emphasize that this form of cancer is intimately associated with a variety of social factors that need further elucidation. The patients studied came to the clinic as a routine measure and were subsequently referred for definitive diagnosis on the basis of the abnormal cell studies. Certainly some of the invasive carcinomas could have been detected by physical examination and biopsy, without benefit of cell studies. It is noteworthy, however, that these people were patients in our clinics and cytological studies did in fact call attention to the necessity of a pelvic examination and a cervical biopsy by a physician.

Summary

A group of Negro women was compared to a group of Caucasian women as to prevalence of squamous carcinoma of the cervix and related cervical atypias. Both groups had routine cervical studies in a cancer survey project and did not have previously diagnosed or treated cervical cancer. Both groups were of similar economic status and were patients of a charity hospital. The prevalence of invasive carcinoma, intraepithelial carcinoma, and dysplasia was found to be higher in the Caucasian women than the Negroes. The remarkably higher relative frequency of cervical cancer in the Negro previously reported[2-5,7] is not the result of racial susceptibility but rather is associated with factors relative to the lower socioeconomic status of the Negro in the United States.

REFERENCES

1. Clemmesen, J., and Nielsen, A.: Social distribution of cancer in Copenhagen, 1943 to 1947. *Br J Cancer*, 5:159–171, 1951.

2. Dorn, H.F., and Cutler, S.: *Morbidity from Cancer in the United States, Variation in Incidence by Age, Sex, Race, Marital Status, and Geographic Region.* Public Health Monogr No. 29. Washington, D.C. U.S. Govt Print Off, 1955, Pt. 1.

3. Dunn, J.E., Jr., Rowan, J.C.; Erickson, C.C., and Siegler, E.E.: Uterine cancer morbidity data; Memphis and Shelby County, Tenn., 1950–51. *Public Health Rep, 69:*269–274, 1954.

4. Kaiser, R.F., and Gilliam, A.G.: Some epidemiological aspects of cervical cancer. *Public Health Rep, 73:*359–367, 1958.

5. Kennaway, E.L.: Racial and social incidence of cancer of uterus. *Br J Cancer, 2:*177–212, 1948.

6. Public Health Service, Federal Security Agency: Cancer Morbidity Series, 1–10. Public Health Service Publ. No. 13, 65, 67, 112, 126, 152, 178, 216, 217, 244. Washington, D.C. U.S. Govt Print Off, 1950–1952.

7. Robinson, B.W.: Malignancy in Negro; statistical review. *Am J Roentgenol, 66:*783–790, 1951.

8. Stocks, P.: Cancer of uterine cervix and social conditions. *Br J Cancer, 9:*487–494, 1955.

9. Wynder, E.L., Cornfield, J., Schroff, P.D., and Doraiswami, K.R.: Study of environmental factors in carcinoma of cervix. *Am J Obstet Gynecol, 68:*1016–1052, 1954.

PART FIVE
ALCOHOLISM AND DRUG ADDICTION

Ethnic or racial patterns in alcoholism and drug addiction can be traced only when the data record these factors. Unfortunately, while there is a great deal of material on alcoholism and drug addiction, there is a dearth of material delineating racial or ethnic group affiliation.

Robert Strayer's study of the Negro alcoholic is both quantitative and qualitative. On the one hand he attempts to give a statistical picture of white and black alcoholics over a decade. On the other hand, he attempts to analyze the personalities of those who become alcoholics. Strayer's conclusions, however, may not be the basis for widespread generalizations inasmuch as his sample was relatively small.

M. M. Vitols has attempted a similar survey of alcoholism. It is of value to compare the two studies, inasmuch as Strayer's was done in a northern city, Bridgeport, Connecticut, while Vitols' was based on patients admitted to North Carolina State Hospitals.

The study of drug addiction of young Negro men by Lee N. Robins and George E. Murphy was done in St. Louis. The variables of absent father, delinquency, and dropping out of high school were considered to be significant factors for predicting future addiction to heroin.

Milton Helpern's technical study of fatalities due to narcotic addiction in New York gives a figure of about 100,000 persons addicted to hard drugs out of a population of eight million. The ratio of deaths per 10,000 deaths from narcotism between blacks and whites is twelve to one. This documents (at least in New York City), the disparate rates of addiction between blacks and whites.

Chapter 14

STUDY OF THE NEGRO ALCOHOLIC

ROBERT STRAYER

Study of the alcoholic population of any ethnic or racial minority group can contribute to a better understanding of the forces which make for interaction and conflict. These forces may in some measure condition the use of alcohol as a means of accommodation to the problems created by conflicting cultural or racial patterns. This understanding can be especially helpful for developing client-therapist relationships and in the effective treatment of the alcoholic. This may be particularly true with respect to the American Negro, who represents one of the oldest and least assimilated of minority groups in the land, long exposed to discriminatory practices resulting in economic and social problems strongly reflected in day-to-day living.

The purpose of the present study was to gain some understanding of the manner in which the Negro alcoholic might differ from or resemble his white counterpart, and particularly to note anything in the clinical material which illumine the motivational forces in his drinking. It was thus important to study the Negro alcoholic not only in the interrelationship of his subculture to the larger American society but also as an individual presenting a problem in treatment, and to consider the manner in which this problem might reflect itself in that interrelationship.

Description of the Sample

The subjects consist of all the Negro alcoholics admitted to the Bridgeport Clinic of the Connecticut Commission on

Reprinted with permission from the *Quarterly Journal of Studies on Alcohol*, Volume 22, 1961.

Alcoholism over a period of nine and a half years ending in December, 1958. During this time, in a total of 1,308 patients, 44 were Negroes—26 men, and 18 women. Of the 1,264 white patients 1,077 were men and 187 women. All the Negro patients resided in the Greater Bridgeport Area, compared to 975 of the 1,264 white alcoholics. The Greater Bridgeport Area contains a population of approximately 260,000, including some 11,500 Negroes. Thus the clinic appears to have drawn nearly proportional segments from the two populations (white 0.5 percent, Negroes 0.4 percent). How this relates to the total alcoholic population of the respective racial groups in the area is impossible to say in the absence of other statistics.

It is particularly interesting that 41 percent of the Negro patients were women, compared to 16 percent among the whites—the latter being close to the national sex ratio. It seems important to examine the 18 Negro female cases for features which may be peculiar to the Negro family structure as possibly accounting for the drinking pattern of these women, and perhaps providing clues for their treatment. For this reason comparison will be made not only between the Negro and white clinic population but also between the females of both groups.

The data were gathered from the case records of the patients. Some items were not available in all the records. Often this was due to the fact that the patient had been too inebriated to give the information at the first visit and never returned thereafter. The cases with incomplete data never exceeded 30 percent of the white sample and 7 percent of the Negro sample. For most of the items studied information was available in all the case records.

Conclusive generalizations are severely inhibited by the limitations of the sample. These limitations include the large discrepancy in the size of the two populations, the fact that the sample came from only one clinic, and the small number of Negro cases. Whatever interpretations may be drawn from the data can only be related to the specific sample studied and should not be applied indiscriminately to Negro alcoholics in general. The lack of previous studies of Negro alcoholic samples precludes comparative evaluations. In a sense, then, this must be considered an exploratory attempt.

SOURCE OF REFERRAL. Of the entire case load, 18 per cent of the Negroes and 17 per cent of the whites were referred by social agencies. Other referring sources, by percentage, included relatives (18 percent Negroes, 12 percent whites), self (14 percent Negroes, 12 percent whites), Alcoholics Anonymous (no Negroes, 17 percent whites), courts (7 percent Negroes, 10 percent whites), physicians (9 percent Negroes, 9 percent whites), hospitals (7 percent Negroes, 8 percent whites), friends and patients (20 percent Negroes, 9 percent whites), clergy (6 percent Negroes, 4 percent whites), employers (no Negroes, 2 percent whites). It is notable that A.A. represents the largest single source of referral, along with social agencies, of the white patients, yet while the social agencies referred an equal proportion of Negroes, not one Negro was referred by A.A. The explanation appears to be that there is not a single Negro member in any of the A.A. groups in the Greater Bridgeport Area.

RESIDENCE. A large majority of both the Negroes (73 percent) and the whites (65 percent) were living with their families, while 21 percent of the Negroes and 22 percent of the whites were living in rooming houses, 4 percent of the Negroes and 9 percent of the whites were homeless, and 2 percent and 4 percent respectively were living in local missions. Four out of five of the Negroes had been born and raised in the south and a goodly number of them still maintained regular contact with their southern relatives either through correspondence or by periodic visits.

AGE. The greatest numbers in both groups fell within the 36 to 45-year age category (Negroes 59 percent, whites 38 percent). There was little difference in the proportions below 35 years of age (Negroes 30 percent, whites 27 percent). The remainder were over age 46.

MARITAL STATUS. Half the patients in each group (Negroes 50 percent, whites 49 percent) were married; 11 percent of the Negroes and 18 percent of the whites were single;

39 percent of the Negroes, and 33 percent of the whites were divorced, separated or widowed. In the latter category, the largest percentage in both groups (Negroes 21 percent, whites 16 percent) were separated.

Among the Negroes only 39 percent of the women were married, compared to 58 percent of the men; and 50 percent of the Negro women, compared to 30 percent of the men, were either divorced, separated or widowed.

In every instance the marital status of the Negroes in the sample had been legalized. Separation, in most instances, implied desertion by the husband and there were twice as many Negro broken homes involving children (39 percent) as white (17 percent).

EDUCATIONAL STATUS. Among the Negroes 48 percent had only an elementary school education; 17 percent had graduated from high school and 28 percent had some high school education, while 7 percent had from one to three years of college. Among the whites the corresponding percentages were 35, 21, 30 and 9, and 5 percent had finished college.

OCCUPATIONAL STATUS. Applying the classification of the *Dictionary of Occupational Titles*, 46 percent of the Negroes and 17 percent of the whites were unskilled workers, 26 percent of the Negroes and 32 percent of the whites were semiskilled, 5 percent of the Negroes and 18 percent of the whites were skilled workers, and 20 percent of the Negroes and 7 percent of the whites were in service occupations. The latter excess was in part accounted for by the large number of Negro women employed as domestics. No Negroes fell within the clerical, sales, professional and managerial classifications, compared to 20 percent of the whites.

DRINKING PATTERNS. An attempt was made to evaluate drinking patterns in terms of frequency, behavior changes, and duration of addiction. Among the Negroes 68 percent drank daily; among the whites 59 percent; and 22 percent of the Negroes were weekend drinkers compared to 15 per cent of the whites. The greatest difference appeared in the pattern of periodic drinking: 10 percent of the Negroes and

26 percent of the whites. The proportion of periodic drinkers is greater among the Negro women (18 percent) than among the Negro men (4 percent), while the proportion of weekend drinkers among the Negroes is reversed: 29 percent of the men and 12 percent of the women.

In an attempt to discover the extent to which the patients used alcohol as a tool in social intercourse, it was found that 58 percent of the Negroes and 51 percent of the whites customarily drank with others, 27 percent of the Negroes and 26 percent of the whites had no habitual preference between drinking alone or with others, and 15 percent of the Negroes and 23 percent of the whites customarily drank alone.

The tendency to drink in company is more pronounced in the female patients. Of the Negro women 47 percent customarily drank with others, compared to 23 percent of the white women. The Negroes more commonly drank at home with friends or relatives, visiting by friends and relatives being often the occasion for heavy drinking. Use of the tavern in drinking was much less evident in the Negro sample than in the white.

BEHAVIOR WHILE DRINKING. Information obtained from the patients indicates that the Negro alcoholic when intoxicated is more likely to be gregarious, talkative and gay than his white counterpart. There is no noticeable difference in the frequency of acting out of aggressive behavior. In all instances of assaultive behavior by the Negroes the victims were Negroes; most commonly it was the wife.

Other behavioral observations indicate that 5 percent of the Negroes and 14 percent of the whites are passive and withdrawn when intoxicated, while 2 percent and 14 percent, respectively, are argumentative and irritable. Among the Negroes men and women are equally gregarious and gay while drinking, but the women are more often passive and withdrawn (women, 12 percent, men, 0) and less given to assaultive behavior (6 percent versus 12 percent).

BEVERAGES. The following large differences in beverage preference were recorded: 30 percent of the Negroes and

6 percent of the whites drank wine exclusively; 30 percent of the Negroes and 9 percent of the whites drank whiskey exclusively; 15 percent of the Negroes and 40 percent of the whites drank whiskey and beer, the latter often as a "chaser" for the whiskey.

DURATION OF PROBLEM. The length of time that an alcoholic has been drinking to excess may reflect the depth of the behavioral pattern and the use of alcohol in adjusting to daily living. This knowledge can then help in formulating both a diagnosis and a prognosis.

The Negroes in the present sample had been drinking excessively for somewhat shorter periods of time than the white patients. This might be accounted for by the age difference between the groups. Of the total Negro sample, 56 per cent had been drinking excessively less than 10 years compared to 42 percent of the whites, while 38 percent of the whites compared to 15 percent of the Negroes had been drinking to excess over 15 years. The remainder in both groups had been drinking excessively from 11 to 15 years at the time they came to the clinic.

ATTENDANCE AT CLINIC. The ability to sustain contact with the clinic may be an expression of the strength of the patient's motivation to get well. Repeated contact enhances the likelihood of establishing a meaningful therapeutic relationship through which the problems related to the patient's drinking can be resolved or minimized. Proportionately twice as many of the Negro patients (41 percent) had 10 or more interviews as whites (22 percent). The Negro women demonstrated a much more sustained interest in treatment than did the men—only 24 percent of the men compared to 61 percent of the women were seen in ten or more interviews. By comparison, 48 percent of the white women were seen in ten or more interviews.

RESPONSE TO TREATMENT. The patient's drinking pattern at the time he came to the clinic was compared with his pattern when he terminated clinic contact. If the patient was completely abstinent or if the intensity or frequency of his drinking was reduced he was rated improved. If no change occurred or the drinking had become worse, he was rated unimproved. No evaluation was made if the patient had been seen for less than four interviews. Because it was impractical to attempt to evaluate the more than 1,000 white male case records, only the two female samples and the Negro men were rated. These groups were regarded as especially important because of the excess of Negro women in the patient load.

Of the Negro women, 50 percent were rated as improved and 22 percent unimproved; the remaining 28 percent could not be rated. Of the Negro men, 35 percent were rated as improved and 27 percent unimproved, the remainder being unratable. The greater ability of the women to sustain contact apparently was reflected in their response to treatment. The response of the white women to treatment was less favorable than that of the Negroes: 32 percent were rated as improved and 34 percent as unimproved, while another 34 percent could not be rated.

Discussion

As indicated previously, the small size of the Negro sample severely restricts the possibility of drawing inferences from the statistical material. In good measure, however, the findings reinforce certain clinical impressions based on therapeutic contacts with the Negro patients of the Bridgeport clinic. It is essential to reemphasize, however, that these impressions relate to the sample studied and should not be applied to Negro alcoholics generally unless confirmed by additional evidence.

A consistent impression derived from contact with the Negro patients in the sample is the status striving of the better educated and those who have acquired some property. Typically this takes the form of frequent and spontaneous expression of the respectability of the patient's family background. It appears to be related to his need to maintain an ideal of his self-image and to impress this upon the therapist. He tends to emphasize the value placed in his home upon a good education, that he or she was exposed to "proper" religious training, and that the family was never involved in antisocial behavior. In some instances Negro patients stressed the sacrifices they had made in helping their children achieve a better education.

Although the occupational statistics revealed no Negroes in the middle class, this does not imply a lack of identity with middle-class strivings and morality. Class structure within the Negro subculture is not exclusively based on occupation. "Rather the middle class is marked off from the lower class by a pattern of behavior expressed in stable family and associational relationships, in great concern with front and respectability and in a drive for getting ahead."[1] The clinical material as well as the statistics indicate the Negro's identity with family and the striving for status. The legalization of marriage and divorce represents in part the attempt to achieve a middle-class morality. This is particularly significant if the type of marital ties which existed in the rural south is considered. These stemmed from historical forces which gave rise to certain cultural practices as seen in the common-law partnership. With the urbanization of the Negro and the breaking down of some racial barriers marriage has assumed a more institutionalized form:

> Among the middle-class families the breaking of marital ties is a matter for the divorce court, while the Negro from the isolated areas of the South has only vague knowledge of the meaning of divorce. It is part of the middle-class Negro's conformity to moral codes and maintenance of respectability to have his marital relations rest upon legality.[2]

The legalization of marital relations and the Negro's reiterated verbalization of respectability of family background reflects this identification.

This identification is also shown in other ways, particularly in the role of patient at the alcoholism clinic. The alcoholism is looked upon as a falling from grace, so to speak, not only in the patient's relationship with his family but also in the relationships within the Negro community. The apparently strong motivational forces to achieve sobriety, indicated in the superior ability of the Negro patients to sustain treatment contact, may reflect the attempt at reestablishment within the family and community. This is oftentimes made explicit by the Negro patients when they verbalize the reason why they want to stop drinking.

In all the cases seen at the clinic, never has a Negro patient presented as part of his defense structure that the therapist does not understand him as an alcoholic or as a Negro. Rather does the Negro seek understanding of his needs in relation to his frustrated drives and the acceptance of his desire to reestablish himself as a respected individual. Nor does the Negro verbalize, as the basis for his frustrated drives, the discrimination to which he has been subjected. Whether this is related to the fact that he is dealing with a therapist of another race is an unresolved question. Yet the very fact of his inability to verbalize as a defense his position as a Negro in a white society puts him in a favorable therapeutic situation in which the therapist can focus upon those immediate reality situations which are creating stress, which initiate drinking episodes, and which are most susceptible to change.

Frequently the Negro client looks upon treatment and the treatment relationship as an unwritten contract which he is obligated to observe. A certain formality tends to mark his adherence to the contract. Thus, he rarely presents himself at the clinic without telephoning and making an appointment. Promptness is a fetish and broken appointments are cause for profuse apologies. When the Negro is able to pay a fee he recognizes the need to do so, as symbolizing his striving for independence, and he does so regularly and consistently. These are not common behavioral practices of alcoholic patients. The element of responsibility that the Negro stresses in the treatment relationship appears to be part of his desire to maintain his concept of self and his need for status. This latter need, interestingly enough, finds expression even in his drinking. The Negro whisky drinker makes it a point to stress, and this quite spontaneously, the expensive brand he drinks.

Frazier has emphasized:

> The important position of the mother in the Negro family in the United States. . . . In the absence of institutional controls, the relationship between mother and child has become the essential bond in the family and the woman's economic position has developed in her those qualities which are associated with a matri-archal organization.[2]

This statement seems to have a good deal of applicability to some of the clinical observations on the Negro woman alcoholic. The relatively strong position of the woman in the family household is manifest in many ways. She enjoys an economic independence which is not equally evident in her white counterpart. Of the 18 Negro women in the sample, 56 percent were employed at the time of referral to the clinic, compared to 28 percent of the whites. Also, 52 percent of the wives of the married Negro men were working compared with 23 percent of the wives of the white men patients. Frequently this represented an attempt on the part of the wife to supplement the husband's earnings not only as a means of making ends meet but also to secure additional advantages for the children. The weak economic position of the Negro man has necessitated that the woman go to work. This has placed her in a position of advantage, but has also created added burdens in her role as mother and supplemental provider. Negro women patients oftentimes expressed their feelings of responsibility for the children, and spoke of the burden they carry in relation to the family. They are aware of their key role in keeping the family together. This seems particularly significant since half of the Negro women were divorced, separated or widowed. In a number of cases the husband of the woman patient was also a heavy drinker, but showed a complete lack of interest in treatment for himself and saw his wife alone as having a drinking problem. When the wife in this sort of couple achieves sobriety, the husband often attempts to seduce her into drinking, and failing, he will sometimes express his frustration in punitive aggressive behavior against her. In several such instances the wife expressed the feeling that the responsibility for doing something about her problem was hers as she represents the only hope for continuity and survival of the family, and that the husband's behavior would not serve as a deterrent to her objective.

The matriarchal feature in American Negro family living has historical antecedents in the slavery period. This background was later reinforced by the mass migration of the Negro men to the North in search of better job opportunities and escape from discriminatory practices. The women, frequently deserted, were left with the responsibility of caring for the children. How much the legacy of the matriarchy has been perpetuated in the Negro sample seen at the clinic should be carefully evaluated as a means of understanding motivational forces in relation to the Negro woman's alcoholism. The material makes amply clear her preoccupation with family and her strong motivation for sobriety as a means of keeping the family together. Most important is her expression of feeling that this is her responsibility, apart from the role of the husband where one is present in the home. In other areas, too, decisions within the home are frequently made by the woman, and the children seem to see her as the symbol of authority.

This latter fact is particularly manifest in the Negro male alcoholic's attitude toward the mother figure. He sees her as the character-shaping force within the family. This, in itself, may become a source of conflict within the male alcoholic. Cross-currents of dependent-independent strivings pull him in both directions, making it difficult for him to resolve his role. In a good number of instances the alcoholic is a man who married a very strong, assertive woman, whom he identifies with the mother figure and toward whom he expresses his hostility, particularly when drinking. In several instances the alcoholism appeared to be not so much an expression of dependency *per se* but a revolt against it, yet driving the man into a deeper dependency role.

Another apparently pertinent fact is that the wife of the Negro alcoholic seems to have a greater feeling of independence in relation to her husband's drinking than the wife of the white alcoholic. She is frequently employed and has had to assume the role of breadwinner within the family. She is less likely than her white counterpart to express interest in the patient's treatment and very rarely becomes involved in the total treatment process.

> The case of Mr. T illustrates some of these facts. Born and raised in Mississippi, his mother was a school teacher, with tremendous ambitions for her children. She was the strong, controlling force within the family, while the father was passive and ineffectual. She laid great stress upon education and attempted to manipulate the children to follow her pattern. Three older sisters of the patient were university graduates and worked as nurses and teachers. The patient rebelled against his mother's domination. After teaching school for several years he came to Bridgeport where he worked as a porter. He started drinking heavily, married a woman twelve years his senior, herself a university graduate and a professional worker. Like his mother she was manipulative and controlling. His drinking increased, and his functioning ultimately was affected. He found himself torn between his desire for emancipation and the assertion of his masculinity and his deep-seated dependency needs. He was floundering helplessly and in deep conflict at the time he came to the clinic for help.

> His wife, seen at that time, seemed more concerned with her own status needs than her husband's drinking problem. She frankly indicated that it was his responsibility to stop drinking and that the perpetuation of the marriage was contingent on his doing so. She showed little interest in maintaining contact with the clinic and, although encouraged to do so, failed to make another appointment or to express any further interest in her husband's progress. She quite bluntly revealed that she could manage for herself and would not feel any economic hardship if the relationship were terminated.

Although the Negro sample is small, it gives a decided impression of the strength of the matriarchal element in the families of these patients. This feature could well serve as a catalyst for the development of strong dependency patterns in the male Negro in accommodation to the family culture. A problem is then created when the Negro is exposed to another culture which places conflicting demands upon him. It seems significant that every Negro man in the sample, with one exception, started his heavy drinking only after he moved to Bridgeport. There are, of course, other causative factors involved, many of a purely individualistic nature. But this factor is pervasive. It is frequently expressed as hostility toward the wife, with various ramifications, from blunt verbalization of castration anxieties, to conflicted feelings over the need for independence, to attempts to impress the therapist with their good performance as fathers and providers. This claim, however, cannot tolerate reality testing.

The strong dependency trait in the male Negro alcoholics is, of course, not peculiar to them but is widely evident in the white alcoholic men as well. In the former, however, it seems to be derived essentially from the matriarchal family background and in this sense it differs from the maternal dependency of the white men. In the latter, the dependency is expressive of emotional pathology within the mother-child relationship. In the Negroes it expresses the cultural mores of a people, with deep-seated historical antecedents.

Accompanying the dependency of the Negro male alcoholic may be very strong narcissistic feelings, and preoccupation with self and with somatic complaints. He tends to place great emphasis upon what alcohol is doing to his health. Thus the focus in treatment must be partially geared to this attitude, although emphasis may also be placed upon day-to-day problems which are producing tension and pressure. Medication has real meaning in the total treatment program of these patients, who see sobriety essentially in relation to physical well-being and improved functioning.

More recently, Frazier has noted:

> The Negro family has developed [also] as a patriarchal organization similar to the American family as the male has acquired property and an interest in his family and as the assimilation of American attitudes and patterns of behavior has been accelerated by the breaking down of social isolation, sometimes through physical amalgamation.

The effect of the developing patriarchy has been evident in only two or three of the Negro alcoholic patients. In each instance the man has acquired both property and education, exhibited steady work habits, strong status strivings both for himself and his children, pride around family and related traits, as well as a strong superego and strong motivation for sobriety. These men represent the figure of authority within the home and their wives have shown real concern and interest in the patient's problem in treatment. In each instance the family has come from an urban area in the south and has been living in the north more than ten years.

The Negro woman alcoholic patient brings into treatment the tensions and pressures arising out of her responsibilities in the management of the family and the problems of her relationship with her husband if he is present. Her relatively strong superego and motivation for achieving sobriety as a means of sustaining the family represent very positive factors in treatment. It seems that the very factors which induce the excessive drinking also serve as a motivating force in seeking sobriety.

Treatment of the Negro, as with all alcoholics, must be on an individualized basis. The therapist, however, should be aware of the cultural forces which reflect themselves in the Negro's attitude and living, particularly where they evoke conflict and resulting psychopathology. The therapist must be able to utilize constructively the motivational forces which bring the Negro patient into the clinic and build upon that which is positive in the character structure of the individual. This also involves an ability to communicate with the Negro as well as an interest in his problem. He is quick to sense the basis upon which he is accepted and reacts to it accordingly. The therapist must also guard against the pitfall of thinking in terms of stereotypes and recognize the need for a highly individualized, flexible approach. The penetration of the barriers between therapist and Negro patient are contingent upon the therapist's elimination of ghetto thinking, first as it applies to the therapist in relation to psychotherapeutic practice, second as it applies to the Negro's own isolation which has arisen from external discriminatory practices reinforced by self-imposed insulation from a hostile environment.

Summary

The records of the Connecticut Commission on Alcoholism Clinic in Bridgeport were reviewed and from the extracted data a statistical description was compiled of all white and Negro male and female admissions during a nine-and-a-half year period. In a total of 1,308 admissions there were 1,077 white men and 187 white women, 26 Negro men and 18 Negro women. The race distribution was approximately proportional to the area population, but Negro women were heavily overrepresented. The sample was described in terms of age, source of referral, type of residence, marital status, educational status, occupational status, drinking patterns, behavior while drinking, beverage preferences, duration of problem, attendance at clinic, and response to treatment.

The Negro patients, more especially the women, tended to show stronger motivation to achieve sobriety as manifested by superior capacity to sustain contact with the clinic.

Particular features of the American Negro subculture, as reflected in patterns of interaction and conflict, were discussed in their possible relation to the development of patterns of excessive drinking and motivation for recovery. The Negro patients were seen to exhibit strong strivings for middle-class status and morality. Particular emphasis was given to the significance of the matriarchal organization of most Negro families. This legacy from the slavery period was seen as catalyzing the development of dependency patterns in the men, with resulting conflict, tensions and pressures evocative of resort to excessive drinking; and as imposing added tensions and pressures on the women, with similar effect. The strong feeling of responsibility for maintaining the family, however, was seen as a highly favorable prognostic factor.

It is concluded that while the treatment of Negro alcoholics must be as individualized as that of white patients, awareness of the special cultural forces and motivational elements involved, together with the avoidance of stereotypical thinking, can result in more effective therapeutic function.

REFERENCES

1. Drake, S. and Cayton, H.R.: *Black Metropolis.* New York, Harcourt, Brace, 1945, p. 661.

2. Frazier, F.E.: *The Negro in the United States.* New York, Macmillan, 1957, p. 368.

Chapter 15

CULTURE PATTERNS OF DRINKING IN NEGRO AND WHITE ALCOHOLICS

M. M. Vitols

In the evaluation of a patient not everything can be explained on purely psychodynamic grounds. The emotionally and mentally ill person can only be understood by considering the state of health of the social field in which that particular patient lives.[1] This applies even more when we are dealing with persons who have problems of alcoholism. Not only is the use of alcoholic beverages different from one country to another; it is also quite different among people living in the same country. It is stated that the use of "alcoholic beverages in a group or society is primarily a cultural phenomenon and it is in the light of the culture of the group or society that the uses of such beverages are to be understood."[2] There are also papers and books published dealing with society, culture and drinking patterns.[3] The drinking patterns in such ethnic and cultural groups as Irish,[4,5] Jewish,[4-6] and Italian[7] have been discussed. However, little has been reported on the Negro alcoholic.[8] This paper deals with the cultural and dynamic factors in the makeup of the Negro alcoholic.

The data and observations have been derived from alcoholic patients admitted over a period of years to the North Carolina State mental facilities. During the fiscal year 1962–63, only two State mental institutions admitted alcoholics—one white and the other Negro alcoholics (Table 15-I).

Table 15-II lists the number of admissions of alcoholics from 1961 through 1965.

Abridged and reprinted with permission from *Diseases of the Nervous System*, June, 1968.

TABLE 15-I
Alcoholic Admissions July 1962-June 1963
N.C. State Hospital System

	White	Negro
Alcoholic Admissions	1148	92
% of total population		
in N.C.	75%	25%

In 1965 the State of North Carolina Mental Health Department regionalized the hospitals and Cherry Hospital, serving Eastern Carolina, admitted a total of 1039 alcoholics, of which 132 were Negroes and 907 white, the population of the catchment area being 45 percent Negro and 55 percent white.

These data do not reflect the true incidence of alcoholism and, as can be seen in Table 15-II, they show only that there are more alcoholics referred and treated in the state mental health facilities. Many alcoholics are treated in other psychiatric facilities, general hospitals, Veterans Administration hospitals or on out-patient basis. However, the data indicate that the Negro is referred less for treatment of alcoholism to the state mental facilities. This does not necessarily indicate that there is less or more alcoholism among Negroes. Due to specific social-cultural patterns there is greater tolerance of abnormal behavior in the Negro family and community, especially in the lower socioeconomic class, and the Negro alcoholic is no exception. In general the attitude towards the Negro alcoholic is different. He is either placed in jail to sober up and/or regarded as not needing any specific treatment.

TABLE 15-II
Alcoholic Admissions to N.C. Mental Hospitals

Year	Negro	Total
1961	48	903
1962	64	1070
1963	92	1240
1964	135	1707
1965	132 (regional)	2702

The Social-Cultural Differences

With the development of this country, drinking customs were brought over from Europe to the American Colonies. At first the use of alcoholic beverages was accepted and approved by the colonists; however, drunkenness was not tolerated. From the early period of the history of America the Indians, Negroes and other servants were prohibited from drinking alcohol. The main reason given was a fear of violence when intoxicated. When the Negro later became a slave he was too valuable to be permitted to use alcohol, and only twice a year, after the summer crop was brought in and at Christmas, was he allowed to have alcoholic beverages. In spite of the strict laws regarding the sale and use of alcoholic beverages by this group they did not prevent the Negroes, Indians and servants from obtaining alcohol. Besides the slaves there were also the so-called free Negroes, but by the middle of the century the status of the free Negroes had deteriorated to such an extent that there was no distinction between them and slaves.

Reports of the time indicate that the Negro was considered childish, irresponsible, shiftless, lazy and addicted to excessive use of alcohol.[9] This belief about the Negroes and their irresponsibility, and love of alcohol, continued after the Civil War. General Robert E. Lee stated "The Negroes as a race were spend-thrifts and gullible and had a liking for tobacco and whiskey."[10] After the Civil War there was considerable and excessive use of alcohol among some of the freed slaves. However, a large number were steady in their work habits and temperate in their use of whiskey.

With the beginning of the twentieth century there was an overall concern about the use of alcohol by the total population, and also concern about drinking among Negroes. The Negro leaders—ministers—started to speak up, pointing out that alcoholism had hurt the Negro greatly.[11] Later during the mass migration of Negroes from rural to urban areas in the South and from the South to North and Midwest, many of the Negroes in their environment with less restrictions indulged themselves in excessive use of alcohol. A noted

Negro sociologist and authority on Negro life offered a theory "excessive drinking and sex seems to provide a means of narcotizing the middle class of Negro against a frustrating existence."[12] Another stated that among the most serious problems confronting the Negro communities is the disproportionate number in the grip of alcohol, the Negro communities being the greatest consumers of alcoholic beverages.[13]

It is stated by many researchers and workers in the field of alcoholism that alcohol is used to escape from day to day living and its problems. The position of the Negro in America has been such as to lead him to engage in excessive use of alcohol and therefore the admission data to the mental health facilities do not truly reflect the real extent of alcoholism among the Negroes. The estimated occurrence of alcoholism in the population area (Table 15-III) served by Cherry Hospital is estimated at 22,000 or 2 percent but only 1039 alcoholics have been treated on in-service basis.

Other data concerning Negro and white alcoholics have been derived from psychiatric interviews, social histories and direct contact with alcoholics in group therapy.

Onset of Drinking

Our data demonstrate that the onset of acute and persistent alcoholism addiction starts at an earlier age in the Negro than in the white. While the white alcoholic is experimenting with his drinking patterns between the age of 15 and 20 or later, the Negro alcoholic might show a fairly consistent and many times severe addiction during the early or middle teens. We became interested in this pattern and conducted a survey

TABLE 15-III
Alcoholic Admissions–Cherry Hospital
(Regional) July 1965–June 1966

	White	*Negro*	*Total*
Alcoholic Admissions	907	132	1039
% of population in Catchment area	55%	45%	1,083,000 (population)

in the local, and at that time all Negro high school, and the interviews brought out that there was already established dependence upon alcohol between the ages of 12 and 14 in about one third of the class. Three of these high school students have had at the age of 15 the first occurrence of delirium tremens. Among the Negro alcoholics the admitted occurrence of delirium tremens was encountered in the early twenties, while the white alcoholics showed delirium tremens in the late twenties or older.

A similar survey in an almost all white high school (400 students) showed 0.5 percent of the students experimenting with alcohol and only three students with some dependence on alcohol.

Patterns of Drinking

Experience with Negro alcoholics shows that they drink alcoholic beverages along social class lines, the lower socioeconomic class preferring, mostly out of necessity, boot-leg whiskey. However, the middle and upper class Negro also may purchase expensive alcoholic beverages and serve costly foods and beverages, largely as a status symbol. Usually an ethnic or social group has a special national drink, like the English, Italian, French or even the American hillbilly. The Negro appears not to have preference for any special drink, and in his drinking pattern he is predominantly a weekend drinker. This was brought out in the data here. It has created a pattern that led many employers of Negroes to have Monday as pay day in order to reduce the high rate of absenteeism on Monday. However, this arrangement has never worked satisfactorily, for pay day is still a pay day regardless of when. In the purchase of the whiskey, the Negro has coined a new word "spike" to refer to two or more Negroes buying a bottle together and dividing it equally among the group. Weekend drinking is the common pattern among the Negroes, because of vocational necessity and it is considered an exclusively male activity. Male Negro alcoholics in our observation rarely mentioned social drinking. However, the few female Negro alcoholics we have treated mentioned social drinking.

Behavior during Hospitalization

The Negro alcoholic accepts his hospitalization, even being put in jail prior to admission, much more gracefully than his white counterpart and when hospitalized he is less demanding and less manipulative. It is interesting that the Negro alcoholic appears to show fewer psychosomatic complaints or other neurotic defenses during the hospitalization. There have been few requests from the patient or the families for release prior to the prescribed length of treatment—in our state 30 days. The alcoholic as such is part of the family and if a person is drinking, his immediate family is involved, so in case of alcoholism we actually are dealing with the whole family. The white alcoholic, after being sobered up, very often not only demands but also many times manipulates the family into demanding a release as soon as possible. It has been noted during the past year, that in a fully integrated alcoholic ward, the Negro alcoholic has started to assume much of the white alcoholic's behavior and has joined the "game of manipulation."

Dynamic–Cultural Aspects

Much has been written and discussed about the role of the mother in the formation of alcoholism in the child. Narvatil[14] has stated that the mothers of alcoholics are either separated from their children, resulting in deprivation or have been excessively indulgent, and as a result the alcoholics choose women with whom sex life is sparse with rigidity or lack of interest. He considers alcoholism a psychological disturbance of married life, rooted in psychological disturbance in childhood. This is a psychodynamic approach and our observation with the Negro alcoholic also indicates a strong dependent hostile relationship with the mother, with the father being rarely mentioned or emotionally involved.

These psychodynamic findings are closely related to a specific cultural factor in the Negro. The family structure of the American Negro is traditionally matriarchal. As far back as slavery times the mother was more or less the center of the family. She actually held the family together and the marriage usually was unstable, the father feeling very little emotional attachment to the family. Also, the Negro woman, until the recent past, had a better chance for steady and sustained employment and was recognized as a responsible member of the family. This is especially true in the lower class.[15] The Negro as a husband and father plays a secondary role and is usually regarded by the woman as unstable and unreliable. This has created quite a pronounced hostile dependency on the mother in the Negro male alcoholic. This specific Negro family structure, especially in the lower class, together with the interaction of the interpersonal cultural and socioeconomic factors, have been pointed out as possible etiological factors for high incidence of schizophrenia in Negroes.[16]

In a preliminary report comparing the white and Negro alcoholic it was shown that the marital instability was 28.6 percent in the Negro but 51.7 percent in the white alcoholic, the control group showing 7.7 percent.[17] On a superficial glance it appears that the Negro is more stable in marriage. However, this is a misconception for the marital instability is based on data about divorce and separation.

The Negro male, especially in the lower socioeconomic group, is emotionally separated from the wife and family. The wife is aware of this and regards his instability and absence as natural phenomena. The emotional impact of separation is quite different in the Negro family. A Negro male may be absent for weeks, months and at times even years but he still will be regarded as married and accepted as such by his wife and family. The divorce is actually often regarded as an unnecessary expenditure and procedure in this matriarchial unit.

Therefore, the data centered on separation and divorce rates alone do not reveal the true incidence of male absences and instabilities in the Negro family.

Blackouts

The so-called alcoholic blackout appears to be less prominent or frequent in the Negro alcoholic. In comparing a group of 100 Negro alcoholics only 20 (20%) admitted or described a definite and somewhat prolonged alcoholic blackout. In a group of 200 white alcoholics the incidence appeared to be about 70 alcoholics (35%). Assuming that guilt plays a psychological role in the alcoholic blackout it appears that the guilt of using alcohol and the concomitant behavior is less in the Negro than in the white alcoholic. Also, we have observed less depression and less suicidal ruminations and suicidal attempts in the Negro than in the white. Through the years reported in this paper we have had only three depressions and suicidal attempts among the Negro alcoholics. This would be consistent with the findings pointed out by the author in another paper dealing with depression in the Southern Negro.[18]

Summary

Data have been presented concerning the admission of white and Negro alcoholic patients to the North Carolina Mental Health facilities. They indicate that the Negro alcoholic is referred less to the state mental health facilities for treatment; however, this does not reflect the true incidence of alcoholism or different rate of alcoholism in both races. The pattern of drinking in the Negro reflects the inseparability of the historical social and cultural factors from the psychodynamic aspect. One may say that the drinking is not actually the basic problem. The problem is the man's adaptive mechanisms to the inner and outer stresses to which he is exposed. The Negro shows a specific adaptive mechanism and at the same time one might predict that the more the Negro comes to share fully the white man's culture and society the more he will also share the patterns of drinking of the white alcoholic.

REFERENCES

1. Kellam, S.G., and Chassan, J.B.: *Psychiatry*, 25:370, 1962.
2. Patrick, C.H.: *Alcohol, Culture and Society.* Durham, N.C., Duke, 1952, p. 5.

3. Pittman, D.G., and Snyder, C.R.: *Society, Culture, and Drinking Patterns.* Somerset, N.J., Wiley, 1962.

4. Bales, R.F.: Unpublished Doctoral Dissertation. Cambridge, Mass., Harvard University, 1944.

5. Bales, R.F.: *Q J Stud Al,* 6:480–499, 1946.

6. Glad, D.D.: *Q J Stud Al,* 8:406–472, 1947.

7. Lolli, G., et al.: *Alcohol in Italian Culture.* New York, Free Pr, 1958.

8. Larkins, J.R.: *Alcohol and the Negro.* Zebulon, N.C., Record, 1965.

9. Johnson, G.G.: *Ante-Bellum North Carolina.* Chapel Hill, N.C., U of NC Pr, 1937, p. 56.

10. Coulter, E.M.: *The South During Reconstruction.* Baton Rouge, La., La State U Pr, 1949, vol. 8, p. 49.

11. Garland, I., and Bowen, J.W.E.: *The United Negro: His Problems and Progress.* Atlanta, Ga., D.E. Luther, 1902, p. 260.

12. Frazier, E.F.: *Black Bourgeoisie.* New York, Free Pr, 1957, pp. 231–232.

13. *The Pittsburgh Courier,* Dec. 14, 1957.

14. Navratil, L., Chafetz, M., and Demone, H.W.: *Alcoholism and Society.* Fair Lawn, N.J., Oxford U Pr, 1962.

15. Frazier, E.F.: *The Negro Family in Chicago.* Chicago, U of Chicago Pr, 1952.

16. Ewing, J.A., Cochran, C., and Leonard, D.L.: Preliminary Report —Racial and Social Factors in Alcoholism. Unpublished.

17. Vitols, M.M.: *NC Med J,* 22, no. 3, April, 1961.

18. Prange, A.J., and Vitols, M.M.: *Int J Soc Psychiatry,* 8, no. 2, 1962, p. 104.

Chapter 16

DRUG USE IN A NORMAL POPULATION OF YOUNG NEGRO MEN

LEE N. ROBINS, AND GEORGE E. MURPHY

The study reported here is the first attempt, as far as we know, to describe the drug use of a normal population, as ascertained by interview and record research. Previous studies have been restricted to narcotics users known to the police or to hospitals. Those have shown the population of known addicts to be disproportionately young, male, Negro, and from large urban centers.

The normal population we have studied consists of Negro men now in their early thirties, born in a large city, and living in the city of their birth during the last five years. These men were selected from elementary school records beginning approximately 25 years ago. On the basis of earlier studies, this population is one which could be anticipated to have a high rate of narcotics use. The use of a sample from a population in which narcotics use is so prevalent has permitted taking a sample small enough to allow intensive interviewing and yet has provided a substantial yield of narcotics users. Selection of the sample at an age in childhood at which *none* of them will have started using drugs (on entry into elementary school) provides a sample which is unselected for drug use and which does not exclude cases who have been institutionalized (either because of addiction or for other reasons). Institutionalized cases would not have been interviewed had we used an area sample of adults.

Abridged and reprinted with permission from the *American Journal of Public Health*, September, 1967.

The research was supported by US Public Health Service grants MH-07126, MH-5938, MH-5804 and MH-7081.

Starting with a sample unselected for narcotics use permits exploring some of the questions raised by earlier studies:

1. Can the extent of drug use be accurately ascertained by interview with a normal population?

2. What are the chances that an addict will be known to the police or the Federal Bureau of Narcotics?

3. What proportion of addicts receive treatment in the federal hospitals?

4. What proportion of a highly susceptible population ever uses drugs at all?

5. What drugs do they use and at what age do they begin to use drugs?

6. What proportion of drug users ever become addicted?

7. How is age of first drug use related to the extent and seriousness of use?

8. Do drug users specialize in the use of one type of drug, e.g., opiates, or do they use a variety of types?

9. What is the rate of recovery from addiction and of cessation of nonaddicted regular use?

10. What characteristics, observable prior to first use, permit the prediction of use, and of addiction once introduction to drugs occurs?

Methods

This study has obtained interviews and searched records to evaluate the adult adjustment of 235 young Negro men whose names were selected from public elementary school records beginning 26 to 30 years ago. When interviewed as adults between the ages of 30 and 35, these men have been asked whether they have ever taken marijuana, barbiturates, amphetamines, or opiates (offering them vernacular as well as technical terms), the age of first use for each type of drug, maximum dosage, regularity of use, evidences for physical dependence at stopping use, their opinion as to whether or not they had been addicted and date of last use. In addition (but not reported in the present paper), they were asked whether any of these drugs had been prescribed by a doctor, and whether they knew how to obtain these drugs, even if they were not currently using them.

Records indicating involvement with drugs were sought for every subject in the files of the St. Louis office of the

Federal Bureau of Narcotics and the St. Louis police, the admission summary of any prison to which he had been admitted, probation and parole records, his Armed Forces medical records, his Veterans Administration claims and treatment folders, and the records of the five hospitals and three outpatient clinics which serve the medical needs of the vast majority of Negroes in St. Louis.

The Sample

The criteria for eligibility for the study were: being male, born in St. Louis between 1930 and 1934, attending a Negro St. Louis public elementary school for six years or more, having an IQ score of at least 85 while in elementary school, and guardian's name and occupation appearing on the school record. The total population of eligible boys was 930. From these 930, 240 names were initially selected for follow-up. The sample was designed to provide 30 men in each of the eight categories created by taking all permutations of three dichotomized variables: father's presence or absence, guardian's occupation at the lowest level *versus* a higher level, moderate or severe school problems *versus* mild problems or none.* The distributions of IQ scores, year of birth, and number of addresses at which the boy was known to have lived during elementary school were matched across all eight groups. The level of breadwinner's occupation and the distribution of the nature and seriousness of elementary school problems were matched across the four groups composing each half of a dichotomy. This was to avoid, for example, one school problem group's containing predominantly grade repeaters and another's containing predominantly truants. Additional matching was done within the halves of the father present and absent dichotomy for the father's continued

---

* These three variables were selected because of their importance for testing hypotheses growing out of a study comparing the adult outcome of white child guidance clinic patients and normal school children. This study[7] found poor school achievement and truancy to be highly related to poor adult outcome, and antisocial behavior in the father related to poor outcome for children who were not themselves severely antisocial. Guardian's occupation was not found to be significantly related to outcome when the child and his father's antisocial behavior were held constant.

absence or presence when the boy reached high school. The sample design selected only the upper half of the IQ range, and within that population oversampled within the high occupation and father absent categories.

When, in the course of locating these men as adults, a man was found not to have lived in the St. Louis area at all during the last six years, he was discarded from the sample and replaced by the best matching case from the remaining pool of eligible cases. A statement by a relative or by the man himself, or a death certificate before 1959, was required as evidence of a man's not meeting the residence criterion.

For the category with father absent, high occupation, and no school problems, all eligible cases were exhausted, leaving us with 25 instead of the desired 30 cases in this category. The final sample, then, consists of 235 men whose elementary school records showed half with school problems, half without, half with father in the home, half without; half with guardians who were unemployed, domestic servants, or laborers, and half with guardians in better jobs; all with IQ's of 85 or higher and all born in St. Louis between 1930 and 1934. The study has been limited to men who lived in St. Louis between 1959 and 1964 to insure that they all had exposure to the same drug market and all had a risk of being known to local law enforcement and health agencies. We have included men away in military service or in prison who consider St. Louis as their home, because their service or prison records permit relatively complete assessment of drug problems.

By weighting the sample, the proportions found in the total eligible population can be reconstituted. It is important to remember, however, that the findings of this study apply strictly only to the eligible population: Negro men of normal IQ, born and reared in St. Louis.

For all of the 235 cases finally chosen, we searched the records of a variety of agencies. We obtained interviews for 95 per cent of them between June, 1965, and August, 1966. Interviews were not obtained with 12 men (5 percent). Five of these 12 were not located, three refused interviews, three were in the Armed Forces and stationed overseas or at army posts difficult to reach, and the mother of one prevented our contacting him. While most interviews were conducted in St. Louis, about 12 percent were conducted in other towns and cities. Several took place in prisons. Two men who were alive in 1959 died before we began interviewing in June, 1965. Although we obtained interviews with relatives about them, in the current paper we will not use these interviews because the relatives may not have been completely informed about their use of drugs.

Findings

Narcotics Records

Despite the fact that the population studied was expected to have a high rate of drug use, it was nevertheless surprising to find that 33 men, or 14 percent, had an official record for selling, use, or possession of narcotics.

Percentages are identical, whether compiled for the total sample or for the interviewed sample. Among the 14 men without personal interviews, we found official records for two (14 percent), the same proportion as in the interviewed sample. We expect, therefore, that drug use among the 14 men not personally interviewed follows approximately the same patterns as does drug use among the interviewed men.

All but three men of the 33 for whom we found any public records concerning drugs had records with the police. Two of the three without police records were probably not drug users. One of those records was a report by a relative to a hospital that "maybe he's on drugs"; a second resulted from self-report by a man in the Army, presumably in an effort to get out, since he has subsequently denied drug use at hospital admission as well as in interview. The third man was an amphetamine user, whose record resulted from his reporting his use to a doctor in the Veterans Hospital.

Of the 30 men with narcotics arrest records, 22 were found in the FBN files. Two of the men with arrests who were not in the FBN files had been arrested only out of St. Louis, and a third had been released by the St. Louis police for insufficient evidence. Twenty of the men in the FBN files had official addict reports. These reports are based on admissions of addiction (to heroin in every case) to the police, the FBI, or to an agent of the Bureau of Narcotics. Only half of these admitted addicts have so far been hospitalized at a Public Health Hospital.

Validity of Interview Information

For obvious social and legal reasons it might be expected that users and former users of drugs would tend to deny these practices in an interview with a stranger. It is therefore interesting to see how open the respondents were in their reporting. Among the 31 men interviewed who had a public record concerning drugs, 26 or 84 percent reported that they had at some time taken drugs. Of the 190 men *without* a record, 44 per cent reported having taken drugs.

It is quite possible that all five of the men with an official record who did not report narcotics use to us were telling the truth. Two were the men without arrest records mentioned above: one who had told an Army medical officer he was an addict (as well as an alcoholic and homosexual), and one whose relative had expressed the suspicion to a doctor at the hospital that the man "might be" a user. The other three had been arrested. But two had been convicted as sellers only, and nothing in the FBN records suggests that they were users as well. The other man had been arrested on suspicion of narcotics violations and released for lack of evidence. He has no record with the FBN. Thus in none of these five cases does the official record show the man to have lied to us (even though this is not ruled out).

Every man with an official record *as an addict* reported in interview that he had used heroin, and 16 out of 19 official addicts (84 percent) reported in interview that they had been *addicted* to heroin. In addition, three men *without* official addict reports admitted addiction in interview.

The high validity of the information obtained in interviews is particularly impressive when it is realized that the interviewers had absolutely no knowledge as to whether the man being interviewed did or did not have a narcotics record. Nor did the interviewer intimate in any way to respondents that records were being sought. This finding tends to confirm the impressions of the interviewers that nearly all of the respondents were quite open about all information asked of them. Because of the apparent reliability of the information given in interview, the remainder of this paper will deal with information from interviews, assuming it to be accurate. In discussing heroin addicts, however, we will include the three heroin users who had addict reports with the FBN and who, while admitting heroin use, denied addiction to heroin in interview.

Prevalence of Drug Use and Addiction

One hundred and nine respondents reported having tried at least one of the four types of drugs inquired about in interview (Table 16-I). This is 49 percent of the interviewed

TABLE 16-I
HISTORY OF DRUG USE

| | Interviewed sample (221) | | |
	f	%	Weighted %
Ever tried any drug	109	49	51
Marijuana	103	47	49
Heroin	28	13	12
Addicted	22*	10	10
Used more than six times without addiction	0	0	0
Used less than six times	6	3	2
Amphetamines	37	17	16
Addicted	5*	2	2
Regular (several times weekly) without addiction	14	6	7
Rarely	16	7	6
For weight loss only	2	1	1
Barbiturates	32	14	15
Addicted	0	0	0
Regular (one/week or more)	7	3	2
Rarely	25	11	13
Used any drug regularly (excluding marijuana)	30	14	14

* Official records note 19 heroin addicts, two of whom were also amphetamine addicts. Three additional men reported addiction to both drugs in interview. Therefore, all five amphetamine addicts have also been heroin addicts.

sample, or 51 percent of the weighted sample. Of these, 103, or nearly all, had tried marijuana.

Twenty-eight men or 13 percent of the sample reported having tried heroin. *Ten percent of the sample had been addicted to heroin.* This means that four-fifths of the men who said they never used heroin even once became addicts. Every man who reported using heroin *more than six times* had been addicted.

Amphetamine use was even more common than heroin use, but seemed less serious: Thirty-seven men or 17 percent had taken amphetamines, but only 8 percent had ever used it regularly (51 percent of the men using it). Five men thought they had been addicted to amphetamines. *Each of these five had also been addicted to heroin.*

The use of barbiturates was also fairly common (32 cases or 14 percent), but was even less associated with habituation than was amphetamine use. Only seven men reported using barbiturates as regularly as once a week or more (22 percent of the barbiturate users), and none reported ever having been addicted to barbiturates.

Coming to Public Attention for Drug Use

We mentioned previously that only three men out of 28 with a narcotics arrest record denied drug use, but we also noted that 44 percent of the men *without* public records admitted drug use. We are interested, then, to know under what conditions drug users get official records. We will take as our simplest measure of public records the presence of an arrest for a narcotics violation. As pointed out above, only one self-reported drug user who took amphetamines had any public record without having a police record.

Of all self-reported drug users, only 24 percent have narcotics arrest records. But of self-reported *heroin* users, 79 per cent have arrest records, and *every* man who by self-report used heroin more than six times has a narcotics arrest record. This would suggest that *no heroin addict fails to come to police attention.*

Only six of the 28 men with arrests were other than heroin addicts. Three of these men claimed never to have used drugs.

Three used marijuana, one of them also using amphetamines occasionally while another used barbiturates occasionally. The rate of arrest for drug users who were not heroin addicts (3%) was no higher than the rate of narcotic arrests among men who claim never to have used drugs at all (three out of 112 or 3%). Thus it appears that the illegal use of drugs *rarely* leads to arrest unless the user is a heroin addict.

Current Drug Use and Addiction

Men were asked in interview when they last used drugs. Twenty-two men or 10 per cent of the sample said they had used drugs within the last year. The drug most commonly in current use by our sample is marijuana. All but one of the current drug users said they had used marijuana in the last year, and 13 had used *only* marijuana this recently. Only three (1 per cent) had used *heroin* in the past year, although a fourth man, interviewed in prison, had been using heroin occasionally up to the time he was incarcerated. Among heroin addicts, 84 per cent (including the man in prison) claimed no heroin use in the last year.

Another way of evaluating current heroin use is the method used by the Federal Bureau of Narcotics. The bureau keeps addicts on their active list for five years after the last addict report.[10] Of the 19 men for whom an addict report was found in the bureau files, only five were found in the active file.* Therefore, 74 percent (14 out of 19) of the addicts may be presumed to be inactive. Whether we accept the figure of 84 percent of heroin addicts free of heroin in the last year, or 74 percent of addicts now inactive by the FBN criterion, it is apparent that heroin addiction has a high remission rate.

Even though the great majority of heroin addicts had stopped using *heroin,* they were much more often *current*

---

* While finding only five out of 19 as active addicts is encouraging, the rate this produces, based on a 235-man sample, is still startlingly high. These five cases divided by 235, give an active addict rate of 21.27/1,000 (weighted=26.98/1,000). Weighted or unweighted, this is much higher than the rates ordinarily computed on the basis of FBN files, even taking into account the fact that we are studying a young, male, Negro, urban sample.

drug users than was any other category of drug user. Half
the heroin addicts were currently using some drug. Eighteen
per cent were using only marijuana, and the remainder were
using various combinations of marijuana with heroin,
amphetamines, and barbiturates. *No* heroin addict had taken
only heroin in the last year.

The current drug user typically had a history of multiple-
drug use. Only three of the current users (14 percent) were
men who had used only one drug in their lives (marijuana),
while almost two-thirds (63 percent) of men who had given
up drug use had used only one type of drug (p<0.001).

These results suggest three things: first, that heroin addiction is associated with the use of other drugs; second, that
when heroin addiction remits, the use of other drugs often
continues; and third, that unlike teenagers and men in their
twenties who use drugs, drug users in their early thirties
include a large proportion of men with a history of heroin
addiction. Current or former heroin addicts made up *half*
of the *current* drug users, but only 13 percent of the ex-drug
users.

Regular use of amphetamines and barbiturates showed little
or no relationship to the current use of drugs. As many or
more occasional users of amphetamines and barbiturates had
used drugs in the last year as had regular users.

Patterns of Drug Use: Number of Types, Order of Use, Age at First Use

(a) Number of Types—There were few "specialists" among
drug users in this population, with the exception of marijuana
users. Half of the marijuana users reported using no other
drug. Among users of heroin, amphetamines, and barbiturates,
on the other hand, only 4, 5, and 6 per cent respectively
had not used another drug. Since nearly every drug user had
used marijuana, this necessarily means that nearly every user
of heroin, amphetamines, or barbiturates had had experience
with at least two drugs. But their experience was not limited
to marijuana and one other drug. Nearly two-thirds of amphetamine and barbiturate users had used either three
or four types of drugs, while four-fifths (82%) of those who

tried heroin tried drugs of three or four types. Two-thirds of heroin users used amphetamines, and over half used barbiturates. Conversely, half of amphetamine and barbiturate users had used heroin as well.

(b) Order of Use—In this pattern of multiple drug use, which comes first? Three out of four beginning heroin users had already used marijuana and only 7 percent were introduced to it later. This is in keeping with the commonly held belief that marijuana is a stepping stone to heroin, although it must not be forgotten that half of the marijuana users never used any other drug. There was little apparent pattern to the encounter of heroin users with barbiturates, either with respect to frequency or to timing. On the other hand, heroin users usually began amphetamines *after* they had used heroin.

(c) Age at First Use—Another way of looking at this progression is in terms of age at first encounter with the various drugs. Twenty-five percent of those who ever used marijuana tried it before age 16, and 69 percent before age 20. Only 9 percent were 24 or older at first use. Heroin was tried before age 20 by just half of the users, but only 11 percent started it either before age 16 or after age 24. Thus, the age range for introduction to heroin tends to be narrow. Over three-fourths of heroin users were between 16 and 23 when introduced. Amphetamines tend to be tried later, and barbiturates earlier, than heroin.

Although age at first use varied from drug to drug, *whenever* drug use began, it usually began with marijuana. Among boys beginning drugs before 16, 95 percent used marijuana in their first year of drug use. Boys beginning between 16 and 19 used marijuana in the first year in 85 percent of cases. Every man starting drugs between 20 and 23 used marijuana the first year. Only for men beginning drugs after 23 did a sizable minority (39 percent) *not* use marijuana in the first year. Marijuana, then, is typically the drug of initiation, whatever the age at beginning use.

Although drug use tends to begin with marijuana at all ages, the age at initiation turns out to be a powerful predictor of the seriousness of involvement with drugs. The earlier drug use begins, the greater the risk of going on to heroin ($p<0.02$) or amphetamines ($p<0.01$), the greater the variety of drugs eventually used ($p<0.001$), and the greater the risk of addiction or regular use ($p<0.01$). There also appears to be a somewhat greater risk of continuing drug use into the early thirties, although differences are not significant.

Elementary School Variables and Drug Use

It will be recalled that the subjects of this study were selected according to three dichotomous variables obtainable from elementary school records. Nearly equal numbers of men were selected for each of the eight possible permutations of (a) high or low occupational status of the guardian; (b) father's presence or absence from the home; and (c) presence or absence of school problems. Not only is there no statistically significant difference in use versus nonuse of drugs with respect to these variables, but the proportions of persons using each drug is almost identical with respect to each variable. These variables are clearly unrelated to the probability of drug use.

However, there were 27 percent of cases in which a dis-agreement was found between father's presence as indicated on the school records and as reported in interview. Most of the difference (75%) was in the direction of the subject's reporting the father as absent at some time during elementary school, while the school record did not indicate his having left. If we use the interview report, rather than the school record, we continue to find no difference in the probability of using *some* drug (51% when the father was present and 49% when he was ever absent), but an increased risk of using drugs *other* than marijuana when the father was absent (17% versus 5% for heroin, 20 versus 11% for amphetamines, and 18% versus 9% for barbiturates). The difference is statistically significant only for heroin use ($p<0.05$).

High School Variables and Drug Use

While elementary school records were not predictive, high school variables were strikingly related to drug use. Nearly twice as many high school dropouts as high school graduates used drugs. The difference is significant beyond the 0.001 level of confidence. Both heroin use and heroin addiction are higher in the dropouts, at the same level of statistical significance. It is interesting to note, however, that boys *not beginning* high school used drugs almost as infrequently as did graduates, and much less frequently than boys entering high school and then dropping out. It is perhaps surprising to find that even among high school graduates, 39 per cent had some experience with drugs.

High school attendance and graduation are related not only to initial exposure to drugs, but also to the risk of moving from marijuana to one of the more serious drugs. More than one-third of the high school dropouts who used marijuana also used heroin. But among graduates, only one in eight who tried marijuana then tried heroin. Again, boys not entering high school resembled the graduates more than they did the dropouts, with only one out of six trying heroin after marijuana.

Juvenile Delinquency and Drug Use

It is well known that drug use is most common in high delinquency areas of the city, and that treated addicts frequently have records as juvenile delinquents. Not surprisingly, then, boys who had police or juvenile court records before age 17 in the present study were significantly more frequently ($p < 0.02$) drug users than were nondelinquents. With respect to heroin use and heroin addiction, the difference is significant beyond the 0.001 level of confidence. Delinquents are more likely than nondelinquents to start taking drugs, and once started, are much more likely to use heroin. At the same time, 36 percent of the 62 delinquents reported no drug use at all, and 43 percent of the nondelinquents *did* use drugs. Exposure to drugs was evidently high in the entire population studied, whether delinquent or not.

Delinquency might be associated with drug use only because drug use itself is grounds for a juvenile arrest or because youths who are using drugs either steal to finance their use or act while under the influence of drugs in a fashion which leads to arrest. To demonstrate that delinquency *predicts* drug use, and is not merely its result, we need to limit our comparison to men who were not yet using drugs at the time they first became delinquent. When men whose drug use began before their first delinquency or in the same year are excluded, there is still a significantly greater rate of heroin use ($p<0.05$) and heroin addiction ($p<0.01$) for delinquents than for nondelinquents, although the difference between proportions using *any* drug is not significant.

Relationship of Dropout, Delinquency, Father's Absence, and Drug Use

It was shown that more high school dropouts used drugs than did either nonentrants or high school graduates. Delinquency, however, is well known to be associated with dropping out of school, and might explain the difference in the drug use between high school graduates and dropouts. This familiar pattern is found in our sample. Almost half (46%) of the high school dropouts were delinquent, while only 14 percent of high school graduates were delinquent. Children not entering high school, however, had about the same proportion of delinquents (44%) as did high school dropouts. The lower rate of drug use in the nonentrants could not, therefore, be attributed to a lower delinquency rate.

When we look at delinquency and high school completion simultaneously, we note that high school dropouts were equally likely to *try* drugs, whether or not they were delinquent. However, the *delinquent* dropouts who tried drugs were much more likely to continue into heroin addiction ($p<0.01$). Almost half of the delinquent dropouts who ever used drugs eventually became heroin addicts.

Among delinquents, almost the same proportions of dropouts and graduates used drugs, while among nondelinquents, graduates were only a little over half as often drug users as were dropouts ($p<0.01$).

Among both delinquents and dropouts, the interview report that the father had been absent at some time during elementary school continued to be unrelated to the use of *some* drug, but was rather sharply related to the risk of heroin addiction when any drug had been tried. Among delinquent drug users, 56 percent of those without a father in the home (at least part of the time) because addicts, compared with only 14% of those with fathers never absent ($p<0.05$). Among dropout drug users, 37 percent of those without a father in the home became heroin addicts, compared with 17 percent of those with a father (not statistically significant). Among the 18 drug users who were delinquent, dropouts, *and* whose father was absent, 61 percent became heroin addicts. With a father present, the addiction rate was 22 percent.

Being a dropout seems to be a major determinant of experimentation with drugs, while delinquency and having no father in the home seem to be major determinants of going on to heroin addiction once drugs are tried.

Discussion

Previous studies of drug addiction have started with addicts known to the police or to hospitals. From such studies,[1,4,5,9] demographic characteristics of drug addicts, such as age, sex, race, and areas of residence, can be determined. But other important questions cannot be answered by this method: what proportions of addicts are known to the police, how prevalent is drug use in the population from which the addicts come, what proportion of drug users ever become addicts, and how does the personal and social background of the addicts differ from that of their nonaddict neighbors of like age, sex, and racial characteristics who share their urban-slum environment. Although it would be possible to conduct a population survey of a random sample of adults to answer these questions, such a survey would miss those individuals who are institutionalized either as a result of addiction or for other reasons. The findings would then give a spuriously low estimate of the number of drug addicts originally living in the target area.

The present study investigates drug use in a normal population. It has selected subjects from elementary school records made prior to their first exposure to narcotics so that

no drug users have been missed because of institutionalization. Therefore, this sample was unselected with
respect to drug use. As adults, their drug use has been ascertained by record research and interviews. Records were
sought for all the sample, and personal interviews obtained
with 94 percent. Relationships were examined between their
drug use as adults and factors ascertained from their pre-drug
childhood records in school, with the police, and with the
juvenile court.

The methods used in this study give us an approximation
to the lifetime prevalence of drug use and drug addiction
for our sample. Although only in their early thirties at
interview, they are old enough so that few who are not now
addicted are likely ever to become addicts. Negro male drug
addiction seldom begins after 35. This is attested to by the
findings that over 97 percent of all Negro male addicts
admitted to Lexington for the first time are under 39 years
of age[3] and that addiction typically precedes hospitalization
by several years.*

While we believe that our methods have achieved a fairly
accurate count of the drug users and addicts in the sample,
it must be pointed out that the sample represents only a
limited population: Negro men of normal IQ born in a mid-
western city and still (or again) living there in their early
thirties. Our estimates are probably too high for the total Negro
male population of such a city. St. Louis, like other metropolitan areas, includes in its adult Negro population many persons
from smaller cities and from rural areas, who have had little
exposure to drugs during the vulnerable years of late adoles-
cence and early adulthood.

Although city-born Negro men were expected to have a
comparatively high rate of drug addiction, it was surprising

---

* A follow-up study of Puerto Rican addicts[2] found that the average age of starting
heroin was 18, with addiction following within three months. The average age at
arrest was 20, but the average age at discharge from the hospital was 30.7. These
figures and the fact that the average age on admission to Lexington for Negro men
is 29 years[3] suggest a lag of 11 to 12 years between addiction and hospitalization,
and a lag of two to three years between addiction and first arrest for narcotics
use.

to find that one out of every ten of our sample had been addicted to heroin. Four per cent had been treated for addiction in a U.S. Public Health Service hospital. This is a higher rate than would have been anticipated on the basis of any published figures which relate number of addicts to base populations. But this high rate cannot be explained by our having discovered addicts who had failed to come to official attention. Indeed, it is a finding of considerable importance that no regular heroin user in the present population had escaped official attention, and that 86 percent had reports as addicts with the Federal Bureau of Narcotics.

Of equal importance is the fact that very few men who denied drug use had had narcotics arrests. It has been commonly observed that the burden of both arrests and convictions rests more heavily upon the poor and upon Negroes, for offenses of whatever gravity. The finding that Negro men who deny drug use have rarely been arrested for narcotics violations gives us additional confidence in arrest records as a reliable index of the extent of narcotics addiction. Our findings indicate that fairly reliable lifetime prevalence figures for heroin addiction can be obtained from an unduplicated cumulative list of men arrested for drug law violations. It should not be necessary to do further interview studies in a general population in order to identify most heroin addicts, at least among urban Negro men.

Only 14 percent of the addicts in this study reported having used heroin in the last year (or 18%, including the man whose drug use was interrupted by imprisonment). This finding is in keeping with observations by others[6,7,9] that heroin addiction is often a remitting illness. While our rate of current addiction is somewhat lower than figures found by others, this difference can be accounted for in part by our having included addicts who never went to a public health hospital. Among men in our sample who had been in a USPHS hospital, 22 percent reported current heroin use and 44 percent reported current use of other drugs only. These figures (34% using no drugs) are similar to O'Donnell's and Vaillant's figures[6,7] for rates of use at follow-up by men discharged from Lexington. These slightly higher figures for current use by men treated in hospitals do not of course, indicate that hospitalization is detrimental, or even that it is not helpful. Presumably, the hospitals receive the most seriously addicted members of the addict population.

We also found, as did O'Donnell and Vaillant, that heroin addicts and ex-heroin addicts commonly are using a variety of types of drugs at follow-up. The variety of drugs used, combined with the frequent giving up of the use of heroin, suggests that the problem of drug addiction is not simply one of physical dependence on heroin *per sé* but is rather the general readiness of the addict to use drugs that alter mood or level of consciousness.

Not only had 10 percent of this population been heroin addicts, fully half had used *some* drug illegally. Virtually everyone who used any drug used marijuana. Thus marijuana must have been both widely available and widely acceptable. It served as the introduction to drugs for most of those who went on to other drug use. Marijuana use by no means always had serious consequences, however. Half of the marijuana users never used any other drug, and one-third did not even continue the use of marijuana itself for more than one year. When marijuana use did not lead to heroin addiction, the user rarely became known to the police. The younger the age when marijuana use began, the more likely was the user to go on to heroin addiction. This agrees with Vaillant's observation[8] that opiate use before 20 predicts that the user will become a chronic addict.

Although marijuana was almost always the drug of initiation, it was by no means solely a youth's drug, used in the teens and discarded after beginning to use the addicting drugs. It was used by all but one of the men currently using drugs in their thirties, and over half of the current users were using marijuana exclusively. In addition, many of the men not using drugs currently said that they could readily get marijuana if they wished to. Marijuana thus appears to be the most widely available and widely used drug among both Negro teenagers and adult Negro men.

One of the surprising findings of our study is the apparent lack of relationship between drug use and occupational status of the guardian or the presence or absence of school problems prior to age 15. Chein[4] has shown that the majority of drug users known to the police live in areas in which the heads of households have low status occupations. But he too found no difference in the social status of households within the area which did or did not include drug users. Rather, households of low status appear to be endemic in those areas in which the susceptible minority group populations live.

While socioeconomic status and elementary school performance did not prove predictive of drug use, we did find that dropping out of high school predicted experimenting with drugs, and that delinquency and absent fathers predicted going from marijuana use into heroin addiction. The combination of the absent father, delinquency, and dropping out of high school characterized the group of boys most vulnerable to heroin addiction. This vulnerable group of Negro boys would be the reasonable target for a program hoping to prevent addiction.

REFERENCES

1. Ball, John C.: Two patterns of narcotic drug addiction in the United States. *J Criminal Law, Criminology, and Police Science, 56*:203–211, 1965.

2. ——: The Onset of Heroin Addiction in a Juvenile Population. Read at the annual meetings of the American Sociological Association, 1966.

3. Ball, John C., and Bates, William M.: Migration and residential mobility of drug addicts. *Social Problems 14,* Summer, 1966, p. 60.

4. Chein, Isidor, Gerard, D.L., Lee, R.S., and Rosenfeld, Eva.: *The Road to H.: Narcotics, Delinquency and Social Policy.* New York, Basic, 1964.

5. Dai, Bingham.: *Opium Addiction in Chicago.* Shanghai, China, Commercial Press, 1937.

6. O'Donnell, John A.: A follow-up of narcotic addicts: Mortality, relapse, and abstinence. *Am J Orthopsychiatry, 34*:948–954, October, 1964.

7. Robins, Lee.: *Deviant Children Grown Up: A Sociological and Psychiatric Study of Sociopathic Personality.* Baltimore, Williams & Wilkins, 1966.

8. Vaillant, George E.: A twelve-year follow-up of New York narcotic addicts: I. The relation of treatment to outcome. *Am J Psychiatry,* *122:*727–737, January, 1966.

9. ———: A twelve-year follow-up of New York addicts: IV. Some determinants and characteristics of abstinence. Read at the American Psychiatric Association meetings, 1966.

10. Winick, Charles: Maturing out of narcotic addiction. *Bull Narc,* *14:*1–7, 1962.

Chapter 17

FATALITIES FROM NARCOTIC ADDICTION IN NEW YORK CITY

Incidence, Circumstances, and Pathologic Findings

MILTON HELPERN

The spiraling increase in the incidence of addiction to narcotic drugs, especially heroin, particularly in the younger groups of the population of large urban centers in the United States, is of great concern to the community and has been the subject of many surveys and reports. Federal, state, and municipal branches of government, the medical and legal professions, social welfare, and educational, law enforcement, and correctional agencies are deeply troubled by this disturbing major social and public health problem.

During the period between the end of World War I and the beginning of World War II, the mode of utilization of drugs by narcotic addicts underwent a significant change. The subcutaneous injection of solutions of morphine or of heroin, a synthetic derivative of morphine, and the inhalation or sniffing of dry mixtures of heroin or cocaine were replaced by the intravenous injection of crudely prepared solutions of drug mixtures of heroin diluted with other substances. The powdered drug, formerly mixed with large quantities of lactose and more recently with mannitol and quinine, is dissolved in a small amount of water heated to a boil by match flame in a crude receptacle such as a teaspoon or bottle cap. The injection apparatus ("the works") is usually improvised

Abridged and reprinted with permission from *Human Pathology*, March, 1972.

from an easily obtainable medicine dropper, its tip fitted tightly with a paper flange into the hub of a hypodermic needle, the latter usually obtained either by theft or illegal purchase. More recently, addicts have come into possession of discarded, disposable plastic syringes, preferring to use only the needle in combination with a medicine dropper, the rubber bulb of which is easier to manipulate than the rigid plunger of a syringe, for self-injection into a vein. The injections are most often self-administered into the superficial veins of the elbow fold and adjacent part of the forearm, but other convenient areas on the upper and lower extremities are also selected for the intravenous injection of heroin. The solution is drawn up into the improvised syringe through a small wad of cotton, which filters out solid particles of undissolved material.

In recent years the powdered diluents with which heroin is mixed have varied, and bitter-tasting substances like quinine have been added, according to some to disguise the strength of the sample and the presence of fraudulent substitutes. Another explanation for the quinine seems to be that it was first added to the mixtures as a diluent during the 1930's, a period when falciparum malaria was rampant in New York City among intravenous heroin addicts who had become infected directly as the result of the common use of unsterilized unwashed syringes. The addicts and those who prepared the drug mixtures soon learned that quinine was a cure and preventive of malaria and began adding it as a diluent in the heroin mixtures. The remarkable fact remains that despite the marked increase in intravenous addiction, there have been no cases of artificially transmitted malaria in intravenous addicts since 1943 in New York City.

Interestingly, a small outbreak of vivax malaria was reported in 1971 in Bakersfield, California, among addicts who were infected by addicted soldiers returning from Vietnam with malaria that they had acquired there naturally. Addiction to heroin had developed during their military service in Vietnam where the method used was not by intravenous injection but by smoking and sniffing. After acquiring malaria naturally they returned to the United States where their addiction continued but by intravenous injection with resultant transmittal of the malaria to other addicts. Drug mixtures in California do not contain quinine.

The admixture of other poisonous substances like nicotine, strychnine, and cyanide also must be considered and is another reason for careful toxicologic analysis in fatal cases. Diluted heroin mixtures sold to addicts by pushers are dispensed in glassine envelopes. These contain 3 to 5 grains (0.2 to 0.3 gm) of diluted drug of which about 18 percent is heroin. There is considerable variation in total weight and strength of samples. The result of a recent extensive detailed analysis of so-called "street" samples sold to addicts in New York City and confiscated by the police before or after sale are contained in a report by Fulton.[1]

The practice of taking heroin intravenously is believed to have begun in Cairo, Egypt, in the 1920's, and the method was copied by addicted seamen and in turn by other addicts in maritime cities. It soon became the method of choice almost everywhere for the utilization of narcotic drugs. The indiscriminate sharing of unsterilized improvised syringes for the intravenous injection of heroin was the basis for an epidemic of fatal falciparum malaria among the narcotic addict population of New York City and other urban centers in the United States in the 1930's.[2]

Prior to 1943 there were relatively few acute deaths of addicts from a direct reaction to the injected drug interpreted as overdosage. In addition to the fatalities from malaria, occasional deaths were caused by sepsis from large subcutaneous abscesses secondary to infected needle punctures in the skin, by bacterial endocarditis from septic thrombophlebitis in the injected veins, by viral hepatitis, and by tetanus in subcutaneous addicts.

During World War II heroin was practically unobtainable in the United States. Some addicts continued with the use of addictive substitutes, such as the amphetamines and the barbiturates, and there were some fatalities among them from septic infection originating in the injection sites, but the number of deaths from this type of addiction was relatively small.

With the end of the war in 1945, and subsequent resumption of unrestricted travel and commerce, the very lucrative organized illegal traffic in heroin was resumed, and the drug was again smuggled into the United States from other countries in ever increasing quantities.[3] With this renewed supply there has been an alarming increase, especially in urban centers, of which New York is the largest, in the incidence of intravenous heroin addiction, an extremely expensive habit for the addicts who, in order to satisfy the rapidly recurring intense craving for heroin, become involved in other sordid criminal activities ranging from theft to the selling of drugs, burglary, robbery, assault, homicide, and prostitution.

Although there are no precise figures on the incidence of narcotic addiction today, it is estimated that in New York City with a resident population of 8,000,000 there are about 100,000 persons addicted to hard drugs of which heroin is the most abundant. The estimates vary, but there is ample evidence from law enforcement, social welfare, health, hospital, and voluntary agencies that it has been increasing steadily despite the concern and the diligent efforts of these groups to combat it.

The ratio of deaths per 10,000 deaths (1950 through 1961) from narcotism in black as compared with white persons is about 12 to 1. The ratio of deaths in male blacks compared with male whites is 10 to 1; the female ratio, black to white, is greater, almost 15 to 1. The figures for white persons include approximately 34 percent males and 20 percent females of Puerto Rican extraction.

The average mean age at death from narcotic addiction for both sexes over the 12 year span from 1950 through 1961 was 29 years. There has been a definite decrease in the average mean age of persons whose deaths resulted from narcotics over the 20 year period from 1950 through 1969. In 1969 the average mean age was 25 years. In 1970, in the five boroughs comprising New York City, there was a total of 884 deaths from narcotic addiction to heroin. One hundred ninety-nine occurred in teenagers or adolescents 14 through 19 years of age, with 685 deaths occurring in addicts above the age of 20. Of the latter older group, 624 were between 20 and 40 years of age. The greatest number of deaths —275—was in the age group 20 through 24. The next to the largest—179—was in the group between 25 and 29. There were 95 deaths in addicts between 30 and 34 years of age and 75 in those between 35 and 39 years.

Also in 1970 a total of 312 narcotic addicts died of other causes, mostly by homicide. These included 37 adolescents, 14 through 19 years of age, and 275 adults. The total number of deaths in which narcotic addiction was the direct cause or an associated finding in deaths from other causes, mostly homicide, was 1204.

The situation in New York City with regard to fatalities from narcotic addiction did not change in 1971. The age distribution of fatalities was the same.

The race and sex distribution of deaths in the first nine months of 1971 for the adolescent and adult groups is shown in Table 17-I. The highest percentage of addiction deaths and presumably of total addiction during the period from 1950 through 1961 occurred in the unskilled worker or laborer group, with a lower incidence in the semiskilled and skilled worker groups. An analysis of the narcotic deaths in 1969 revealed 20 percent unemployed and 28 percent with unknown occupation in contrast to the 44 percent of semi- and low-skilled laborers. Students comprised 8.4 percent of the deaths, a fairly large number.

Geographic Distribution

In New York City the greatest number of narcotic deaths occurred in the Borough of of Manhattan. Approximately 75 percent of all such deaths in New York City formerly took place in this borough. A comparison of the total number of deaths in each borough indicates that the Manhattan incidence was more than twice that of The Bronx, which had the second highest percentage of narcotic addiction fatalities. In recent years the incidence of fatalities has increased in all the boroughs.

It is probable that many deaths from acute narcotism have gone unrecognized because of failure to study the scene of

TABLE 17-I
RACE AND SEX DISTRIBUTION
OF NARCOTIC DEATHS, JANUARY 1 TO
SEPTEMBER 30, 1971

	Age	
	14–19	20 and above
Race		
Black	86	429
White	57	208
Puerto Rican	26	119
Oriental	0	2
Total	169	758
Total adults and adolescents		927
Sex		
Male	138	641
Female	31	117
Total	169	758

death and recognize the subtle findings, which are easily overlooked or misinterpreted by the inexperienced observer. A thorough autopsy is necessary to rule out competing unsuspected violent, especially homicidal, and also natural causes of death.

The subcutaneous rather than intravenous injection of narcotics, when encountered, is more prevalent among women addicts and more apt to be complicated by relatively less rapid sepsis with abscess formation and other complications. Thus, more women addicts are likely to get to the hospital while still alive. Tetanus is also more likely to occur in such addicts, and the manifestations of this complication usually lead to hospitalization.

Pathologic Findings and Causes of Death

The largest number of deaths result from acute reactions, and in the compilation for the 12-year period from 1950 through 1961 the percentage of these cases was 48. Although this constituted about half the total, it is important to point out that in the recent years of the study, with a considerably higher death rate from addiction, the acute reaction deaths have greatly exceeded the incidence of such acute deaths in the earlier years and of other less rapid fatal complications of narcotic addiction. The acute reaction type of death now occurs in about 80 percent of the deaths.

REFERENCES

1. Fulton, C.C.: An analytical study of confiscated samples of narcotic drugs. *Int Microfilm J Legal Med* Fall, 1965, vol. 1.

2. Helpern, M.: Epidemic of fatal estivo-autumnal malaria among drug addicts in New York City. *Amer J Surg, 26:*111, 1934.

3. Helpern, M., and Rho, Y.-M.: Deaths from narcotism in New York City: Incidence, circumstances, and postmortem findings. *NY J Med, 66:*2391–2408, 1966.

PART SIX
MENTAL ILLNESS

A most controversial and sensitive area in social science today is the evaluation of mental development along comparative racial lines. In Chapter Eighteen, Maurice V. Russell reviews a recent work on mental illness among Negroes. He considers this area largely unexplored and stresses the need for more basic research.

The study by Mayer Fisch, Ernest M. Gruenberg and Cynthia Bandfield focuses in on the services rendered by the psychiatric unit of a municipal general hospital in New York City. Negroes and other nonwhites show a consistently higher rate of admission to mental hospitals during a one-year period. However, since the study deals with emergency situations, the higher rate of admission for nonwhites again may very well be due to socioeconomic factors.

Chapter 18

MENTAL ILLNESS AMONG NEGROES

MAURICE V. RUSSELL

The subject of mental illness among urban Negro populations has been more unexplored than one would expect in
the literature of social psychology. With a handful of exceptions, notably Kardiner and Ovesey's pointed study, *The Mark
of Oppression* (W.W. Norton, 1951), most of the research has
concentrated on white or undifferentiated samples.

The book, *Mental Illness in the Urban Negro Community*, New York, The Free Press, 1966, grew out of
some very interesting findings that the authors, Robert J.
Kleiner (Temple University) and Seymour Parker (Michigan
State University), made on migratory studies. They discovered from the list of Negro patients using psychiatric services
in Philadelphia (the location of the present study, also) that
Southern migrants had a lower rate of mental illness than
the natives of the city. Such statistics not only conflicted with
the common-sense assumption of the great strain that an
adjustment to a new environment creates, but also with a
good proportion of research on migration and mental illness.

The authors tried to account for this reversal of the expected
outcome with a few hypotheses: 1) that the situation of the
American Negro is unique, in that he takes on the ideals
of the rest of American society, believing in the free, open
system of opportunity while coming up against a relatively
closed structure; 2) that this discrepancy between his aspirations and his achievements produces great stress; 3) that goal-
striving stress is an important factor leading to mental illness;
and 4) that Southern Negro migrants, coming from a semi-caste

Abridged and reprinted with permission from *The Crisis*, December, 1966.

structure, will have less belief in an open society, will make fewer demands on themselves, and their goals will be more in line with the realistic choices offered them.

Kleiner and Parker decided to investigate these ideas by administering a questionnaire to as large a section of the Philadelphia Negro community as possible. Unfortunately, the questionnaire, no matter how objectively its inquiries are chosen, can never be the finest instrument for scientific investigation; and the results of this research are not as clear or significant as the migratory studies, which were based on statistics of hospital and private clinic admissions. It should be added that the present study did set out to find evidence dealing with much more complex concepts.

There are difficulties at the very start in undertaking such a venture; the problem of questioning the mentally ill and eliciting valid responses from them was minimized, according to the authors, by a comprehensive training period for the interviewers. The classification of the mentally ill is further complicated in the Negro population by the fact that, until recently, Negroes have not tended to seek out psychiatric services. In my own experience, as Director of Psychiatric Social Service at Harlem Hospital Center, this situation has been changing quickly; with the expansion and improvement of facilities, applications have multiplied as the community became increasingly aware of our existence. This greater willingness to use public psychiatric services may appear statistically in the next few years as a jump in mental illness; while in fact, the increased number of persons receiving treatment could well produce the opposite trend.

The sampling taken in Kleiner and Parker's study is certainly large enough, and was drawn from both the regular Negro community and the mentally ill segments in it. An attempt has been made to divide the sample into a mental health continuum of four groups—low symptom and high symptom (among the community respondents); neurotics and psychotics (among the ill respondents). The division among the community was made according to a list of psychosomatic symptoms (dizzy spells, headaches, stomach trouble, etc.)

which are regarded as an indication of susceptibility to mental illness.

The exclusive use of psychosomatic symptoms is a somewhat questionable method for classifying the tendency towards mental illness; not that these symptoms have no relation to psychological disturbances, but the problem is far too complex to rest there. It may be that psychosomatic symptoms are at times a more healthy outlet than no release; and therefore some of the subjects in the low symptom group, which is treated as the standard of normalcy in this study, might become mentally ill as easily as the high symptom respondents. In any case, this division, which has a crucial relation to the findings, is entirely hypothetical, since both groups at the time of the research were healthy and one would need a longitudinal study over a period of five or ten years to discover whether more mentally ill cases came from the high or low symptom group. Similarly, the evidence for a four-step continuum—low symptom, high symptom, neurotic, psychotic—is not conclusively established.

The main concern of the book has to do with the relation between goal-striving stress and mental illness, and strong data are produced to support this connection. The method for determining goal-striving stress is rather complicated, involving the discrepancy between achievement and aspiration, the degree of satisfaction a person expects from achieving a goal, and the probability he would predict of failing or succeeding. The majority of items asked on the questionnaire were designed to provide measurements for goal-striving stress: they dealt with the subject's self-image contrasted to his self-ideal; his position (below or above); his close friends; and the occupational, income and educational levels that he was situated in as opposed to those he wanted to achieve.

The mentally ill were shown to have both higher and lower stress scores, indicating that many took their failure extremely hard, while others set too modest goals for themselves in order not to be disappointed. If the first reaction can partially be explained by the self-hate which many Negroes feel as a result of their racial membership, the second is an equally common response: to become apathetic and refuse to participate in striving for goals. The authors assert with probable correctness that this apathy is feigned, and indicates a painful compromise with one's aspirations rather than a characteristic laziness or indifference—the stereotype which is drawn of many Negroes of the lower socioeconomic classes. The ill subjects who had low goal-striving stress scores also showed lower self-esteem, and judged themselves further below their reference group (close friends) than other respondents, supporting the idea that they were not happy with their goal-less existence.

The relation between goal-striving stress and mental illness leads one to wonder: if Negroes are more prone to this kind of stress, will they have higher rates of illness than whites? There are no comparative statistics of the two groups, since such a study has been considered beyond the scope of the subject. But eventually these comparisons may have to be included to understand the full implications of the goal-striving factor.

One of the weakest points in the demonstration has to do with perception of opportunity structure. The authors' hypothesis, a stimulating one, is that the mentally ill will believe more in an open society, while the low symptom group will consider the society relatively closed, in keeping with the realities of Negro life in America. (It should be recalled that this thesis derived from the Southern migrant studies.) Disappointingly, none of the correlations between the attitudes of Southern migrants and Negroes on this subject reach statistical significance. It may even be argued that the very act of migration indicates some belief in an open opportunity structure, although this idea is never raised.

The burden of comparison between the mentally ill and community segments of Philadelphia seems to rest largely on the question: "It has been said that if a man works hard, saves his money, and is ambitious, he will get ahead. How often do you think this really happens?" (p. 51). The authors show that their data strongly support the assumption of greater optimism on the part of the ill respondents. However, they

fail to relate this to the findings of another question on perceived barriers to occupational aspirations: the community
disclosed a much higher proportion of perceiving no barriers
than did the ill sample. The mentally ill group reported illness
and negative personality traits as large barriers, indicating
that they understood their disorder would hold them back
(p. 129). In short, the ill might have more belief in an open
opportunity structure for others, while not for themselves.
The authors, in another context, admit that "the responses
of the patients change somewhat when the question deals
with another reference individual . . ." (p. 135). The concept
of open vs. closed society is so enormous in any case, that
it would require a much finer breakdown than the crude
measurements employed in this study.

There are a good number of questions on the individual's
feelings about being a Negro, and the responses are milder
than the authors had expected. Large numbers of both community and ill samples condone the idea of "passing" and
feel that being a Negro has been only somewhat of a barrier
or none at all. Parker and Kleiner point out that these figures
were gathered in 1960, before the current developments in
the civil rights revolution. The theoretical base from which
the authors are working is that a healthy Negro feels ambivalent about his membership, while a mentally ill person, by
denying that his race has been an important barrier, would
actually be refusing to identify with other Negroes or to accept
Negro norms and values. Although the data bear out these
responses for the two groups, there is an attempt to lean over
backwards to clinch the point. For instance: "The community
subjects are 'Ambivalent' about passing and at the same time
recognize that being Negro has been 'Very Much' or
'Somewhat' of an obstacle to goal achievement" (p. 162). The
actual breakdown of their data on the "obstacle of being
Negro" shows that 8 percent of the community answered
"Very Much," 57 percent answered "Slightly, or to Some
Degree," and 35 percent answered "Not at all" (p. 161).
In other words, 35 percent of the replies was dropped from
their analysis!

Much stronger responses were found in an area where the

authors had not given much emphasis: the person's feelings about success or failure as a husband or wife. Of the various categories under self-image, the most serious discrepancies between the rating of self-performance and ideal were found under the spouse sub-identity in the mentally ill sample. This area also revealed the largest discrepancy between answers given by the mentally ill and the community groups, showing that "the spouse role is evidently one of the major determinants of low self-esteem among the mentally ill" (p. 182). This would suggest that, had there been a higher percentage of questions on interpersonal tensions and not quite so many on occupation, income, race or status, the investigation might have produced a more faithful picture of goal-striving stress.*

* For the reader with patience the book is rich in hypotheses and directions to follow. So rich, in fact, that the authors should be encouraged to write a more basic theoretical work on mental illness and the urban Negro community, which this book is straining to become at times, and not to confine themselves so tightly to their data.

Chapter 19

THE EPIDEMIOLOGY OF PSYCHIATRIC EMERGENCIES IN AN URBAN HEALTH DISTRICT

MAYER FISCH, ERNEST M. GRUENBERG, AND CYNTHIA BANDFIELD

This paper reports an exercise in community diagnosis. Epidemiological data are frequently demanded by those engaged in planning community health services, and they are entitled to the best available information regarding the incidence and prevalence of conditions requiring service.

In the mental health specialties, such planning has depended very heavily on mental hospital admission rates; to these data have recently been added information about clinic utilization patterns. When these data are combined with prevalence surveys, such as that recently reported by Srole and Langner[1] in the midtown area of New York, a rather confusing picture emerges. Admission rates which are, in all conscience, high enough, are contrasted with enormously higher prevalence rates of significant psychiatric disorder.

A cooperative venture by the School of Public Health and the Department of Psychiatry at Columbia University has led to a number of studies which seek to provide more information of practical value to those who are organizing services in our immediate health district. Each year some 700 residents of this district are admitted to all state, private and voluntary

Abridged and reprinted with permission from the *American Journal of Public Health,* April 1964.

The authors would like to express their appreciation to the Bellevue Psychiatric Hospital, represented by: Arthur Zitrin, M.D., director; and with particular acknowledgment to Lawrence A. Cove, M.D., and Richard A. Markoff, M.D., who performed most of the examinations on which this report is based.

This investigation was supported by Public Health Service Research Grant 5-R11 MH 478-3 and a grant from the Foundations' Fund for Research in Psychiatry.

psychiatric hospitals within New York State. Of these, approximately 300 are admitted directly to these institutions, while
the other 400 go via the psychiatric unit of the municipal
general hospital which serves the district, as well as a much
larger part of the city. This hospital is not located within.
the district. However, an additional 500 patients per year
from the district pass through the municipal general hospital
psychiatric unit without being referred to state hospitals. This
group of patients does not appear in statistics available from
any administrative source at this time.

Even when we have hospital statistics, they tend to give
us information only about age, sex, color, and diagnosis. But
as in other fields of medicine, diagnosis leaves the thoughtful
student of community health problems uncertain as to the
level of severity and the nature of the service problems that
the particular patients present.

We wondered whether it was possible to get some idea
of the number and nature of emergency situations which were
being presented by psychiatric patients. There are many presenting syndromes representing acute states of abnormal mental functioning, as illustrated in psychiatric textbooks and in
the American Public Health Association's "Guide to Control
Methods of Mental Disorders."[2] It is believed that each of
these syndromes is capable of being manifested by patients
in different diagnostic groups. Likewise, most of the diagnoses
in psychiatry may be manifested by almost any one of the
acute emergency syndromes.

We decided to explore the frequency of the different acute
syndromes presenting emergency situations and the relationship of these emergency situations to diagnosis. We assumed
that a very large proportion of these emergencies would
appear at the municipal hospital psychiatric unit. As noted,
most psychiatric hospitalizations from the district occur at
this point, and it is the only facility to which there are channels
of virtually automatic referral and admission in case of need.

The health district is on the periphery of Manhattan Island
and is almost purely residential in character. It consists virtually exclusively of apartment houses and the commercial

AUTHOR: SHILOH A

TITLE: ETHNIC GROUPS OF AMERICA

PUB DATE: 1973

COMPLETE APPLICABLE BLOCKS	AGE AT REGISTRATION	NO. OF YEARS AT PRESENT ADDRESS		YEAR DISCHARGED FROM MILITARY	STATE FROM WHICH MILITARY WAS ENTERED			STATUS
		YOURSELF	SPOUSE			YES ☐	NO ☐	

COMPLETE THIS SECTION IF MARRIED	NAME OF HUSBAND OR MAIDEN NAME OF WIFE	AGE OF SPOUSE	YEARS MARRIED

COMPLETE THIS SECTION IF ACTIVE MILITARY OR DEPENDENT	ACTIVE DUTY MILITARY	DEPENDENT OF ACTIVE DUTY MILITARY	MILITARY DUTY STATION	LETTER FROM C.O.
	☐	☐		YES ☐ WILL FURNISH ☐

CHECK THE CORRECT BLOCKS

	YES	NO	
A	☐	☐	Have you resided continuously for more than one year at your current address?
B	☐	☐	Have you (as a civilian) continuously resided in the State of Texas for more than one year?
C	☐	☐	Do you (or your parents if under age 22) maintain a legal residence (domicile) within the boundaries of the college district?
D	☐	☐	Do you certify that you are a legal resident of Texas?

I CERTIFY THAT ALL INFORMATION GIVEN IS CORRECT AND COMPLETE

_____ SIGNATURE   _____ DATE

IT IS THE POLICY OF THIS COLLEGE TO ADMIT STUDENTS WITHOUT REGARD TO RACE, COLOR OR NATIONAL ORIGIN.

FOR OFFICE USE ONLY

RESIDENT CLASSIFICATION FOR TUITION PURPOSES

FORM RECEIVED BY _____

STATE CODE _____   BY _____

REMARKS:

establishments which serve the local population. In 1960, this population comprised 269,000 persons. It contains representative segments of most of the ethnic groups that constitute New York City, and its economic range is from lower class to upper middle, with only few representatives of either extreme of the social scale. The population is about one-quarter Negro, a proportion which is gradually increasing.

Age, Sex, Race Groupings

Table 19-I presents the overall admissions statistics from our health district to the municipal hospital psychiatric unit, for the year ending June 30, 1962. (There were 923 patients from the district who went to this hospital; as noted earlier

TABLE 19-I.
ADMISSIONS TO PSYCHIATRIC UNIT
RATES PER 1,000 POPULATION BY SEX, RACE, AND AGE

Age in Years	Total	Male	Female	White			Nonwhite		
				Total	*M*	*F*	*Total*	*M*	*F*
Less than 15	0.3	0.4	0.2	0.2	0.2	0.3	0.7	1.2	0.2
15–24	4.8	5.0	4.6	2.9	3.2	2.7	11.0	11.5	10.5
25–34	6.3	6.9	5.8	4.3	5.1	3.5	11.6	12.2	11.1
35–44	5.0	5.4	4.7	3.2	3.1	3.3	8.5	10.2	7.3
45–54	3.1	3.4	2.9	2.1	2.2	2.0	6.1	6.6	5.6
55–64	2.2	2.6	1.9	1.9	2.4	1.5	3.3	3.1	3.5
65–74	3.2	2.4	3.8	3.2	2.2	3.9	3.0	3.0	3.0
75 and over	5.4	5.9	5.1	4.4	5.2	3.9	12.9	10.9	14.1
Total	3.4	3.6	3.3	2.4	2.5	2.3	6.6	6.9	6.2

NUMBER OF ADMISSIONS BY SEX, RACE, AND AGE

Age in Years	Total	Male	Female	White			Nonwhite		
				Total	*M*	*F*	*Total*	*M*	*F*
Less than 15	16	10	6	8	3	5	8	7	1
15–24	146	71	75	69	36	33	77	35	42
25–34	223	114	109	108	62	46	115	52	63
35–44	185	87	98	80	34	46	105	53	52
45–54	133	63	70	65	30	35	68	33	35
55–64	88	48	40	61	36	25	27	12	15
65–74	78	26	52	67	21	46	11	5	6
75 and over	54	23	31	39	18	21	15	5	10
Total	923	442	481	497	240	257	426	202	224

about 300 other patients went directly to other more remote psychiatric facilities.)

This table is divided into age, sex, and race groupings, with the admission rate per 1,000 inhabitants of the district in each corresponding bracket. Population figures are derived from the 1960 census.

This table shows a rise in rates with age through age 30, succeeded by a marked decline in the 40's and 50's, with a rise in rates again after age 65. Analysis by five-year age groups revealed a pattern no different from that shown here by the ten-year groupings. It will be noted that there is no outstanding sex difference in admission rates, but that the rates of nonwhites or Negroes of both sexes are quite consistently more than twice those of whites. This differential is found in nearly all mental hospital admission rates. A similar contrast has been shown between the economically priviledged and deprived segments of white populations.

The total minimal incidence of psychiatric hospitalization per year, 3.4 per 1,000, is notably high. By contrast, admission rates to New York State psychiatric hospitals for the last available year are as follows: For New York State as a whole, 1.6 per 1,000; for New York City, 1.8; for Manhattan, 2.8; and for this health district, 1.7. This admission rate of 3.4 per 1,000 to the psychiatric unit of the municipal hospital appears to depict a different situation from that experienced by the more remote state hospital. The subgroup of greatest risk consists of males in the 25-to-34-year-old age bracket where the rate is 6.9 per 1,000, 5.4 for whites, and 12.2 for Negroes.

In order to qualitatively describe this flow of admissions and to focus on psychiatric emergencies arising in the community, we chose to concentrate on patients in the 15-to-44-year-old age group. Patients in this age bracket constituted over half of the total admissions (544 out of 923), and their admissions are most apt to arise in a crisis situation. All patients in this age group who were admitted from the health district were therefore given a direct psychiatric examination as soon after admission as possible, usually within one or two days, either by one of the authors or by one of two other psychiatrists who are members of this research team. This examination was completely apart from the usual procedures of the hospital. It was not done to arrive at a specific diagnosis or treatment recommendation, but to describe the general nature of the problem and the principal reason for admission to the hospital. However, two groups of patients within this age group were systematically not examined:

1. Those patients returning from convalescent care, but who were still on the rolls of a state hospital. Such patients may pass through this municipal psychiatric unit if return to full inpatient status is required; however, they are already in a treatment channel and will usually be returned within a day or two to the state hospital from which they had been released.

2. Prisoners or patients under court remand. These patients are generally sent in for psychiatric "clearance," as it were, pending some legal action. They were not examined because of their unique administrative status.

Admissions in these two categories have been included in our count and rates of total admissions, but were not examined by a member of our group and are not included in the tabulations which follow. There were 394 admissions of patients between the ages of 15 and 44, who were not prisoners nor on the rolls of another hospital. These 394 admissions were accounted for by 175 males and 219 females; 185 whites and 208 Negroes. Nearly all of these patients were examined by us. In those few instances where examination was missed for one reason or another, the hospital chart yielded sufficient information for inclusion in this report.

A review of the diagnosis of these cases, as made by the regular hospital staff after their normal series of examinations, revealed that there were only three clinical categories which accounted for a substantial number of admissions in this age group. These were, in order of frequency, schizophrenia, 177; conditions associated with alcohol, 107; and psychoneurotic depressive reaction, 64. All other diagnostic categories accounted for only 46 admissions.

Concerning the diagnoses associated with alcohol, it is the policy of the hospital not to admit patients for simple alcoholic intoxication; some other complication or feared complication must be present to warrant admission. The majority of the cases in the grouping of alcohol received a final diagnosis of acute brain syndrome due to alcohol, while far fewer received the diagnosis of alcoholism. There were only eight diagnoses of simple alcoholic intoxication. Diagnoses associated with alcohol were, as expected, more frequent in males, but were also far from rare in females, the numbers being 69 and 38, respectively. Illness attributed to alcohol was more frequent in Negroes, but the sex ratio was about the same in both races. Psychoneurotic depressive reaction was diagnosed more than twice as often in females as in males, and more often in whites than in Negroes. Schizophrenia accounted for substantially more female than male admissions, but veterans hospitals may be treating many of the men who would otherwise come to this hospital with this condition.

Table 19-II shows these admissions divided by sex and race but tabulated by the principal reason for admission to the hospital. This table is presented only in terms of absolute numbers. However, an approximation of population rates of any particular category in these tables can be derived by cross reference with Table 19-I. Many cases presented several of the phenomena listed in this table. In such instances, we selected the single most outstanding reason, or the sine qua non, for the person being in the hospital at this time. We have been speaking of emergencies, but efforts to adequately define this concept, so that each admission could be reliably and independently judged as to whether or not it represented an emergency, led to increasing ambiguity. We have therefore chosen to divide the reasons for hospitalization into two categories—those which inherently represent an emergency situation, and those which do not. A review of the type of situations included in the former category will probably best define the nature of the emergencies of which we are speaking. It will be noted that these constitute well over half the admissions. However, a great many of the cases in the lower part of the table also constituted emergencies, in that the need for hospitalization was equally pressing.

TABLE 19-II.
PRINCIPAL REASON FOR HOSPITALIZATION BY SEX AND RACE
PATIENTS 15–44 YEARS OF AGE*

	Total			White			Nonwhite		
	Total	M	F	T	M	F	T	M	F
Emergency Situations									
Suicide attempt, gesture, or major threat	94	24	70	58	15	43	36	9	27
Assaultive or violent behavior	35	17	18	17	11	6	18	6	12
Bizarre, obviously "crazy" behavior	45	22	23	21	10	11	24	12	12
Unmanageable household behavior	17	8	9	11	6	5	6	2	4
Acute confusion	11	5	6	5	3	2	6	2	4
Delirium tremens	34	27	7	4	4	0	30	23	7
Total	236	103	133	116	49	67	120	54	66
Other Problems									
Delusional ideation	31	11	20	18	6	12	13	5	8
Hallucinations	25	11	14	7	4	3	18	7	11
Simple withdrawal	9	4	5	2	2	0	7	2	5
Subjective emotional complaints	38	16	22	16	7	9	22	9	13
Subjective somatic complaints	15	7	8	7	5	2	8	2	6
Other and unknown	40	23	17	20	14	6	20	9	11
Total	158	72	86	70	38	32	88	34	54
Total Admissions	394	175	219	186	87	99	208	88	120

* Not including prisoners and patients of other hospitals returning from convalescent status.

This classification is obviously not intended as a new, competing scheme of psychiatric nosology. It does, however, add a vivid and relevant dimension for describing the frequency of phenomena which bring people to psychiatric attention. It is purely descriptive, and in some ways is reminiscent of the classifications used by psychiatrists of more than a century ago, before the clinical entities of our current nomenclature were recognized. Delirium tremens is of a somewhat different descriptive level than the other categories to which the reasons for admission have been reduced. It was retained in the grouping because of its relatively idiosyncratic constellation of symptoms, and its high incidence.

The largest number of cases admitted for suicidal behavior received the diagnosis of psychoneurotic depressive reaction. In most of these cases the diagnosis was made only because of the one act which led to hospitalization. Most denied any continuing suicidal intent or significant depression after they were at the hospital and were soon discharged. Many of the acts were probably attention getting devices or indirect forms of aggression.

This psychiatric unit of the municipal general hospital can offer little active treatment. Because of the constant stream of new admissions, it must make some disposition of most of its patients within less than two weeks. They are then either discharged back into the community, in nearly all cases then receiving no further treatment, or they are sent on to a state hospital.

It will be noted that except for the schizophrenics, nearly all are soon discharged. Schizophrenia is not a homogeneous diagnostic category, and the term has come to be used with ever increasing latitude. Many of the patients who received this diagnosis did not manifest the clinical characteristics attributed to schizophrenia by the European psychiatrists of the turn of the century who first described the syndrome. However, among the 30 percent of the schizophrenics who were discharged into the community there were several who had experienced episodes of florid psychosis, but with rapid disappearance of symptoms, so that no protracted hospitalization was deemed necessary.

Examination of the relationship between disposition and reason for hospitalization indicates that a higher proportion of the emergencies than of the other cases are soon discharged into the community. We do not know their subsequent fate. These emergency admissions, by and large, probably occur in people less profoundly ill than those presenting the other problems. They often represent acute, impulsive reactions against an environment which the individual at that point perceives as intolerable. These crises were in many instances probably preventable. We are left to speculate as to the effect of this crisis and hospitalization upon each patient. We suspect that hospitalization is not usually perceived by these patients as beneficial and rarely channels them into a therapeutic situation. A broader availability of community services, particularly facilities which might be equipped to handle these problems on an outpatient basis and to follow through on their treatment, might reduce the incidence of such crises.

Conclusions

Overall admission rates to mental hospitals from this urban health district are extremely high as compared to most published data about defined populations. We believe that this is attributable to several factors. First, the area is one of high density apartment residences; second, the usually published data do not include admissions to readily accessible acute psychiatric services without certification procedures; and third, the high level of acceptability of utilization of psychiatric hospitalization by the New York City population. The degree to which such services are occupied with the treatment of acute crises associated with alcohol in men and with the management of suicidal behavior in women is particularly striking.

We have confirmed that the syndromes of acute psychiatric emergencies are widely distributed in different diagnostic groups and that the different diagnostic groups are represented in almost every acute emergency syndrome. Despite a high level of mental health education during the past few decades, over half of the patients in early and middle adult life who appear for in-hospital psychiatric care at a municipal facility still present severe syndromes of a crisis nature, which require immediate, and sometimes drastic, response by service agencies. Any clinical service to be offered to such a metropolitan district must be prepared to deal with a large volume of severe psychiatric emergencies.

REFERENCES

1. Srole, L., Langner, T.S., Michael, S.T., Opler, M.K., and Rennie, T.A.C.: *Mental Health in the Metropolis.* New York, McGraw, 1962.

2. Program Area Committee on Mental Health, APHA. *Mental Disorders: A Guide to Control Methods.* New York, The Association, 1962.

PART SEVEN

TOWARDS THE DELIVERY OF
EFFECTIVE HEALTH SERVICES

In the preceding chapters we have considered patterns of poor health correlating to race, ethnicity, and socioeconomic conditions. Once a profile has been delineated, we confront the problems of alleviating the situation through the delivery of medical services and preventive medicine.

Ann F. Brunswick and Eric Josephson go to the heart of the matter—the attitudes and perceptions of young people in Harlem which affect their health. These adolescents show considerable awareness of what it is to be healthy.

For many years, drinking a certain amount of milk daily was considered a prerequisite for keeping children well. School lunch programs, especially for poor children, included milk automatically. However, as David M. Paige, Theodore M. Bayless, and George C. Graham report, recent studies have shown that there are racial factors in lactose tolerance which may make emphasis on milk drinking for Negro children harmful rather than helpful.

Victor W. Sidel faces the crucial question of the physician-patient ratio in the ghetto. He is quite critical of the idea that increasing numbers of physicians will necessarily lead to improvement of health care. He suggests, instead, "radical changes in the kinds of personnel who provide health care . . . and in the elimination of the ghetto itself."

In the concluding chapter, George A. Silver reviews what has been learned of the attitudes toward health care in the ghetto, and the inadequacies in the delivery of health services. He suggests the need for reevaluation by all individuals and agencies involved. The neighborhood health centers which have recently been developed have shown the efficacy of the health team approach. Silver suggests further study along these lines.

Chapter 20

HEALTH ATTITUDES AND BEHAVIOR OF ADOLESCENTS IN HARLEM

ANN F. BRUNSWICK, AND ERIC JOSEPHSON

A dolescents' views about health—what they consider important health problems, how they perceive health itself, what they believe to be good and bad health practices, the things they themselves do (apart from getting medical care) which may affect their health—these will be discussed here. The source for these data was the personal interview, during which considerable attention was given to health attitudes and practices.

This emphasis needs little justification. It is now considered axiomatic that planning for improvement in the delivery of medical care is not just a matter of determining health care needs and then providing the resources to meet those needs; also to be taken into consideration (for all but infants and young children) are attitudinal and behavioral factors with significance for the maintenance of health. What does "health" mean in a particular population—here, young blacks? What is perceived as threatening to health? What do adolescents do to maintain their health? These questions have rarely been touched upon in the literature on adolescent health.

Perceptions of Neighborhood Health Problems

This information was obtained by means of an indirect technique frequently used in survey research. Youngsters

Abridged and reprinted with permission from the *American Journal of Public Health*, Supplement, October, 1972.

were asked, "What do you see as some of the biggest health
or medical problems for young people like yourself living
around here?" There were four problems mentioned by at
least one in ten of those interviewed: drug abuse, smoking
cigarettes, drinking, and unsanitary living conditions. First,
in order of importance, was drug abuse. This was mentioned
by approximately *half* of the 12 to 15-year-olds, with girls
somewhat more likely to mention it than boys. Just how salient
the question of drug abuse was to youngsters is illustrated
by the following comments made to interviewers:

> Everybody seems to be taking dope around here. (12-year-old boy)
> You have to grow up around here with all these addicts. And if
> you see someone else doing it, it may seem like fun and you try
> it. (13-year-old boy)
> Young boys and girls of 15 and 16 [are] taking dope. (13-year-old
> girl)
> The worst problem around here is trying to get young people off
> drugs. (15-year-old boy)

Cigarette smoking was mentioned by one fifth of the sample
as a major health problem of their contemporaries. Drinking
and drunkenness were cited as major health problems by
one tenth of the boys and girls. Illustrative of their comments
are the following:

> A lot of people like to get drunk or high and it affects their health
> by slowing them down. (13-year-old boy)
> The men get drunk and fall out in the streets and bust their heads.
> (13-year-old boy)

Unsanitary living conditions were cited by another tenth
of the sample in comments like these:

> There are too many roaches, rats and flies in the projects. . . . The
> streets are always dirty. (15-year-old boy)
> People live in buildings that are all messed up. (14-year-old boy)
> Most of the little children go outside and play right on the avenue
> with the trash and garbage spilled all over. (13-year-old girl)

Conceptions of Health and Personal Health Concerns

The first question using the word "health" in the personal
interview was, "How would you describe a healthy person?"
The behavior most frequently associated with being healthy

was physical activity, endurance, agility, and stamina, as the following replies suggest:

> A person who has a lot of energy—someone who plays around a lot—plays tennis and swims.
> They have more loose joints.
> Like activities keep them healthy—they take gym, go swimming.
> He isn't short-winded—he could do a lot of things without getting so tired.

Four in ten youths, and boys (48%) more than girls (32%) mentioned some aspect of physical activity when describing a healthy person. Three in ten youths associated being well-built with being healthy, boys (32%) slightly more than girls (26%). Closely allied was the concept of strength, an idea expressed by a quarter of the 12 to 15-year-olds, and boys (28%) more often than girls (18%). High on the list of ideas associated with being healthy were matters relating to diet: nearly a quarter mentioned eating the right food or a balanced diet; one in eight talked about eating the right amount and having a good appetite.

Resistance to disease (not getting sick) and the absence of either disease or physical impairment were mentioned by 20 percent and 16 percent, respectively. Cleanliness—about the person and his living conditions—was a theme mentioned by about one in ten when he described a healthy person.

These same themes appeared in replies to a question concerning what adolescents would like to discuss with a doctor if they had the chance to ask him anything they wanted. Foremost on the list, mentioned by one in five of all 12-to 15-year-olds and by boys (23%) more than girls (14%), were questions concerning their general state of health:

> How is my health coming along?
> Ask him how I feel.
> Ask him was I in shape—do I have any disease or anything?
> Am I healthy now?

Nine percent would like to discuss their weight with a doctor:

> To look at my stomach to see if I'm overweight.
> I have been trying to lose weight—I would like to ask him if I should and, if not, why not? About weight—losing weight and gaining—how it works.

How to avoid illness and stay healthy were questions that 7 percent of these youths said they wanted to talk over with a doctor.

When youngsters were asked how often they thought about their health, three-quarters said they thought about it "often" or "sometimes." These youngsters then were asked what they thought about and their replies provide additional insight into adolescents' conceptions of health. One in six thought about his health in general:

> Will I ever be sick like some children I know?
> I think about me and what's going to happen to me—I can't say my health don't bother me.
> I think about how healthy I am or should be—I try to think about why I am so lazy at times.
> I think about getting a medical check but then I don't go.

A similar proportion thought about getting sufficient exercise and keeping in shape (22% of the boys and 7% of the girls); their weight, usually about not getting fat (10% of the boys and 20% of the girls); eating the right food (10% of the boys and 17% of the girls); and about ways of protecting their health and avoiding illness (10%).

Adolescent health concerns are reflected in responses to another question that did not ask about health but rather what, if anything, adolescents would like to change about themselves. Among that half of the sample who would like to change themselves in some way, nearly one-quarter said they would like to change their weight; one-sixth—boys and girls equally—said they would like to change their height; one-eighth mentioned changing their general appearance; and approximately one-tenth—almost all of them girls—said they would like to change their hair.

Important in people's conceptions of health are their beliefs about the preventability of illness and/or the inevitability of illness. Three questions in the personal interview tapped these attitudes. Nine in ten Harlem adolescents believed that being healthy was mainly a matter of taking proper care of themselves. However, three-quarters believed that, regardless of how careful a person is, he could expect a considerable amount of sickness in his lifetime; better than half felt that there was not much a person could do to avoid illness.

Personal Health Behavior

Given these conceptions of and attitudes toward health, what do youngsters regard as "good" or "bad" about their own health practices and what are they doing from day to day to maintain their health?

In the personal interview, adolescents were not asked about their own use of drugs. However, it is worth noting that when they were asked about things they themselves did that were not good for their health, one percent—boys and girls alike—volunteered the information that they were using drugs.

There were no such constraints in asking about cigarette smoking and drinking. Boys and girls were quite alike in the proportions who said they smoked; about one in six of the 12- to 15-year-olds and a much greater proportion of the 16- to 17-year-olds (50% of boys and 62% of girls) said they were smoking cigarettes. Indeed, both the proportion of smokers and the number of cigarettes smoked grew steadily with age. Approximately three out of ten smokers (representing one in twenty of all 12- to 15-year-old black youngsters) reported smoking at least half a pack of cigarettes a day. (This may be compared with national data on teenage smoking for 1970, according to which 8% of 12- to 18-year-old boys and 5% of girls this age were smoking half a pack or more of cigarettes daily: unpublished data from the National Clearing House for Smoking and Health.) The proportion of older adolescent girls in Harlem who smoke is higher than generally found (Public Health Service, 1969).

The salience of cigarette smoking as a health problem to youngsters in Harlem is illustrated by their responses to a question about things they did that were not good for their health. One in ten mentioned his own smoking. After eating habits, this was mentioned most frequently as behavior which was bad for health. Responding to another question, among those youngsters who reported that they think about their health, one in twenty was sufficiently concerned about his smoking to mention it as something he thinks about; practically all who gave this reply were boys.

As to their own drinking behavior, more girls than boys in the 12- to 15-year-old age group (20% and 12%, respectively) reported that they drank wine, beer, or other alcoholic beverages. As may be expected, drinking increased with age—and 16- and 17-year-old boys were considerably more likely to drink than girls: 56 percent of the boys this age and 34 percent of the girls drank some alcoholic beverage. Regarding the salience of drinking as a health concern, when asked what they do that might be bad for their health, one percent volunteered that they drank too much.

What do youngsters do that they consider *good* for their health? Themes they expressed when describing a healthy person and their personal health concerns recurred in accounts of their own health practices: exercise and physical activity, bodily appearance, diet and weight, resistance to disease, and cleanliness.

Physical activity was most prominent among the things they reported doing that were good for their health. Four in five youngsters mentioned something in the way of physical exercise:

I play basketball almost every night—I walk a lot.
Exercise—perhaps for one hour.
I play—I dance.
Track, swimming—improve your muscles—build you up inside—make your muscles stronger.
I go with my friend to the park—climb mountains and stuff like that.

The difference between boys and girls was not as great as might be expected with regard to the frequency of mentioning exercise as one of their good health practices (87% of boys and 72% of girls).

The association of physical activity and health was demonstrated also in replies to an inquiry about poor health practices—things youngsters said they did that were *not* good for their health. In contrast to the 80 percent who mentioned getting exercise as something that contributed to their health, one in twenty felt that he did not get sufficient exercise.

Evidence has already been presented regarding young people's concern about bodily appearance and body image, a consideration which might properly be recognized as underlying certain other replies—for example, the frequent references to exercise and physical activity already described and the emphasis on weight, diet, and eating patterns to be discussed next.

In their descriptions of a healthy person there was more frequent reference to the *kind* than to the amount of food eaten. In talking about their own health practices, adolescents again referred more often to the kind than to the amount of food they ate—although both were mentioned with frequency. Four in ten of 12- to 15-year-old youths said that one of the good things they did for their health was to eat the correct food. Girls more often than boys mentioned that they ate the right amount of food (32% and 20%, respectively).

Yet, in terms of criticizing their own health habits, one in five (22%) felt that he ate too many sweets—girls (25%) slightly more often than boys (18%); almost 10 percent referred to other improper foods that they ate (again girls were more likely to refer to eating the wrong food than boys). When asked about things they did that were harmful to their health, equal proportions of girls and boys, about one in fourteen, reported that they did not eat enough or that they skipped meals.

The interview also included direct questions about eating patterns. About half of the 12- to 15-year-olds were satisfied with the amount of food they ate; four in ten thought they ate too much; one in ten that he did not eat enough. About half of the girls and better than a third of the boys reported that they ate more in snacks than in meals. More girls (19%) than boys (8%) reported eating about the same amount in snacks as in meals. Thus, in answer to direct questions, it appears that more girls than boys had inadequate eating patterns; or perhaps girls were more aware than boys of such patterns. Hardly any of these youngsters (7%) reported that they had ever been on a special diet—either medically or self-imposed.

Special questions were included to obtain a picture of

nonalcoholic beverage drinking patterns. About six in seven of these youths said they drank some milk daily; four in ten drank at least three glasses a day. Daily consumption of soft drinks was slightly lower than that of milk. Almost equal proportions had at least one soft drink daily (82% drank soda compared to 85% who drank milk); one-fourth had three or more soft drinks daily.

One in seven said he drank coffee daily, and 3 percent drank more than one cup of coffee in a day. More tea was drunk than coffee, with four in ten reporting daily tea consumption, girls more than boys. One in seven drank two or more cups of tea a day. Only one in twenty reported no regular pattern of drinking water daily; four in ten said they drank at least five glasses of water in a day.

One in eight of the youngsters cited cleanliness among their good health practices. As noted earlier, in addition to associating personal cleanliness with being healthy, unsanitary living conditions were also identified as a health problem. The interview included three direct questions that bear on living conditions. One inquired about the frequency of garbage removal: 15 percent did *not* report daily garbage collection or access to an incinerator. Another question dealt with the adequacy of heat in the winter time: three in ten said they did *not* have enough heat. The third question asked about the supply of hot water in the buildings: about a quarter reported insufficient supplies of hot water.

In discussing their health practices, youngsters sometimes talked about the amount of sleep they got. One in five, somewhat more girls than boys, mentioned sleep as something they did that was good for their health. Insufficient sleep was mentioned third most frequently as one of their poor health practices, after diet and smoking. Seven percent of all the 12- to 15-year-olds were critical of their own sleep patterns.

How much did they actually sleep? The mean number of hours on weekday nights was close to nine hours and almost two thirds slept this much. Boys were somewhat later risers than girls.

Nine in ten of these youths slept in a bedroom; about one-third slept in a room by themselves; four in ten slept in a room with one other person. About one in twelve slept in a room with at least three other people. Concerning sleep disturbance in connection with psychosomatic indicators of emotional problems, more girls reported trouble falling asleep (35%) than boys (22%), and slightly more girls reported being disturbed by bad dreams (22%) than boys (18%). Since girls were *not* more likely to sleep in rooms with others (78% of the girls slept in a room by themselves or with just one other person compared to 69% of the boys), their greater sleep problems would not appear to be a function of less comfortable sleeping space.

Summary

This investigation into conceptions of health, health concerns and health practices among 12- to 15-year-old adolescents in Harlem showed considerable awareness of these matters. Drugs, smoking, drinking, and sanitary conditions were foremost public health concerns to them. Physical activity, bodily appearance (including strength and weight), diet, resistance to disease, cleanliness and sleep were matters most likely to be discussed in connection with personal health practices and behavior. All but sleep figured prominently in adolescents' ideas of what it is to be healthy.

Chapter 21

MILK PROGRAMS: HELPFUL OR HARMFUL TO NEGRO CHILDREN?

David M. Paige, Theodore M. Bayless
and George G. Graham

INTRODUCTION

Low levels of intestinal lactase activity are found in many otherwise healthy adults and children. Attention in recent years has focused on this problem in American Negroes,[1,4] Asians,[5,8] Bantu tribes,[9,10] South American Indians,[11] Thais,[12,14] and other groups.[15,17] Current evidence indicates that low lactase levels are the norm in the majority of adults in most populations in the world.[18] Notable exceptions are Scandinavians and those of northern European extraction.

As the problem is further refined, it is becoming evident that lactose intolerance exists in significant numbers of Negro children.[19] Milk has traditionally been embraced as an important staple of the diet for these children who so often represent the target population of much public health nutrition input. It is therefore exceedingly important to know the acceptance or rejection of this product and the physiological basis for this, if any, in populations of children destined to be lactose intolerant.

It appears that there are no long-term biological effects on the growth and development of healthy children who manifest lactose intolerance and lactase deficiency. The potential

Abridged and reprinted with permission from the *American Journal of Public Health*, November, 1972.

This paper was presented before the Food and Nutrition Section of the American Public Health Association at the Ninety-Ninth Annual Meeting in Minneapolis, Minnesota on October 14, 1971.

difficulty seems to rest with the nature of the diet presented to these children. For if lactose is present to a large extent in the diets fed to Negroes, and there is rejection because of an underlying enzymatic deficiency with its resultant discomfort of gas, bloating, cramps, and diarrhea, then a problem would indeed exist. The paradox would be that we are attempting to upgrade the nutritional status of disadvantaged Negroes with food products that a large number of individuals cannot physiologically tolerate.

In this paper we report on: 1) the number and racial profile of those elementary school children who do not consume their one-half pint container of free, unflavored whole cow's milk during the lunch period; 2) their family history of milk consumption; 3) symptoms induced by an oral lactose load; and 4) the blood sugar rise during the oral lactose tolerance test.

Materials and Methods

Two independent observations of milk consumption were carried out in each of two Baltimore City elementary schools. One school is predominantly Negro and one predominantly white; both are located in lower socioeconomic census tracts and are under the medical aegis of Baltimore City Children and Youth Projects. Three hundred twelve Negro and 221 white children in the first through sixth grades were observed during the school lunch period.

The standard federally supported "Type A" school lunch is served at both schools, with which a one-half pint container of unflavored whole cow's milk is served. All children observed were participating in this program. There was no opportunity for these children to obtain beverages from other sources, nor were optional beverages served in the food line.

Milk consumption was observed as follows: Each child was given a self-sticking name tag in the morning. At lunch, they passed through the food line and ate their lunches without interference from the observers. As the child returned his tray to the "bussing" window, the name tag was removed from his person and attached to his milk carton. Observers remained behind the bussing window, completely out of sight, where they weighed each carton on a Chatillon food scale and recorded in quarters, by weight, any milk left in the carton.

The observed children were categorized as either milk drinkers or nonmilk drinkers. A milk drinker was defined as one who consumed 50 percent or more of his one-half pint container of milk; on the other hand, a nonmilk drinker was one who consumed less than 50 percent of his milk.

A random sample of children who performed in a similar manner on both observations was drawn to have a lactose tolerance test performed; they were chosen so as to provide approximately equal numbers in each category. All children were in apparent good health, free of overt gastrointestinal or allergic disorders, with no previous history of gastroenteritis or malnutrition.

The parent of each child was interviewed to determine the child's consumption or nonconsumption of milk and milk products.

Results

Twenty percent of the Negro children observed consumed less than one-half of their milk. In contrast, 10 percent of the white children consumed less than half of their milk. Overall, the failure to consume moderate amounts of milk in Negroes was twice that of whites.

Lactose tolerance tests were abnormal in 17 percent of the white nonmilk drinkers, and in 20 percent of the white milk drinkers tested.

Among the Negro milk drinkers, 35 percent had flat lactose tolerance curves (blood sugar rise less than 26 mg/100 ml). Symptoms associated with lactose intolerance were noted in three of the five.

In the Negro nonmilk drinkers who had lactose tolerance tests, 77 percent had an abnormal rise in blood sugar, with symptoms of lactose intolerance in 85 percent of these children. The difference between Negro nonmilk drinkers and milk drinkers was significant (p.<.025).

The history of milk consumption (more than four ounces

of milk consumed per 24 hours) obtained from the family revealed that 53 percent of the nonmilk drinkers in school were described by their mothers as nonmilk drinkers at home: contrasted with 93 percent of the Negro milk drinkers in school consuming milk at home.

Among white children 42 percent of the nonmilk drinkers in school were reported by their parent as being nonmilk drinkers at home; while all milk drinkers at school consumed milk at home.

All children categorized as nonmilk drinkers had been able to drink milk as infants. There was no past history of milk allergy or milk feeding problems.

Seventy-nine percent of the mothers of Negro school children categorized as nonmilk drinkers did not consume milk at home; compared to 33 percent of mothers of Negro milk drinkers rejecting milk. There was no significant difference in milk consumption by the mothers in either white group.

Of all Negro mothers not drinking milk, 40 percent stated that they did not consume milk because it provoked one or more symptoms associated with lactose intolerance. Only one mother cited the lack of money as the reason her family was not consuming milk.

Discussion

It appears that milk rejection by Negro elementary school children in an organized school feeding program is significantly higher than in similarly matched white children. Overall, the frequency of nonconsumption of moderate amounts of milk in Negroes is approximately twice that of whites.

An association has been demonstrated in the Negro nonmilk drinkers between poor consumption in the lunchroom and at home, lactose induced symptoms, and lactose malabsorption.

Moreover, it is important to note that 58 percent of all Negro children studied were shown to inadequately digest lactose as demonstrated by a flat lactose tolerance curve. Even though many of these children may continue to consume milk, they are probably not realizing its full nutritional value.

It therefore appears that race and nationality influence milk consumption. In addition to our own data on Baltimore City schoolchildren, domestic surveys reinforce the fact that native white Americans and northern Europeans consume more milk than people of southern European extraction, Negroes, and Orientals.[20] A Boston survey[21] has shown that the Boston Irish population consumed 0.794 pint of milk per day, while Negroes consumed only 0.362 pint of milk per day. Even at equal income, total per capita fluid consumption by whites in South Carolina was nearly twice that of Negroes.[21] These racial differences have usually been attributed to inadequate financial and educational resources on the part of Negroes.

We believe a number of factors are operating to affect milk consumption: lack of finances, poor education, and inappropriate consumer purchasing habits are certainly important factors. This importance is reflected in subsidized milk programs, nutrition education, and consumer guides to appropriate buying habits. However, in addition to the factors enumerated above, one should recognize that lactose malabsorption may be an additional factor contributing to milk rejection on the part of Negro children. One may not, therefore, assume that a half-pint carton of milk, if made available and placed on a lunch tray, will be consumed. Current results suggest the need to reconsider the rationale of attempts to reinforce the nutritional status of Negroes through heavy emphasis on milk consumption and milk distribution.

Conclusion

In conclusion, it appears that Negro children who reject milk are different from the other children studied. The significant differences manifest themselves in a consistent pattern of milk rejection at school and at home, intolerance to lactose, and an inability to split lactose as measured by the lactose tolerance test. This constellation of events suggests that beyond the social and economic determinants that contribute to or militate against the consumption of milk, Negro children who fail to drink milk do so because of the additional biological fact of low/levels lactase. It appears, too, that the numbers of Negro children unwilling to consume milk are sufficiently great to call for a reevaluation of the efficacy of our present milk programs.

REFERENCES

1. Bayless, T.M. and Rosensweig, N.S.: A racial difference in incidence of lactase deficiency. *JAMA, 197:*968–972, 1966.
2. Cuatrecasas, P., Lockwood, D.H., and Caldwell, J.R.: Lactase deficiency in the adult: A common occurrence. *Lancet, 1:*14–18, 1965.
3. Huang, S.S. and Bayless, T.M.: Lactose intolerance in healthy children. *N Engl J Med, 276:*1283–1287, 1967.
4. Bayless, T.M. and Rosensweig, N.S.: Incidence and implications of lactase deficiency and milk intolerance in white and negro populations. *Johns Hopkins Med J, 121:*54–64, 1967.
5. Huang, S.S. and Bayless, T.M.: Milk and lactose intolerance in healthy Orientals. *Science, 160:*83–84, 1968.
6. Chung, H.M. and McGill, D.B.: Lactase deficiency in Orientals. *Gastroenterology, 54:*225–226, 1968.
7. Bolin, T.D., Crane, G.G., and Davis, A.E.: Lactose intolerance in various ethnic groups in Southeast Asia. *Aust Ann Med, 17:*300–306, 1968.
8. Davis, A.E. and Bolin, T.D.: Lactose intolerance in Asians. *Nature, 216:*1244–1245, 1967.
9. Cook, G.C. and Kajubi, S.K.: Tribal incidence of lactase deficiency in Uganda. *Lancet, 1:*725–729, 1966.
10. Jersky, K. and Kinsley, R.H.: Lactase deficiency in the South African Bantu. *S Afr Med J, 41:*1194–1196, 1967.
11. Alzate, H., Gonzales, H., and Guzman, J.: Lactose intolerance in South American Indians. *Am J Clin Nutr, 22:*122–123, 1969.
12. Keusch, G.T., Troncale, F.J., and Miller, L.G.: Acquired lactose malabsorption in Thai children. *Pediatrics, 43:*540–545, 1969.
13. Keusch, G.T., Troncale, F.J., Thavaramara, B. et al.: Lactase deficiency in Thailand: Effect of prolonged lactose feeding. *Am J Clin Nutr, 22:*638–641, 1969.
14. Flatz, G., Saengudom, C., and Sanguanbhokai, T.: Lactose intolerance in Thailand. *Nature, 221:*753–759, 1969.
15. Gudmand-Hoyer, E. and Jarnum, S.: Lactose malabsorption in Greenland Eskimos. *Acta Med Scandia, 186:*235–237, 1969.
16. Elliot, M.B., Maxwell, G.M., and Vawser, N.: Lactose maldigestion in Australian aboriginal children. *Med J Aust, 1:*46–49, 1967.
17. Gilat, T., Kuhn, R., Gelman, E. et al.: Lactase deficiency in Jewish communities in Israel. *Am J Dig Dis, 15:*895–904, 1970.
18. Bayless, T.M., Paige, D.M., and Ferry, G.D.: Lactose intolerance and milk drinking habits. *Gastroenterology, 60:*605–608, 1971.

19. Paige, D.M. and Graham, G.G.: The etiology of lactase deficiency: Another perspective. *Gastroenterology, 61:*798, 1971.

20. Waugh, F.V. The Consumption of Milk and Dairy Products in Metropolitan Boston in December, 1930. Massachusetts Agriculture Experimental Station, September, 1931.

21. Drake, P., and Roach, F.E.: Use of milk by urban and rural families in South Carolina. *Clemson Bulletin 437,* South Carolina Agriculture Experimental Station of Clemson Agricultural College, May, 1956.

Chapter 22

CAN MORE PHYSICIANS BE ATTRACTED TO GHETTO PRACTICE?

Victor W. Sidel

First, it has not to my knowledge been demonstrated that more *physicians*—as contrasted for example, to more specially-trained nurses,[1] more family health workers,[2] more welfare rights activists,[3,4] or more revolutionaries[5,6]—are what the people in the ghetto most need to improve their health and to improve their health care. Second, it has not to my knowledge been demonstrated that the attraction to ghetto practice of more of our *current* physicians—physicians recruited into current medical schools by our current criteria and trained by our current methods—will provide the health care that the people of the ghetto want or need. Third, it has not to my knowledge been demonstrated that it would be better for health care, for health, or for quality of life to attract physicians *into* rather than to transport people *out of* the ghetto; the extension of this point is, of course, that the basic issue is not the attraction of physicians into the ghetto but the elimination of the ghetto. Finally, it has not to my knowledge been demonstrated that a white, middle-class physician has much to contribute to a solution of the problem, especially in a place like Wentworth-by-theSea.

Although there are in my view serious questions about my relevance, and the relevance of my topic, to the search for a solution to the problems, it remains the conventional wis-

Abridged and reprinted with permission from *Medicine in the Ghetto,* edited by John C. Norman, Appleton-Century-Crofts, New York, 1969.

The author is indebted to Carl Cobb, Daniel B. Doyle, Dr. John Kosa, Dr. Roger Sweet, and Dr. Andrew Twaddle for their suggestions on the manuscript.

dom that 1) attracting more physicians into the ghetto will improve medical care and will improve the health of the people of the ghetto and 2) discussion of the problems by people like me in places like this will contribute to their solution.

The evidence that there are relatively few physicians in the ghetto and that they differ in their training and practice patterns from those in other areas is easy to marshal: studies in upstate New York,[7] Chicago,[8] Los Angeles,[9] New York City,[10] and Boston[11] have shown that areas with poor socioeconomic indices have lower ratios of doctors to population than do areas with higher indices. The Boston study further demonstrates that those physicians who are classified as "intermediary physicians"—general internists, pediatricians, and obstetricians-gynecologists—have "almost totally avoided the poor areas:" only 10 percent of all intermediary physicians were located in the lowest groups of census tracts, an area which included 60 percent of the population studied. Furthermore, a survey performed for the Harvard Medical School Commission on Relations with the Black Community[12] of the 40 physicians practicing in the Roxbury and North Dorchester areas of Boston showed that the mean age of these doctors is 66; only six are under 50. Half are graduates of schools which no longer exist: twelve of the Middlesex University School of Medicine, five of the College of Physicians and Surgeons of Boston, and three of Kansas City University School of Physicians and Surgeons.

Although I know of no specific studies on the attitudes and practice patterns of ghetto physicians in the U.S., a study I did last year in London in collaboration with Margot Jeffreys, Professor of Medical Sociology in the University of London, might be relevant.[13] All of the general practitioners of the London Borough of Camden, an inner London borough, were contacted, and 90 per cent agreed to a lengthy interview. Of the 138 general practitioners, 69 were classified as practicing in middle-class districts of the Borough and 69 in working-class districts. Among the differences we noted were: the working-class general practitioners saw more patients per day than did their counterparts in the middle-class districts; fewer took cervical Pap smears (which was one of our measures for preventive medicine practice); fewer made direct use of hospital-based diagnostic facilities and fewer were eager to have hospital beds under their direct control; and fewer were members of academic societies. Perhaps most striking in indicating the attitudinal differences was the response to a check-list question: Which of these aspects of general practice do you like best? The one most frequently chosen response by the practitioners in middle-class districts (chosen by 37%) was "being able to maintain continuing personal relations with patients"; the one most frequently chosen by the practitioners in working-class districts (also chosen by 37%) was "the opportunity to help people."

It appears that ghetto physicians are older, not as well trained, more overworked, less likely to practice preventive medicine, and more paternalistic in their attitude toward their patients than are physicians practicing in other areas.

Turning from the clear evidence that medical care in the ghetto is poor to the less clear topic of my paper, a first step in answering such a question as "Can More Physicians Be Attracted to Ghetto Practice?" might be to make a list of those methods which have been suggested. Such a conventional list would certainly include:

1. *Increasing the income of, or providing other material benefits to, physicians entering ghetto practice;*
2. *Increasing the professional satisfactions of ghetto physicians;*
3. *Increasing the total life satisfaction of ghetto physicians —which would include satisfactions other than income or professional satisfactions, perhaps analogous to the satisfactions of physicians who practice in certain rural areas because they like to hunt or fish; and*
4. *Excusing the ghetto physician from certain other duties in the society which he would find onerous.*

Many different suggestions have been made for implementation of each of the methods on this list. For example:

1. Methods which have been suggested to increase the income of ghetto physicians include: putting more money into the hands of ghetto residents with which they might,

if they wished, purchase more medical care on a fee-for-service or other basis, or pay for it at a higher rate; developing prepayment plans for panel practice at a subsidized per capita rate paid directly by some third party; paying the physician a salary and/or providing him with office facilities to work in the ghetto and permitting him to give care without charge or to charge for it in addition to his salary or subsidization. There are an infinite number of variations on this theme: one of these suggests paying for a student's medical education and giving him a stipend while he is in training, in return for his spending a specified number of years in the ghetto after completion of his training.

2. Methods suggested to increase the professional satisfaction of ghetto physicians include: providing access to hospitals and medical centers of high quality; setting up medical care teams so that the ghetto physicians might work with other physicians and other personnel with high professional skills; and establishing means of helping the physician to provide those things for his patient which he feels the patient needs, including better food, better clothing, better housing, better education, and better jobs.

3. Methods suggested to increase the total life satisfactions of ghetto physicians include: surrounding him, and his spouse, with friends whom they would find congenial; and strengthening features of the urban life, including the positive social, cultural, and recreational aspects of living in the center of a large city.

4. There are so few onerous duties that a U.S. physician must perform that the principal example of the fourth item on the list is, of course, excusing the physician from service in an obscene war such as that in Vietnam in return for his service in the ghetto. The willingness of the federal government to respond to such a suggestion might, it has been suggested, provide a rather direct test of the relative importance of the war on poverty and the war in Vietnam.

But as one examines this conventional list a common factor becomes strikingly clear. We are taking physicians as we currently select them into medical schools and as we currently train them, and then providing inducements which some of these physicians might find seductive in attracting them into ghetto practice. There is little prospect, in my view, that such seduction will work on the scale which is needed, although individual items on the list might help give short-term partial amelioration for specific crisis situations in the ghetto. And even if the seduction did work in the short term, there is little evidence that those seduced would practice successfully in the ghetto or stay in the ghetto.

Examples of the failure of such methods to work in the long run are common. In the Soviet Union medical education is provided free by the state and in addition the student is paid a stipend during his training; in return, after the completion of his training, the student is urged (the Soviet authorities insist that he cannot be forced) to spend a period of practice in a rural area—rural areas being the remaining areas of relative physician shortage in the USSR. The physician receives a higher pay scale and has additional important benefits—such as housing—if he remains in rural practice, but the serious urban/rural differential persists. Why have the inducements not worked? First, the brightest medical school graduates are excused from such service and enter residency training immediately. Second, many of the graduates apparently find methods of avoiding such service entirely and of remaining in the cities. Finally, many of those who indeed perform their assigned service in rural areas return to the cities for practice—or for further training and then practice—after their period of exile is completed.

Closer to home, although a number of physicians have been recruited into rural areas by the community's supplying them with practice facilities, there are no good data to my knowledge on how well these physicians are accepted or how long they stay. It has been demonstrated for example, that although the higher fees supplied by the Medicaid program in New York City succeeded in the short run in bringing dentists into the ghetto, it did not succeed in the short run in bringing physicians into the ghetto.[14] Even upgrading of working conditions, changes in patterns of practice, and availability of excellent staff often do not appear to make a critical difference, as the rapid professional turnover and empty positions in some ghetto health centers would suggest.

Why are such methods not likely to work successfully—or for other than a short period—with physicians who are recruited and trained in the current pattern? If one examines the attitudes of those who are already physicians or those in medical training, it is clear that there is little inclination toward practice in the ghetto or sympathy with the problems of its citizens. For example, Fredericks, Kosa, and Robertson[15] sent a questionnaire to a random sample of physicians in the United States; 76 percent returned the completed questionnaire. Of those responding, less than 20 percent agreed with the statement, "Every doctor should serve for two years in a poor area before settling down" and over 40 percent agreed with the statement, "A dissolute way of life is the cause of many diseases among the poor." In an interview study of 28 pediatric residents, Roth, Kosa, and Alpert[16] found that the "great majority . . . displayed an essentially negative attitude toward the poor," that only two of the 28 "wanted to work in community clinics in poverty-stricken urban areas" (and those two saw themselves as directing such a clinic from an academic base), and that none of the 28 "planned a career that would include personal treatment of the poor patient as the essential part of his medical practice."

In my view the major reasons for these attitudes among physicians and medical students are the way in which students are selected into medical school and the way in which they are trained. The bias in the selection of students toward the higher socioeconomic classes has been repeatedly demonstrated. For example, in a survey of students in two public and two private medical schools in 1965, Rosinski[17] found that 34 percent of the students come from families in the top 3 percent socioeconomically and only 8 percent of the students came from families from the bottom 40 percent. Lyden, Geiger, and Peterson[18] in a survey of graduates of six private and six public medical schools found that 60 per cent of the doctors had fathers who were themselves physicians or other professionals, executives, or small business men, whereas only 15 percent of the total U.S. employed are in such occupational groups; conversely, only 18 percent of the graduates had fathers who were skilled or unskilled laborers, an occupational group that includes 58 percent of those employed in the U.S.

Similar selection biases are seen toward the male sex, toward the white race, and toward the student who is proficient in getting good grades in course work and in examinations. The old bias toward science orientation may be at last shifting toward people orientation, as suggested by data collected by Dr. Funkenstein at the Harvard Medical School.[19] Perhaps the old saw that the major attractions of students to medical school are based on "parents, power, prestige, profits, and prurience" never was a fair generalization; but to the extent that it was—and still is—true, these self-selection critieria and the subsequent medical school selection criteria probably represent a barrier to the attraction of physicians into the ghetto.

Even the data on overall selection bias do not tell the whole story. There is further bias and maldistribution *within* the medical education system. For example, of the 200 black physicians currently graduating from U.S. medical schools each year, three fourths are said to graduate from Howard and Meharry Medical Schools.

Although there is obviously no guarantee that medical students drawn from lower socioeconomic classes or from black parentage or from among women will later be attracted to ghetto practice—in fact, the limited evidence suggests that most of those whom we currently recruit from such pools end up in the same kinds of nonghetto practice as their colleagues—there are at least some analogies which suggest that there may be greater chance that such students will be more willing to practice in the ghetto and that they will be more effective. For example, to return to the USSR as an analogy, the greatest success in providing primary care practitioners for rural practice has lain in the recruitment of *feldsher* candidates from the areas in which practitioners are needed; these *feldshers* are said to be much more comfortable practicing among the people with whom they grew up, whose language they speak, and whose customs they know. The analogy of the *feldsher* to the U.S. primary care physician may seem far fetched, but many of their functions are comparable—and the *feldsher* appears to be much happier performing them in certain areas than is the physician.[20]

After the candidate arrives in medical school, everything possible is done to drive him away from consideration of ghetto practice or from being effective if he were later "attracted" into the ghetto. These carefully nurtured techniques include:

1. The early emphasis on the biochemical and the pathologic, so that the human being becomes interesting only as the bearer of enzymes or of a disease. In fact, if the patient has no definable organic disease the student is taught to think of him as a "crock";

2. The frequently heard derision about the quality of practice of the primary care physician, who is called an "L.M.D." and rarely given even the courtesy of a report on his patient;[21]

3. Making the student dependent on hospital-based services for his professional comfort and satisfaction; and

4. Permitting him little or no contact with, and therefore little or no opportunity to adopt as a role-model, physicians giving primary care or practicing in the ghetto.

Furthermore, in the "professionalization" of the student, he is taught—either implicitly or explicitly—that he is captain of the health team, that he makes lonely life-and-death decisions, and that he knows best and will have to convince the patient that he does. The emphasis, it has been said, is on the production of an "M-Deity." The roles of other health professionals, the right of the patient to make his own decisions, even though they may be wrong in the eyes of the doctor, and the role of the community in making health decisions are concepts which are rarely taught.

Finally, responsibility for providing physician care in the ghetto is diffused. This diffusion takes two forms. First, there is the diffusion which exists because the student is taught that his primary responsibility is to the individual patient rather than to the community; hence, those individuals who have individual doctors may be the objects of considerable concern, but those who do not are the concern of very few. Second, and perhaps even more important, there is the diffusion of responsibility which occurs when many people might act, but do not. The murder, for example, of Kitty Genovese over the course of one-half hour on a street in Kew Gardens while 38 people looked on from their apartments—and not a single one so much as telephoned the police—has generated a number of elegant psychologic experiments.[22] These experiments demonstrate very clearly that an individual alone is much more likely to take action in response to an emergency than is an individual in a group among whom no single person has the clear responsibility for action. In our current medical education the student is taught that he has a personal responsibility for the life and health of his patient and that if no one else is acting, he must act; at no time is he taught that he has a personal responsibility for the health of his community and that if no one else is acting, he must act.[23]

In brief, current selection and training of medical students lead to the production of a population of physicians whose attitudes, values, and life styles make work in the ghetto difficult if not impossible. This suggests that a new list of methods of attracting physicians into the ghetto is needed. This list would not be incompatible with the first list: clearly some of the older methods, such as a fundamental change in the patterns of, and methods of payment for, medical practice in the United States are needed on other grounds. But it would appear to me that those which follow are a *sine qua non* for the long-term attraction of physicians into ghetto practice.

1. Change the recruitment of medical students:
   a. Attract applicants from new pools; and
   b. Accept a higher percentage of poor, nonwhite, female, and people-centered candidates—using these characteristics either singly or in combination—into medical school.
2. Change medical education:
   a. Permit the student to learn that technical competence and intellectual achievement are not the only requisites of the primary care physician, and that compassion and a passionate desire to better the quality of life are at least as important;

b. Permit the student to learn that good medicine can be practiced outside the hospital, and that much of it *should* be practiced outside the hospital if it is to be good;

c. Provide the student with an opportunity to choose as role models those practicing as primary care physicians and those practicing in the ghetto;

d. Encourage acceptance of a new medical ethic which insists that responsibility to the community is as important as responsibility to the individual patient and that each physician bears a personal responsibility for the health and welfare of his community;

e. Provide the student with examples of his medical school working actively and responsibly with the citizens of the ghetto, not only to provide a model for care or a base for teaching or research, but primarily to give good medical care and improve health; and

f. Refrain from actions such as indiscriminate land-taking which are insensitive to broader community needs, and which suggest that *primum non nocere* (first, do no harm) has no application in community medicine.

When these changes are made in the selection of candidates into medical education and in the education of students after they get into medical school, we will be able to talk more realistically and positively of attracting physicians into the ghetto. We will have physicians who are willing and able to live life styles, and enjoy professional and other satisfactions, which are compatible with medical practice in the ghetto. Of course by the time this happens it is likely that the ghetto will no longer exist in its present form: either the same social forces which will have changed the medical education process also will have forced a change in the ghetto or, as is more likely, the process will take so long that other solutions—of a more radical nature—will have been found for the problems of poor health, poor medical care, and a poor life in the ghetto.

In short, to return to where I began, my response to the question "Can More Physicians Be Attracted to Ghetto Practice?" is to recommend further attention to the premises on which the question is based. The considerations I have outlined suggest that the question may be inappropriate in its current form and that the solutions to the problem lie rather in radical changes in the kinds of personnel who provide health care in the ghetto, in the selection and training of physicians, in the sites of care, and in the elimination of the ghetto itself. The problems we face, in my view, are such that mere tinkering with the current system, however imaginatively or with whatever goodwill—and this includes attempting to attract current physicians and medical students into the ghetto—may serve only to perpetuate the evils we have and to delay the radical changes which are necessary.

REFERENCES

1. Silver, H.K., Ford, L.C., and Stearly, S.G.: Pediatric nurse practicioner program. *Pediatrics, 39*:756, 1967.

2. Wise, H.: Medicine and poverty. In Torrey, E.F. (Ed.): *Ethical Issues in Medicine.* Boston, Little, 1968, pp. 347-370.

3. Cloward, R.A., and Elman, R.M.: Poverty, injustice, and the welfare state. Part II: How rights can be secured. *The Nation,* March 7, 1966, pp. 264-268.

4. Paull, J.E.: Recipients aroused: The new welfare rights movement. *Social Work,* April, 1967.

5. Guevara, E.C.: On Revolutionary medicine. In Gerassi, J. (Ed.): *Venceremos! The Speeches and Writings of Che Guevara,* New York, S & S, 1968, pp. 112–119.

6. Allan, T., and Gordon, S.: *The Scalpel, the Sword: The Story of Dr. Norman Bethune.* Boston, Little, 1952.

7. Terris, M., and Monk, M.A.: Recent trends in the distribution of physicians in upstate New York. *Am J Public Health, 46*:585, 1956.

8. Lepper, M.H., Lashof, J.C., Lerner, M., German, J., and Andelman, S.L.: Approaches to meeting health needs of large poverty populations. *Am J Public Health,* 57:1153, 1967.

9. Roemer, M.I.: Health resources and services in the Watts area of Los Angeles. *Calif Health, 23*:123, 1966.

10. Piore, N., and Solal, S.: *A Profile of Physicians in the City of New York Before Medicare and Medicaid.* New York, Urban Research Center, 1968.

11. Dorsey, J. L.: *Physician Distribution in Boston and Brookline, 1940 and 1961.* M.P.H. Thesis, Yale University, 1968.

12. Report of the Harvard Medical School Commission on Relations with the Black Community. Boston, Harvard Medical School, 1969.

13. Sidel, V.W., Jefferys, M., and Mansfield, P.M.: Unpublished data, 1968.

14. Kavaler, F.: People, providers and payment—telling it how it is. *Am J Public Health,* 59:825, 1969.

15. Fredericks, M.A., Kosa, J., and Robertson, L.S.: The doctor and the poor: a study of physicians' attitudes toward treating the poor. Paper pre-

sented at the annual meeting of the Eastern Sociological Society, New York, April, 1969.

16. Roth, J.A., Kosa, J., and Alpert, J.J.: Who will treat the poor? Altruism and entrepreneurship among young physicians. Paper presented at the annual meeting of the American Sociological Association and the Society for the Study of Social Problems, San Francisco, Calif., August, 1967.

17. Rosinski, E.F.: Social class of medical students: a look at an untapped pool of possible medical school applicants. *JAMA, 193:*95, 1965.

18. Lyden, F.J., Geiger, H.J., and Peterson, O.L.: *The Training of Good Physicians: Critical Factors in Career Choices.* Cambridge, Mass., Harvard U Pr, 1968.

19. Funkenstein, D.: Personal communication, 1969.

20. Sidel, V.W.: *Feldshers* and *"feldsherism"*: the role and training of the *feldsher* in the USSR. *N Engl J Med, 278:*934, 981, 1968.

21. Sigelman, J.: Communications between selected North End and East Boston general practitioners and the Massachusetts General Hospital. Paper written by a second-year medical student during elective work in the Community Medicine Unit, Massachusetts General Hospital, October, 1968, (mimeo).

22. Latane, B., and Darley, J.M.: Bystander "apathy." *Am Scientist, 57:*244, 1969.

23. Taylor, C.E.: Ethics for an international health profession. *Science, 153:*716, 1966.

Chapter 23

WHAT HAS BEEN LEARNED ABOUT THE DELIVERY OF HEALTH CARE SERVICES TO THE GHETTO?

GEORGE A. SILVER

For a long time, we had held to the professional position that the poor gave health a very low priority. A poll by Louis Harris[1] recently taught us otherwise. It seems we may have taken some comfort from our failures to supply needed care that we were not entitled to. When we said housing and jobs were more important considerations to the poor than health, we may have been justifying our inactivity. Certainly we have not provided the housing or the jobs either.

Hunger and malnutrition, for example, are surely aspects of health needs. There should be no more question of the fact that they exist among the poor today. Some economists estimate the loss to the American economy as well over $5 billion a year—the people who die, the illness and associated medical care costs, the compensatory education for the deprived and mentally retarded children, losses from work, and the like. Yet the government estimates it would cost less than $3 billion to end hunger in the United States![2]

The ghetto is fighting the basic inhumanity of a society and a culture that does not recognize their needs; that does not care if their babies die, but lets rats live in their decayed living quarters; that lets them be cheated in food prices and rent and puts greater value on death and murder than on life in assignment of national priorities. Our respect has increased for their patience and long-suffering humanity.

Abridged and reprinted with permission from *Medicine in the Ghetto*, Edited by John C. Norman, Appleton-Century-Crofts, New York, 1969.

They continue to expect help of us, believe we are well intentioned, and despite our defective system that poisons them, traps them, and deprives them of health and medicine, they still hope. We have seen with surprise how few of them develop rage and paranoia. They do not see us as deliberate murderers but see the situation only as "accidental homicide."

The ghetto people are sicker, and they have a harder time· getting their needs met. They do not participate in decision-making, so the allocation of resources is rarely in the direction of meeting their needs as they perceive them.

We have come to see that the whole medical care system was inadequate to meet not only their needs but the needs of the rest of us as well.

In reviewing the data on differential health status of our own population and that of other countries, it is clear that not only the poor are at a disadvantage.[3] In spending well over 6 percent of our Gross National Product for health services, more than any other country in the world, we are clearly not obtaining the health dividend of the dollar expenditure.[4] Shortages of personnel and disorganized, or at least poorly organized, marginally productive health services affect us all. As Voltaire noted, "the good is the enemy of the best," and the upper income groups have not yet begun to suffer what the poor suffer, so we are still reluctant to make major change. It is doubtful if the narrow view of dealing with the problem in terms of improving care for the poor can be effective as a long-term solution. It has become clear that our present distribution of resources, expenditures, and organization of services cannot be apportioned to reach more people with medical care services, and to serve them better.

Solutions in terms of simply supplying more, and not in different ways, will not work; and trying to set up such different ways for the poor alone will not work either. In the long run it will mean two kinds of educational tracks, two kinds of organization of health care, two kinds of payment mechanisms, with all that represents in competition, administration, and cost.

If anything is to be done it must be done with reallocation of existing resources for everyone, a better use of our present funds because we know better what to do than we are now doing.

To do this we must abandon the shibboleths of medical care thinking, those things we talk about every day as being basic requirements because they seem so professionally desirable, evaluate their necessity, and review what it is that needs to be done and determine how it might be approached more rationally.

To do this of course will mean a reevaluation by each of the vested interests: the physicians, hospitals, and nursing homes, among the providers; the various professional interest groups; the professional schools; the manufacturers of drugs and equipment; the health officials at every level; the insurance carriers; the whole American people. Efficiency and economy and more equitable distribution of health services are needed. How can this best be achieved? This we have yet to learn.

The special ghetto health services developed in the past few years, like the neighborhood health centers, have taught us that a health team is a practical way of rendering medical care to families.[5] It has taught us that a nurse can undertake to coordinate health services for families and relieve the doctor of a good deal of work for which he is really overtrained. We may not have identified the particularly appropriate role for the doctor yet, but the outlines are there.[6] And the new ghetto health services have demonstrated the value and capability of the family health worker, a new kind of intermediate health worker taking over some of the roles of the doctor and some of the roles of the nurse.

Of course, some of these answers have served to raise new questions, questions about licensure and career ladders, and the role of educational institutions in the training of new kinds of health workers.

Other hard questions have arisen from the experiences to which we have no good answers: vociferous partisan responses, yes—but no good answers. Can we preserve freedom of choice of the physician and still allow for the best mechanism of organization by professional standards? In the economics of medical care can we conserve funds and at the same time offer incentives to economy and efficiency and still provide all the services required?

For example, we know that the most efficient and economical method of delivering medical services is through group practice with prepayment, a modified clinic system, a closed panel. We have the evidence to hand from the experiences of the prepaid group practice systems.[7] This is incompatible with fee-for-service solo practice. There are 60 to 70 thousand general practitioners, the majority in fee-for-service solo practice. Can we bring the bulk of physicians into a prepayment group practice scheme?

We have learned that to meet manpower needs and to organize health services more efficiently we have to attack the two elements simultaneously. Their interrelatedness is such that improved organization of medical practice can only be achieved through a change in the manpower structure in the health field. This means not only the introduction of new types of health manpower but a rethinking of the whole method of selecting and training the constituent elements of the health manpower field.

We have learned that bringing people into the health field at entry level jobs without providing career ladders does not make for suitable recruitment. Yet we have done very little to change the patterns of credentials, licensure, and professional vested interests. In other words, we still need to learn how we can retain the values that are inherent in professionalism without losing out to the kind of rigidity that now afflicts our professional system.

At the same time, we have a great deal to learn about the jobs that are to be done, more in the way of task definition, so that we can determine what kind of training is required, how much training is required, what kind of recruits we can select, and whether academic qualifications are really necessary. In this connection, we have done very little about proficiency testing. Over the years, academic qualifications have superseded proficiency testing. Can we afford to let the pendulum swing back? At the same time we need to ask ourselves other questions about present professional standards of recruitment. Are present prerequisites too high? Are entrance tests suitable?

Moreover, can we afford not to ask ourselves whether there should not be various levels of education even within a specific professional field? It has taken us a long time to get to the point where we have a single M.D. degree.[8] Should we now be thinking in terms of training doctors through career ladders? Should we be thinking of reassuming the responsibilities for apprenticeship training in addition to academic training in medicine?

We have learned a few lessons about money. Total medical care is expensive, but the average expenditure per person at the present time for health care seems adequate to provide a family-centered, comprehensive service if it is efficiently organized, e.g., a neighborhood health center.[9] As a matter of fact, if the money now spent were efficiently channeled, it could probably serve to provide suitable health services for all our people. This does not mean that we have learned to cope with all the problems related to reimbursement. We might say we have learned that there are problems in every method of financing services—general revenues, employer-employee contributions, grants-in-aid—and in every method of reimbursing the practitioners and providers of services—fee-for-service, capitation, salary, reasonable costs.

In the field of professional education, we have learned that a lot still needs to be learned and that much needs to be done that we already know and are not doing.

We do not know, for example, how we can get doctors to do what is socially desirable and socially necessary without compulsion. If we doubled the number of medical schools and turned out twice as many doctors, what guarantee do we have that they would not all become specialists in ophthalmology or surgery so that there would still remain a deficit of family physicians and other scarce specialists; and what guarantee do we have if there were the right proportion of the kinds of physicians and the mix of specialists that we require, that they would practice in the areas where they are needed? We need to obtain information about the impact of a guaranteed salary or of a capitation method in aiding a better deployment and distribution of all kinds of health workers.

Another area in which we have more questions than answers is in the matter of citizen participation. The overriding question in citizen participation is whether we mean control or advice and consent in design and administration of health services. Certainly we have learned that without the participation of the poor and the minority groups, the ghetto dwellers themselves, that professional considerations alone do not give adequate rein for flexibility and innovation required in improving health services for the poor. This also touches directly upon one of the major social issues of our time, which is the need of people to feel that in some degree they have a voice in the control of their own destiny.[10] From the standpoint of planning, design, and operation of health services for the poor it is an absolute necessity that the poor themselves be able to say what it is they want and how they will accept what is designed. In this sense, the citizen in the ghetto is brought in as an expert, the value of whose contribution is as great as that of any other expert in the particular field of his expertise.

Professionals, of course, are very concerned about the kinds of services that would be developed, fearful that the demands of the consumer groups might run counter to the professional and expert judgment in that area. The consumer might want students for the health professions to be recruited without regard to previous training; or the curriculum dominated by factors other than scientific and professional considerations. He may prefer solo practice to group practice, neighborhood store fronts to the most up-to-date technologically equipped clinics, or even the recruitment of cultist practitioners instead of the M.D. With the consumers in control what will be the role of the professional? How should the professional react?

The experience in this regard is illuminating, but not decisive. In very few instances are consumers actually in decision-making roles. They have been selected to serve on advisory boards and urged to set up citizen committees and the like, although even here, representation from the poor as consumers has been minimal; but very rarely do they receive the federal grant money or the local health department funds to operate health services. The stage of development is still too new to be able to say what will happen if consumers are actually in control.

On the other hand, the demands made on the committees where they do serve would not lead one to be excessively fearful. What they are asking of medical educators, of hospital clinics, of health departments have been noted by professionals for many years as serious questions about necessary reforms. It would be hard to fault the consumer as being unreasonable in asking for evaluation of medical education admission and curriculum policies of clinic services.

What may be more to the point in this argument is: Who is a citizen? Who is a consumer? Who is to be the representative that speaks for him? Is he to be elected? Is he to be selected? Is he to be appointed? What steps have we taken to educate the community for service in planning bodies and health service boards? Ghetto dwellers can be brought in and trained in varying periods of time to serve in various capacities on boards and committees. They can also serve in the delivery of health services, to reduce the demand for professionals and to increase the satisfaction of service and its ability to reach the unreachable. In this latter regard, citizen participation should be considered a *sine qua non.* Citizens clearly have a right to participate in the employment opportunities, and it may well be that the services will be all the better for it.

We might add, here, that there are other definitions that ought to be developed.

Having learned that the neighborhood health center can be a very satisfying form of delivery of health services to the poor, we still have to learn what a neighborhood is, we even have to learn what a center is. The hospital, because of its concentration of technologic equipment and personnel, perhaps ought to be the center for the delivery of health services as well as for the education of the health professional. Should we convert the neighborhood health center into just this kind of central focus of activity? Or should it be a limited medical focus, with the hospital supplying support and guidance as a professional resource for a number of centers?

Another lesson we learned is that when poor people come to a public facility like a neighborhood health center they expect all their problems to be handled there: social, familial, legal. Some health centers are now multipurpose centers, offering advice in a number of areas and even help in those areas. Should we not be concentrating on neighborhood multipurpose centers with a wide range of expert services available?

I will conclude with a number of questions related more to social policy than to the delivery of health services in the ghetto. But they arise from those same experiences, so I leave them with you.

In a larger area of concern we need to decide whether we should be spending time and money in a development of health services for the ghetto if we are not going to do something more significant about food, housing, and education for ghetto people. Do we have any evidence that concentrating on health services with the multibillion dollar investment that is required is going to be beneficial enough to justify that investment unless the other kinds of needed investments are made as well?

Many of the poor in urban ghettos are rural immigrants. Their needs go back to the deprivation in the rural areas. As the resources of the city grow, the resources of rural areas are being depleted. Can we provide a two-way flow so that the urban center becomes a supporting base for rural areas? We've seen some examples of this kind of support; we know that the Regional Medical Programs offer a framework within which this could be accomplished. Can the ghetto help itself and the rural community as well?

We have come to think of the situation of the ghetto, with its deprivation, its drained-off resources, as bearing the same sort of relationship to the rest of our society that developing countries do to developed countries on the world scene. Can we make use of what has been learned in the developing countries themselves for the improvement of health services in their applicability to the ghetto? Are there ways in which an exchange of students could provide training abroad and training in the United States for both needs? Could we have a domestic health corps to offset the personnel needs in the ghetto health services?

It seems to me that I have asked more questions than I have answered and it may be that this is the most important thing we have learned: that there are many more questions to be answered than there are answers available to us at the present time.

REFERENCES

1. Harris, L.: Living sick. In *Sources, A Blue Cross Report on the Health Problems of the Poor*. Chicago, Blue Cross Assoc, 1968.

2. Testimony submitted by Department of HEW to Senate Select Committee on Nutrition and Human Needs to be published in the reports of their hearings.

3. Fuchs, V.R.: The contributions of health services to the American economy. *Milbank Mem Fund Quart, 40*:65, 1966, pt. 2.

4. Forbes, W.H.: Longevity and medical costs. *N Engl J Med, 277*:71, 1967.

5. Silver, G.A.: *Family Medical Care*. Cambridge, Mass., Harvard U Pr, 1963.

6. Wise, H., Torrey, E.F., McDade, A., Perry, G., and Bograd, H.: The family health worker, *Am J Public Health, 58*:1828, 1968. See also Ford, P.A., Seacat, M.S., and Silver, G.A.: The relative roles of the public health nurse and the physician in prenatal and infant supervision. *Am J Public Health, 56*:1097, 1966.

7. Roemer, M.I., and DuBois, D.M.: Medical costs in relation to the organization of ambulatory care. *N Engl J Med., 280*:988, 1969; MacColl, W.A.: *Group Practice and Prepayment of Medical Care*. Washington, D.C., Public Affairs Pr, 1966.

8. Silver, G.A.: The Y-plan again. *Lancet, 202*:271, 1961.

9. U.S. Department of Health, Education and Welfare: *Delivery of Health Services for the Poor*. Washington, D.C., U.S. Govt Print Off, December, 1967.

10. Spiegel, H.B.C. (Ed.): *Citizen Participation in Urban Development*. Washington, D.C., National Institutes for Applied Behavioral Science, Center for Community Affairs, 1968, vol. 1.

AUTHOR INDEX

A

Aaron, Sadie, 40, 59
Abbell, L.I., 87, 98
Acheson, R.M., 67, 68, 69, 75
Adelson, S.F., 91, 98
Allan, T., 259, 269
Allen, W.C., 70, 72, 76
Alleyne, G.A.O., 112, 116
Alpert, J.J., 264, 269
Alter, M., 55, 62
Alzate, H., 252, 257
Andelman, Samuel L., 84, 260, 269
Anderson, J.W., 112, 116
Anderson, R.S., 53, 61, 112, 116
Antonovsky, Aaron, 22, 23
Aperia, A.C., 111, 115
Appel, B., 47, 49, 61
Aronson, S.M., 70, 76

B

Bales, R.F., 186, 194
Ball, John C., 209, 210, 213
Ballard, M.S., 143, 145
Banfield, Cynthia, v, 224
Barreras, L., 112, 116
Bass, L.N., 52, 61
Bates, William M., 210, 213
Bauer, Mary Lou, 22, 29, 30, 31, 34
Baumgartner, Leona, 44, 45, 46, 60
Bayless, Theodore, v, 242, 252, 257
Bennett, C.G., 73, 76
Berkson, D.M., v, 56, 62, 66, 67, 75, 84, 85, 96
Berstein, J., 110, 115
Bertles, J.F., 107, 108, 113, 114
Beutler, E., 112, 116
Bigman, S.K., 13, 17
Blache, J.O., 85, 97
Blake, E.C., 91, 98
Blanch, T., 47, 72, 75
Blumberg, B.S., 50, 61
Blumenthal, H.T., 97
Bograd, H., 273, 279

Bolin, T.D., 252, 257
Book, J.A., 40, 59
Borhani, N.O., 67, 75
Borun, E.R., 101, 103
Bowen, J.W.E., 194
Boyle, E.H., 68, 75, 91, 99
Bradess, V.A., 98
Brehm, Henry, 31, 33
Brewster, H.H., 107, 113
Brody, J.I., 112, 116
Bronte, Stewart, B., 91, 98
Bross, Irwin J., 148
Broun, G.O., Jr., 108, 114
Brozek, J., 93, 99
Brunswick, Ann F., v, 242
Buchholz, J.H., 100, 103
Burbank, Fred, v, 148, 149, 150, 160, 161, 162
Burch, G.E., 55, 56, 62

C

Calden, G., 40, 59
Caldwell, J.R., 257
Caldwell, M.G., 39, 40, 59
Camp, F.R., Jr., 118, 120
Campbell, D., 144
Carmichael, C.P., 39, 59
Casper, Julian, 148
Cassell, M., 112, 116
Casserd, F., 108, 114
Castle, W.B., 107, 113, 126, 128
Cayton, H.R., 178, 185
Cerami, A., 113, 116, 138, 145
Chafetz, M., 191, 194
Chaplin, H., Jr., 112, 116
Chapman, J.M., 101, 103
Charache, S., 110, 114, 115
Charney, E., 108, 109, 114
Chassau, J.B., 186, 193
Chein, Isidor, 209, 213
Christopherson, William M., v, 55, 62, 148
Chung, C.S., 121, 122, 128

Chung, H.M., 257
Clemmesen, J., 163, 167
Clemson, S.C., 91, 99
Clifford, G.L., 109, 114
Cloward, R.A., 259, 269
Cobb, Carl, 259
Cochran, C., 192, 194
Cohen, M.E., 73, 76, 101, 103
Collins, S.D., 96
Conley, C.W., 111, 116
Conte, N.F., 118, 120
Cook, G.C., 252, 257
Cornelius, E.A., 110, 111, 115
Cornely, Paul B., v, xiii, 4, 13, 17
Cornfield, J., 163, 168
Coulter, E.M., 188, 194
Crane, G.G., 257
Crockett, C.L., 108, 114
Crosby, W.H., 50, 61
Cuatrecasas, P., 257
Cutler, S.J., 159, 162, 163, 167

D

Dacie, J.V., 50, 51, 52, 61
Dai, Bingham, 209, 213
Daland, G.A., 126, 128
Dameshek, W., 53, 61
Darley, J.M., 267, 270
Davies, J.N.P., 160, 162
Davis, A.E., 252, 257
Dawber, T.R., 73, 76, 86, 98, 101, 103
de Koning, J., 111, 115
Delgado, Beatriz de, 42, 60
Demeny, Paul, 21, 33
Demone, H.W., 191, 194
Deschin, Celia S., 48, 61
Dickson, R.J., 55, 62
Diggs, L.W., 107, 112, 114, 116
diSant Agnese, P.A., 121, 122, 125, 128
Döbler, J., 107, 113
Donegan, C.C., Jr., 109, 114
Doraiswami, K.R., 163, 168
Dorn, Harold F., 148, 159, 162, 163, 167
Dorsey, J.L., 260, 269
Doyle, Daniel B., 259
Drake, P., 256, 258
Drake, St. Clair, 19, 33, 178, 185
Dubach, R., 109, 114
Dublin, Louis I., 30, 33

Dublin, T.D., 50, 61
DuBois, D.M., 274, 279
Dubos, R.J., 48, 49, 61
Duke, T.W., 109, 115
Duncan, Otis Dudley, 19, 22, 23
Dunham, H.W., 41, 59
Dunham, Lucia J., 148
Dunn, J.E., Jr., 163, 167, 168

E

Eastman, N.J., 52, 57, 61
Ederer, F., 121, 122, 128
Edgecomb, John H., 148
Elliot, M.B., 257
Elman, R.M., 259, 269
Epstein, F.H., 68, 75, 107, 111, 114, 115
Erickson, C.C., 163, 167, 168
Erlandson, M.E., 108, 114
Etteldorf, J.N., 109, 114
Evarts, Arrah B., 41, 59
Ewing, J.A., 192, 194

F

Fabrikant, J.I., 55, 62
Faris, R.E.L., 41, 59
Farley, Reynolds, 21, 25, 33
Ferguson, A.D., 115
Ferry, G.D., 252, 257
Fiedler, A.J., 110, 114
Finch, Clement A., v, 106, 108, 109, 110, 114
Fink, A., 110, 115
Finnerty, Frank A., Jr., v, 66, 100, 103
Fisch, Mayer, v, 224
Fiumara, N.J., 47, 49, 61
Flatz, G., 252, 257
Fleischer, R.A., 111, 116
Forbes, W.H., 272, 279
Ford, L.C., 259, 269
Forsham, P.H., 53, 61
Fraumeni, Joseph F., Jr., v, 148, 161, 162
Frazier, E.R., 189, 192, 194
Frazier, F.E., 178, 180, 185, 183
Fredericks, M.A., 264, 269
Frederickson, D.S., 50, 51, 52, 53, 54, 61
Freis, E.D., 35, 96
Freytag, E., 71, 76
Frichsberg, Robert P., 22, 35

Frumkin, R.M., 41, 58
Fuchs, Victor R., 272, 279
Fulton, C.C., 217, 221
Funahashi, T., 110, 115
Funkenstin, D., 265, 270
Furcolow, M.L., 46, 60

G

Garcia, J.S., 161, 162
Gardner, E., Jr., 112, 116
Gardner, G.E., 40, 59
Garland, I., 188, 194
Garrison, G.E., 73, 77
Garrison, G.W., 70, 76
Gay, M.L., 161, 162
Geiger, H.J., 264, 270
Gelman, E., 252, 257
Genienberg, Ernest M., vi, 224
Gerald, D.L., 209, 213
German, J., 260, 269
Giblett, E.R., 108, 114
Gilat, T., 252, 257
Gilliam, A.G., 163, 167, 168
Gingrich, Paul, 33
Girusin, H., 73, 76
Glad, D.D., 186, 194
Glaser, S., 44, 45, 60
Glass, A.G., 161, 162
Glass, B., 37, 58
Gleeson, Geraldine A., 22, 35
Godel, J.C., 110, 115
Gofman, J.W., 98
Goldberg, I.D., 67, 75
Goldhamer, H., 39, 59
Goldner, J.C., 70, 72, 76
Goldsmith, M.H., 112, 116
Goldstein, A., 150, 162
Goldstein, Marcus S., 22, 33
Gonzales, H., 252, 257
Gordon, S., 259, 269
Gordon, T., 73, 76
Gover, M., 96
Gower, Mary, 57, 63
Graham, C.G., 252, 258
Graham, George C., vi, 242
Grant, F.W., 99
Gray, S.H., 97
Gray, W.R., 97
Greenberg, M.S., 107, 112, 113, 116

Griggs, R.C., 107, 113
Grinstein, M., 109, 114
Grisolia, S., 110, 114
Groom, D., 91, 97, 99
Gross, Ruth T., 52, 61
Gross, S., 110, 115
Grove, Robert D., 22, 23, 33
Gudmand-Hoger, E., 252, 257
Guevara, E.C., 259, 269
Gunter, Laurie M., 53, 61
Gunz, F., 53, 61
Guralnick, Lillian, 22, 28, 29, 34
Guzman, J., 252, 257
Gyepes, M., 56, 62

H

Halden, E.R., 110, 111, 115
Hall, Y., vi, 56, 62, 66, 84, 85, 95
Ham, T.H., 107, 113
Hames, C.G., 70, 73, 76, 77
Hames, D., 91, 99
Handler, F.P., 97
Harris, J.W., 107, 111, 113, 115
Harris, Louis, 271, 279
Hartley, H.O., 150, 162
Hathorn, M., 108, 114
Hauser, Philip M., 23, 33
Havlik, R., 67, 72, 75
Heath, C.W., 161, 162
Hejtmancik, M.R., 85, 97
Hellegers, A.E., 110, 114
Hellems, H.K., 109, 114
Helpern, Milton, vi, 170, 217, 218, 221
Henry, R.L., 112, 116, 118, 120
Herrick, J.B., 121, 127, 131, 132, 148
Herring, B.D., 52, 61
Herrmann, G.R., 85, 97
Heyman, A., 109, 115
Heyman, Dorothy, 39, 59
Hill, W., 47, 49, 61
Hilleboe, H.E., 50, 61
Hirayama, Takeshi, 148
Hirota, Y., 69, 75
Hoeber, Paul B., 128
Hokanson, J.E., 39, 40, 59
Hollingshead, A.B., 40, 59
Holman, R.L., 97
Ho Ping Kong, H., 112, 116
Hsia, D.Y., 121, 122, 128

Huang, S.S., 252, 257
Huber, R., 17
Hunt, W.A., 40, 59
Hutcheson, J.M., 97

I

Ingram, V.M., 131, 145
Iskrant, A.P., 45, 60
Itano, H.A., 111, 115, 117, 120, 121, 127, 131, 132, 145
Ivins, S.P., 58

J

Jackson, Dolores E., vi, 106
Jaco, E.G., 38, 39, 59
Jarnum, S., 252, 257
Jeffreys, Margot, 260, 269
Jensen, R.D., 161, 162
Jensen, W.N., 107, 113
Jersky, K., 252, 257
Johnson, G.C., 188, 194
Johnson, L.G., 70, 76
Josephson, Eric, vi, 242
Joslin, E.P., 99

K

Kadushin, C., 22, 33
Kaiser, R.F., 163, 167, 168
Kajubi, S.K., 252, 257
Kallman, F.J., 40, 41, 59
Kane, W.C., 70, 76
Kannel, W.B., 73, 76, 101, 103
Kardiner, A., 42, 60, 225
Karns, J.R., 46, 60
Kashgarian, M., 122, 128
Kasower, E.M., 112, 116
Kasower, N.S., 112, 116
Kass, E.H., 107, 112, 113, 116
Kato, H.L., 70, 76
Katsuki, S., 69, 70, 75, 76
Katz, I., 56, 62
Katz, L.N., 84, 85, 90, 91, 92, 93, 94, 95, 99
Kavaler, F., 263, 269
Keil, P.G., 85, 97
Keitel, H.G., 111, 115
Kellam, S.G., 186, 193
Kennaway, E.L., 163, 167, 168
Kennedy, W.A., 17
Kent, A.P., 97

Keusch, G.T., 252, 257
Keys, A., 90, 92, 93, 98
Kinsley, R.H., 252, 257
Kitagawa, Evelyn, 21, 23, 26, 27, 33
Kjelsberg, M., 84, 85, 95
Kleiner, R.J., 42, 60
Kleiner, Robert S., 225, 226, 229
Kligman, A.M., 54, 62
Knobloch, Hilda, 57, 63
Koehler, P.R., 55, 62
Kohn, M., 39, 59
Kosa, John, 259, 264, 269, 270
Krueger, D.E., 68, 69, 73, 75, 86, 97
Kuhn, R., 252, 257
Kuller, L., 67, 68, 72, 75
Kurland, L.T., 67, 75
Kurtzke, J.F., 67, 72, 75

L

LaCourse, P.C., 112, 116
Lane, J.C., 122, 128
Lange, R.D., 107, 113
Langner, T.S., 231, 240
Lantz, Edna M., 59
la Porte-Wijsman, L.W., 115
Larimore, B.W., 50, 61
Larkins, J.R., 186, 194
Lashof, J.C., 260, 269
Laszlo, J., 112, 116
Latane, B., 267, 270
Lawrence, Philip S., 22, 35
Lawry, E.Y., 90, 92, 98
Leavell, B.S., 108, 109, 114
Lee, E.S., 42, 60
Lee, K.I., 85, 97
Lee, R.S., 209, 213
Lefcowitz, Myron J., 22, 33
Lehman, J.L., 96
Leight, L., 109, 114
Leiken, S.L., 110, 115
Leishman, A.W.P., 74, 77
Lenfant, C., 109, 110, 114
Leonard, D.L., 192, 194
Lepper, M.H., 260, 269
Lerner, A.B., 54, 62
Lerner, M., 260, 269
Lesesne, T.P., 68, 75
Lever, W.F., 54, 62
Levy, R.L., 101, 103

Lew, E.A., 55, 56, 62, 63
Lewis, J.H., 97
Lewis, L.A., 90, 92, 98
Lewis, R., 132, 139, 145
Liddell, H.S., 42, 60
Lilienfeld, A.M., 85, 97
Lindberg, H.A., vi, 56, 62, 66
Livingston, Rockwell, 19, 34
Lockwood, D.H., 257
Loewenson, R.B., 71, 73, 76
Lolli, G., 186, 194
LoPresti, J.M., 110, 115
Lotka, A.J., 30, 33
Luger, N.M., 49, 61
Lunde, Ander S., 22, 23, 33
Lusher, J.M., 112, 116, 118, 120
Lydon, F.J., 264, 270

M

MacIlwaine, W.A., 109, 114
Mahmood, L., 112, 116
Malzberg, B., 42, 58, 60
Manning, J.M., 113, 116, 138, 145
Mansfield, P.M., 260, 269
Mantel, N., 150, 162
Mariategui, J., 42, 60
Marks, P.A., 52, 61
Mason, T.J., 161, 162
Massey, E.J., 101, 103
Maxey, K.F., 45, 46, 47, 48, 60
Maxwell, G.M., 257
May, J.M., 45, 46, 60
McCormick, W.F., 122, 128
McCurdy, P.R.,.108, 112, 114, 116, 138, 145
McDade, A., 273, 279
McDonough, J.R., 70, 73, 76, 77, 91, 99
McElfresh, A.E., 112, 116
McGill, D.B., 257
McNamara, P.M., 73, 76
McPhedran, P., 161, 162
McVay, L.V., 85, 97
Meek, P.G., 97
Mellins, H.Z., 56, 62
Mescon, H., 47, 49, 61
Messer, M.J., 111, 115
Michael, S.T., 231, 240
Miller, G., 108, 109, 114
Miller, Herman, 30, 33

Miller, L.G., 252, 257
Miller, R.W., 121, 122, 128, 161, 162
Miller, W.F., 56, 62, 66, 110, 111, 115
Milner, P.F.A., 108, 114
Miners, E., 129, 145
Minnich, V., 107, 109, 113, 114
Mohmood, L., 138, 145
Monk, M.A., 260, 269
Moore, C.V., 107, 109, 113, 114
Moriyama, Iwao M., 19, 20, 26, 34, 96, 97
Morton, N.E., 121, 122, 128
Mosher, W.E., 121, 125, 128
Motulsky, A.G., 108, 114
Moynihan, D.P., 6, 17
Mullinax, G.L., 112, 116
Murayama, M., 107, 113, 117–120, 131, 132, 145
Murphy, George E., vi, 170
Myers, J.K., 42, 43, 60

N

Nalbandian, Robert M., vi, 106, 112, 116–120
Nam, Charles B., 26, 34
Navratil, L., 191, 194
Nesbitt, Robert E.L., Jr., 27, 28, 34
Newill, V., 73, 77
Nichaman, M.Z., 68, 75, 91, 99
Nichols, B.M., 118, 120
Nielsen, A., 163, 167
Norman, John C., 259

O

Obenour, W., Jr., 112, 116
O'Donnell, John A., 211–213
Oettle, A.G., 160, 162
Oh, Shin Joong, vi, 66, 67
Opler, M.K., 231, 240
Orshansky, Mollie, 21, 34
Ostfeld, A.M., 67, 72, 73, 75, 76
Ovesey, L., 42, 60, 225

P

Pachecho, C.G., 42, 60
Paffenbarger, R.S., Jr., 68, 69, 73, 75
Page, D.L., 110, 115
Paige, David M., vi, 242, 252, 257, 258
Park, S.K., 112, 116

Parker, James E., vi, 55, 62, 148
Parker, Seymour, 42, 60, 225, 226, 229
Parrish, H.M., 70, 72, 76
Pasamanick, B., 39, 59, 63, 91
Paton, D., 110, 115
Patrick, C.H., 186, 193
Patterson, J.C.S., 108, 114
Patterson, J.S., Jr., 109, 115
Pauling, L., 117, 120, 121, 127, 131, 132, 145
Paull, J.E., 259, 269
Pavlov, I.P., 42, 60
Payne, G.H., 70, 72, 76
Payne, H.M., 45, 60
Pearson, E.S., 150, 162
Pearson, H.A., 110, 111, 115
Pennell, M.Y., 96
Perillie, P.E., 107, 111, 114, 115
Perkins, J.E., 47, 60
Perry, G., 273, 279
Perutz, M.F., 107, 113
Peters, H.A., 121, 122, 128
Peterson, J., 17
Peterson, O.L., 264, 270
Pettigrew, Ann Hallman, vi, 4
Pettigrew, Thomas, vii, 4
Phillips, J.H., 55, 56, 62
Pick, R., 84, 85, 90–95
Pillsbury, D.M., 54, 62
Pincus, G., 92, 99
Pinedo-Veels, C., 111, 115
Piore, N., 260, 269
Pittman, D.G., 186, 194
Plunket, D.C., 110, 115
Pollack, H., 86, 98
Prange, A.J., 193, 194
Purugganan, H.B., 112, 116

Q

Querec, Linda, 22, 34

R

Rabinowitz, R., 107, 113
Ranney, H.M., 145
Rapoport, M., 54, 62
Redlick, F.C., 40, 59
Reeder, L.G., 101, 103
Rennie, T.A.C., 231, 240
Renold, A.E., 53, 61
Resch, J.A., 71, 73, 76

Reynolds, J.D.H., 112, 116
Rho, Y.M., 218, 221
Ricketts, N., 54, 62
Ricks, P., Jr., 112, 116
Rider, R.V., 57, 63
Ripley, H.S., 40, 41, 59
Roach, F.E., 256, 258
Robbins, S.L., 53, 55, 61
Roberts, B.H., 42, 60
Roberts, D.W., 97
Robertson, L.S., 264, 269
Robins, Lee, iv-vii, 170, 197, 211, 213
Robinson, B.W., 163, 167, 168
Robinson, M., 110, 115
Roemer, M.J., 274, 279
Roemer, M.L., 260, 269
Rogot, E., 45, 60
Rose, Geoffrey, vii, 66, 69, 75
Rosenfeld, Era, 209, 213
Rosenthal, S.R., 96
Rosensweig, N.S., 252, 257
Rosinski, E.F., 264, 276
Roth, J.A., 264, 270
Rotondo, U., 42, 60
Rowan, J.C., 163, 167, 168
Rowntree, L.G., 40, 59
Rubler, S., 111, 116
Rucknagel, D.L., 107, 113
Russell, Maurice, V., vii, 224

S

Sacks, S., 161, 162
Saengudom, C., 252, 257
Saltzman, H.A., 112, 116
Sampson, C., 54, 62
Sanguanbhokai, 252, 257
Sauer, H.I., 68, 70, 72, 75, 76
Saxena, U.H., 115
Schermerhorn, R.A., 59
Schlesinger, Edward R., 27, 28, 34, 121, 122, 125, 128
Schouten, H., 115
Schroff, P.D., 163, 168
Schulman, I., 108, 114
Schultz, G., 112, 116
Schwartz, A.D., 111, 115
Scott, Robert B., vii, 106, 115, 122, 128, 143, 145
Scotto, J., 121, 122, 128
Seltser, R., 68, 75

Sergeant, B.E., 108, 114
Sergeant, G.R., 108, 114
Shands, A.R., 56, 62
Shapiro, O.W., 97
Shapiro, Sam, 27, 28, 34
Shaw, L.W., 44, 45, 60
Shelley, W.B., 54, 62
Shotton, D., 108, 114
Shuey, A.M., 17
Sidel, Victor W., vii, 242, 260, 266, 269, 270
Siegler, E.E., 163, 167, 168
Sigelman, J.C., 266, 270
Silver, George A., vii, 242, 271, 273, 275, 279
Silver, H.K., 259, 269
Singers, S.J., 117, 120, 121, 127
Sirken, Monroe G., 31, 34
Smillie, W.G., 46, 48, 49, 50, 60
Smith, C.H., 108, 114, 131, 133, 136, 145
Smith, D.T., 46, 60
Smith, E.W., 111, 116
Smith, T.M., 97
Snider, T.H., 109, 114
Snyder, C.R., 186, 194
Solal, S., 260, 269
Soltys, S.D., 112, 116
Spain, D.M., 97
Spencer, R.P., 110, 111, 115
Spiegel, H.B.C., 277, 279
Spiegelman, Mortimer, 24, 26, 30, 34
Sprague, C.C., 108, 114
Sproule, B.J., 110, 111, 115
Srole, L., 231, 240
Stallones, R.A., 67, 69, 75
Stamler, Jeremiah, vii, 56, 62, 66, 67, 75, 84–86, 88, 90–99
Stanbury, J.B., 50–54, 61
Statius van Eps, L.W., 111, 115
Stearly, S.G., 259, 269
Steward, Harold L., 148
Stocks, P., 96, 163, 168
Strayer, Robert, vii, 170
Strong, J.P., 97
Stroud, W.D., 101, 103
Strudwick, W.J., 54, 62
Struyker Boudier, A.M., 115
Stubb, S.C., 70, 73, 76
Sullivan, Daniel, 19, 30, 34
Sultz, H.A., 121, 122, 125, 128

Sutton, Gordon F., vii, 4
Symeonidis, Alexander, 148

T
Taback, M., 57, 63
Taeuber, Irene B., 19, 34
Talamo, R.C., 121, 122, 125, 128
Taylor, C.E., 267, 270
Taylor, W.J., 107, 113
Terris, M., 260, 269
Tharp, C.P., 109, 114
Thavaramara, B., 257
Thomas, Louis B., 148
Thomas, W.A., 85, 97
Thompson, D., 111, 115
Thorn, G.W., 53, 61
Thornton, Russell G., 26, 34
Tinsley, J.C., Jr., 109, 114
Torrey, E.F., 273, 279
Troncale, F.J., 252, 257
Turner, M.D., 109, 114
Twaddle, Andrew, 259

V
Vaillant, George E., 211, 212, 214
Vawser, N., 257
Verter, J., 101, 103
Vigil, C.B., 42, 60
Vitols, M.M., vii, 192–194

W
Walker, A.R.P., 73, 76
Walters, J.H., 107, 114
Walton, J.N., 55, 62
Watson, Janet, 129
Watson, R.J., 110, 115
Waugh, F.V., 256, 258
Weiss, M.M., 97
Weissler, A.M., 97
Wells, I.C., 117, 120
White, Elijah L., 22, 35
White, J.E., 54, 62
White, P.D., 85, 90, 92, 93, 96, 101, 103, 121, 128
Whitten, C.F., 110, 115
Wilder, Charles S., 22, 35
Williams, A.O., 71, 73, 76
Williams, E.Y., 39, 59
Williams, J.L., 68, 69, 73, 75

Williams, R.H., 128
Wilson, D.C., 59
Winick, Charles, 203, 214
Winkelstein, W., Jr., 161, 162
Wintrobe, M.M., 51, 52, 53, 55, 61, 62
Wise, H., 259, 269, 273, 279
Wolf, P.A., 101, 103
Wolf, S., 40, 41, 59
Wolff, P.L., 118, 120
Wolfson, S.L., 111, 115
Woolsey, T.D., 96, 97
Wright, C.S., 112, 116

Wylie, C.M., 69, 75
Wyman, A.H., 44, 45, 60
Wynder, E.L., 148, 163, 168
Wyngaarden, J.B., 50, 51, 52, 53, 54, 61

Y

Yaghmai, H.B., 52, 61
Yates, P.O., 69, 74, 75
Yono, K., 70, 76

Z

Zelson, J.H., 111, 115
Zitrin, Arthur, 231

SUBJECT INDEX

A

"Abolish Charity Medicine," 14
Absenteeism in employment, 190
Absent father, 170, 197, 198, 206, 208, 209, 213
Acidosis, 112
Acute pyelorephritis, 134
Addicts, 211, 215, 216
Adolescent, 243, 245, 247, 248, 251
Adolescent health, 243
Africa, 50, 91, 160
  Bantu (South), 94, 151, 252
  North (descent), 131
African peoples, 37, 50, 51, 119
Alabama, Birmingham, 71
  Selma, 9
Albinos, 54
Alcoholic, 170–173, 175–177, 179–181, 183, 187, 189–193, 235
Alcoholic psychoses, 38
Alcoholics Anonymous (A.A.), 173
Alcoholism, 42, 170–193, 235, 236
American Association of Mental Deficiency, 6
American Indian, 20–23, 26, 27
American Journal of Medicine, 107
American Journal of Public Health, 5, 231, 243, 252
American Heart Association, Thirty-Third Scientific Sessions, 84
American Psychiatric Association, 209, 211, 214
American Public Health Association, 16, 17, 232, 240
American Sociological Association, 210, 213
Amphetamine addiction, 201, 202, 204
Amphetamines, 196, 199, 201, 204–206, 217
Anemia; 51, 52, 108, 133, 134, 136, 137
  congenital hemolytic anemia, 51, 52
  hemolytic, 107–109, 133
  pernicious anemia, 51, 52

sickle cell, 51, 57, 106, 111, 113, 117, 121–125, 127, 133, 135–137, 142
Aneurysm, congenital, 68
Anglo-Americans, 38
Annual Epidemiological and Vital Statistics, 83
Anti-social reactions, 41
Appalachian areas, 69
Arabia, 50
Archives of Environmental Health, 78
Argentina, 8
Armed Forces, 199
Army, 40
Arteriosclerosis, 56, 71, 94
Arteriosclerotic diseases, 84
  heart disease, 56, 78–80, 85, 87
Ascites, 136
Asia, 50
Asians, 252
Association for Research and Sickle Cell Anemia, 123
Association for Sickle Cell Anemia, Inc., Brooklyn Branch, 142

B

Bacillus
  leprosy, 46
  tubercle, 46
Bacterial endocarditis, 217
Baltimore City, 253, 256
Baltimore Study, 70, 72, 76
Bantu, South Africa, 51, 94, 252
Barbiturate addiction, 201, 202, 206
Barbiturates, 196, 201, 202, 204, 217
Basic cell epithelioma, 54
Bellevue Psychiatric Hospital, 231
Birth Control Clinic, 100
Blood conditions, 51
  congenital hemolytic anemia, 51, 52
  hemophilia, 51, 52
  leukemia, 52, 53, 121, 122, 149, 150, 152, 153, 155, 156, 158, 161
  pernicious anemia, 51, 52

289

polycythemiavera (erythremia), 53
RH-negative erythroblastosis, 51, 52
thalassemia, 51, 52, 57
Blood pressure, 57
diastolic, 57
elevated, 100, 101
systolic, 57
Body Build and Blood Pressure Study, 82, 83
Boston Study, 260
Boston Survey, 256
Breast cancer, 148, 152–157, 159
British, 74
Bureau of Census, 149
Bureau of Narcotics, 200

C

California, 217
Bakersfield, 216
Los Angeles, 90, 123, 260
California State Department of Health, 11
Cancer, 148, 163
Cancer, 52–55, 77, 149–154, 157, 158, 160, 161, 167
breast, 148, 152–157, 159
leukemia, 52, 53, 149, 150, 152, 153, 155, 156, 158, 159, 161
skin, 54, 152, 153, 155–158, 160
basic cell epithelioma, 54
Capillary stasis, 133
Carbohydrate metabolism, 53
Carcinoma of the cervix, 163, 165–167, 148
Cardiac enlargement, 136
Cardiovascular disease, 55, 56, 79
Cardiovascular mortality, 82, 83
Caucasian, 37, 45, 51–54, 163–167
Census, 21, 23, 30
Cerebral hemorrhage (CH), 68, 71, 73, 74, 69, 72
Cerebral thrombosis (CT), 68, 69, 73, 74
Cerebrovascular disease (CVD), 67–75
Chancroid, 48
Character disorders, 41
Characteristic protrusion of the central incisors, 139
Chatillon Food Scale, 254
Cherry Hospital, 187, 189
Chicago Board of Health, 84, 87

Venereal Disease Detection Program, 84
Chicago Heart Association, 84
Childhood disease, 43, 49
diphtheria, 49, 57
measles, 49
meningitis, 49
scarlet fever, 49
whooping cough, 49, 57
Chinese, 23, 26
Cholelithiasis, 136
Civil Rights Act, 9
Civil War, 188
Cocaine, 215
Colic, 135
Collagen diseases, 55
College of Physicians and Surgeons of Boston, 260
Columbia University, 231
Communicable disease, 43, 49
childhood disease, 43, 49
gonorrhea, 48
parasitic disease, 43
pulmonary tuberculosis, 43–45
syphilis, 47, 48, 55, 57
Conference on the Health Status of the Negro Today and in the Future, 5
Congenital hemolytic anemia, 51, 52
Congress, 9, 14, 16
Connecticut Commission on Alcoholism, Bridgeport Clinic, 171, 172, 177, 184
Connecticut
Bridgeport, 172, 173, 170, 182
New Haven, 41
Control of Communicable Diseases in Man, 61
Coronary disease, 94
Coronary heart disease (CHD), 85, 87, 90, 93–95, 70
Crises, The, 225
Cross racial group, 37
Cuban, 50, 149
Cyanide, 217
Cystic fibrosis, 53, 121–125, 127

D

Darvon, 139
Darwin, Charles, 51

Death rate, 24, 25, 32, 40, 44, 46, 49, 56, 68, 79–81, 150, 151, 155, 156, 160, 221
Degenerative Heart Disease, 85
Delinquency, 170, 207, 208, 209, 213
Delirium tremens, 237, 238
Department of Health of the Commonwealth of Kentucky, 163
Department of Health, Education and Welfare, 9, 145, 160, 162, 271, 275, 279
Depression, the, 25
Depressive reactions, 41
Desegregation, 36, 37, 58
Diabetes, 70, 73, 95
    diabetes mellitus, 53, 85, 93, 94, 121, 122, 125
Diastolic blood pressure, 57
Dictionary of Occupational Titles, 174
Differential mortality, 20
Diphtheria, 49, 57
Disability Insurance Benefits, 31
    Disability Insurance beneficiaries, 31
District of Columbia Department of Public Health, Health Education Division, 13
District of Columbia, population, 101
Division of Vital Statistics, 84
Downstate Reporter, 141, 145
Dropping out of high school, 170, 208
Drug abuse, 244
Drug addiction, 8, 170, 200–202, 204, 207–213, 215–218
Drug use, 195, 204, 206, 208, 209, 210, 211, 213
Dupuytren's contracture of the palm, 56
Dysentery, 50
Dyspnea, 136

E

Egypt, Cairo, 217
Electrocardiogram, 86
England, 69, 163
    Borough of Camden, 260
    London, 260
English, 190
Enteric infections, 50
    dysentery, 50
    typhoid, 50, 57
Enuresis, 136, 141
Epidemiological data, 231
    epidemiological research, 39

Epistaxis, 136
Erythrocyte sequestration, 110
Erythroid marrow, 111, 112
Erythropoiesis, 109
Europe, 52, 53, 188
    European peoples, 37, 252
    Europeans, 52, 54, 238
    Europeans, northern, 252, 256
    Europeans, southern, 256
Experimental neuroses, 43

F

Family disorganization, 42
Farm Security Administration, 5
Federal Bureau of Investigation, 200
Federal Bureau of Narcotics, 196, 199, 200, 201, 203, 211
Florid psychosis, 238
Food and Nutrition Section of the American Public Health Association, Ninety-Ninth Annual Meeting, 252
Foundation for Research and Education in Sickle-Cell Disease, 123
Foundations Fund for Research in Psychiatry, 231
France, 45
French, 131, 190

G

Gall bladder cancer, 55
Gastroenteritis, 254
Genetic counseling, 126
Genetic isolation, 36
Georgia, Evans County, 73
Geriatrics, 84
Glucose-6-phosphate deficiency, 52
Glycogen storage diseases, 124
Gonorrhea, 48
Granuloma inguinale, 48
Great Britain, 163
Greece, 50
Greek, 131, 133
Gross hematuria, 134
Gross National Product, 272

H

Harlem, 242, 246, 247, 251
Harlem, Central, 6
Harlem Hospital Center, 226

Harvard Medical School, 265, 260, 269
  Harvard Medical School Commission on Relations with the Black Community, 260, 269
Health Services, 6, 7, 8, 10
Health status, 5
Heart disease, 56, 71
  arteriosclerotic, 56, 68, 78, 83
  hypertensive, 56
  ischemic, 82, 83
  rheumatic, 56
Heart Disease Control Program, 84
Hematocrit, 108, 112, 134
Hematology, 139
Hematology Clinic, 130
Hematuria, 136
Hemiplegia, 136
Hemoglobin C disease, 131–133, 143
Hemoglobin production, 51
Hemoglobin S, 118, 119, 131, 132, 143, 144
Hemoglobin value, 108
Hemolytic anemia, 107, 108
Hemophilia, 51, 52
Hemotoma, hypertensive intracerebral, 71
  pontime hemotoma, 71
Hepatitis, viral, 217
Heroin, 200–205, 210–212, 215–217
  heroin addiction, 170, 200–202, 204, 207–209, 211–213, 218
Heterozygous state, 51, 52
High school dropouts, 208
Histoplasmoisis, 46
Hodgkin's disease, 154
Homicide, 8, 219, 272
Homozygous state, 51, 52
Hookworm, 50
Howard Medical School, 265
Howard University-Centennial Observance, 5, 7, 15
  Howard University Dental School, 11
Human Pathology, 215
Hypercholestrolemia, 70, 85, 88–90, 93–95
Hyperplastic erythroid marrow, 111
Hypertension, 56–58, 70, 73, 74, 81–83, 85, 86, 93, 94, 100–102
Hypertensive disease, 84, 87, 95
  hypertensive heart disease, 56, 86

Hypoxia, 111
Hysterical reactions, 41

I

Illegitimacy, 8
Illinois, 44
  Chicago, 41, 84, 85, 87–90, 92, 260
Infant mortality, 27, 28
Infectious peripheral vascular disease, 55
Influenza, 50
India, 50
Indian, 131, 188
Inpatient service, 138
International Classification of Diseases (ICD), 149, 161
International list, 78, 149, 151–153
IQ, 197, 198, 210
Ireland, 45
Irish ethnic and cultural group, 186
Ischemic heart disease, 82, 83
Italian, 131, 133, 190
  Italian ethnic and cultural group, 186

J

Japan, 69, 70
Japanese, 23, 26, 94
Jaundice, 135, 136, 137
Jewish Americans, 42, 148
Jewish ethnic and cultural group, 186
Johnson, L.B., 9
Journal of the American Medical Association, 74, 77, 100, 101, 102, 103, 121
Journal of the National Cancer Institute, 148, 149
Journal of the National Medical Association, 67, 117
Juvenile delinquency, 207

K

Kansas City University School of Physicians and Surgeons, 260
Keloids, 54
Kentucky, 148
  Fort Knox, 118
  Jefferson County, 164
  Lexington, 210, 212
  Louisville General Hospital, 164
Kentucky Division of the American Cancer Society, Inc., 163

Kew Gardens, 267
King's County Hospital-Downstate Medical Center (KCH-DMC), 129, 140, 141, 142, 144

L

Lactase, 252, 256
Lactose, 215, 242, 252–256
Lee, General Robert E., 188
Leprosy, 55
    bacillus, 46
Leukemia, 52, 53, 121, 122, 149, 150, 152, 153, 155, 156, 158, 161
Lincoln Hospital, 11
Liver profile, 139
London Borough of Camden, 260
Lymphadenopathy, 136
Lymphogranuloma venereum, 48

M

Malaria, 50–52, 54, 121, 216–217
Malnutrition, 254, 271
Manhattan, 45
Mannitol, 215
Mantel-Haenszel procedure, 150
Marijuana, 196, 201–207, 212, 213
Mark of Oppression, the, 225
Maryland, Baltimore, 39, 69, 253, 256
Macular hemorrhage of the retina, 139
Massachusetts
    Boston, 260
        Irish, 256
    Boston-Roxbury, 260
    North Dorchester, 260
M.D. degree, 275, 276
Measles, 49
Medicaid, 9, 14, 263
Medic Alert emblem, 139
Medic Alert Foundation, 139
Medical World News, 143
Medicare, 9, 13
Medicine in the Ghetto, 259
Mediterranean peoples, 52, 122
Meharry Medical School, 265
Melanin pigments, 54
Mendelian dominant, 51, 52
Meningitis, 49
Mental illness, 37, 38, 40, 42, 58, 224–228, 230
Mental Illness in the Urban Negro Community, 225

Mental retardation, 6, 8, 54
Metabolic abnormalities, 53
    cystic fibrosis, 53
    diabetes mellitus, 53
    periodic paralysis, 53
    phenylketonuria (phenylpyruric oligophrenia), 53, 54
Metastases, 54
Methemoglobin, 112
Mexican-American, 20, 49
Michigan, 44, 117
    Grand Rapids, 117
Michigan State University, 225
Microvasculature, 107
Middle Eastern descent, 131
Middlesex University of Medicine, 260
Midwest, 188
Migratory arthralgia, 136
Milbank Fund, 5
Mississippi, 8, 182
Mississippi legislature, 36
Missouri, mid, 69
    St. Louis, 84, 170, 197–199, 210
Morphine, 215
Multiple sclerosis, 55
Muscular dystrophy, 121–124, 127
Myocardial infarction, 71

N

Narcotics, 209, 218, 219
National Academy of Science, 86, 98
National Cancer Institute, 163
National Center for Health Statistics, 121, 149
National Clearing House for Smoking and Health, 247
National Heart Institute, 84
National Institutes of Health, 117, 124, 163
National Office of Vital Statistics, 40, 44, 49, 53, 55, 56, 59
National Sickle-Cell Anemia Foundation, 123
Navy, 40
Nephritis, 50
Nephrosis, 125
Neurosis, experimental, 43
Neurotic (neurosis), 37, 39, 40–43, 227
New England Journal of Medicine, 120
New Jersey, 44

New York, 44, 148, 170, 232, 234, 260
    Brooklyn, 129, 142, 143
    Erie County, 125
    New York City, 6, 18, 123, 129, 170,
        216–219, 224, 231, 233
        Borough of Manhatten, 219, 232, 234
        Bronx, The, 219
New York Heart Association, 86, 98
New York Times Magazine, 66
Nicotine, 217
Nocturia, 136, 141
North Carolina, 46
North Carolina Mental Health Depart-
    ment, 187
North Carolina Mental Health Facilities,
    193
North Carolina State Hospitals, 170
North Carolina State Mental Facilities,
    186
North, the, 181, 188
Northwestern University, 84

O

Obesity, 85, 93–95
Obsessive-compulsive   reactions,   41
Ohio, 41
Old Age Survivors Disability and Health
    Insurance (OASDHI), 31
Ophthalmic examinations, 10
Opiates, 196
Oriental, 220, 256
Orthopedic disorders, 56
Overweight, 70, 89, 93–95

P

Pallor, 135
Pap smears, 261
Parasitic anemia, 52
Parasitic diseases, 43, 50
    hookworm, 50
    malaria, 50–52
Paresis-psychoses, 38
Pathogenesis, 117
Peace Corps, 8
Pediatric Comprehensive Care Clinic,
    130
Pediatric Emergency Area, 138
Pediatric Hematology Clinic, 138
Pediatric Outpatient Service, 129
Penicillin, 47

Pennsylvania, 44
    Philadelphia, 125, 225, 226, 228
Peptic ulcer rate, 40
Perinatal, 56, 57
Periodic paralysis, 53
Pernicious anemia, 51, 52
Peru, Lima, 42
Peruvian mestizo, 42
Phenylketonuria (phenylpyruvic oligo-
    phrenia), 53, 54, 121–124
Phylon, 36
Pinta, 50
Pneumonia, 50
Poisson variables, 150
Polycythemia vera (erythiemia), 53
Potassium cyanate, 138
Pregnancy, toxemia of, 100
Priapism, 134
Psychiatric facilities, 38
Psychoneurotic   depressive   reaction,
    235, 236, 238
Psychopathic personality trends, 40
Psychoses
    florid, 238
Psychosomatic difficulties, 40
Psychotic (psychoses), 37–40, 42, 43, 227
Public Health Hospital, 200
Public Health Nurse (PHN), 139
Public Health Report, 93, 99
Public Health Service, 5, 16, 84, 163, 168,
    231, 247
Puerto Ricans, 129, 131, 148, 149, 210,
    218, 220
Pulmonary tuberculosis, 43, 44, 45

Q

Quadriplegia, 136
Quarterly Journal of Studies on Alcohol,
    171
Quinine, 215–217

R

Regional Medical Programs, 278
Report, 24, 67, 74
Research Grants Index, 124, 128
Reticulocytes, 109
Retinal hemorrhage, 134
Rheumatic fever, 56
Rheumatic heart disease, 56
RH-negative erythroblastosis, 51, 52

S

Sarcoidosis, 55
Scandinavia, 55
Scandinavians, 252
Scarlet fever, 49
Schizophrenia, 38–41, 43, 192, 235, 236, 238
  paranoid, 41
Scotland, 45
Sepsis, 217, 220
Serum cholesterol levels, 87, 88, 89, 91, 92
S hemoglobin, 118, 119, 131, 132, 143, 144
Sickle cell, 50, 51, 57, 106–113, 117–119, 121–127; 129–144
Sickle Cell Anemia Clinic, 138
SICKLEDEX, 143
Sickle-Cell Disease Research Foundation, 123
Sickle cell, hemoglobin C disease, 131, 134
Sickle cell, thalassemia, 131, 133, 137, 143
Skin cancer, 54, 152–156, 158, 160
Small pox, 57
Smoking, heavy, 85, 90, 93–95
Social security, 25, 31
Social Security Act, 31
Social welfare, 20, 32
South, the, 39, 44, 49, 50, 57, 178, 188
South Africa
  Bantu, 94, 252
South American Indians, 252
South Carolina, 256
Southern School News, 36, 58
Southern States, 69
Soviet Union, 263, 265
Spanish descent, 21, 131
Splenomegaly, 136, 137
Standardized Morbidity Ratio (SMR), 28, 29
Stasis, 110
Statistics Bulletin, 53, 55–57, 61, 62, 89
St. Louis office of the Federal Bureau of Narcotics, 196
St. Louis police, 197, 200
Strychnine, 217
Suicide, 40, 237
Supremacists, 54

Supreme Court, 36
Syphilis, 47, 48, 50, 55, 57, 86
Systolic blood pressure, 57

T

Target cells, 51
Temple University, 225
Tennessee, Memphis, 123
Tetanus, 217, 220
Texas, 38, 39
Thais, 252
Thalassemia, 51, 52, 57, 131, 133, 137, 143
Thiazide diuretic, 102
Third National Cancer Survey, 159, 162
Thrombosis, 110
Toxemia of pregnancy, 100
Transient ischemic attacks (T.I.A.), 72
Treatment facilities, 38
Tubercle bacillus, 46
Tuberculin skin test, 46
Tuberculosis, 46, 47, 49, 55, 57
Turkey, 50
Turkish descent, 131
Typhoid, 50, 57

U

Union of Soviet Socialist Republics (USSR), 263
University of London, 260
University of Louisville School of Medicine, 163
Urea, 118, 119, 138
Urea therapy, 118
Urinalysis, 86
Urine specimens, 139
U.S. Army Medical Research Laboratory, 118
U.S. Commission on Civil Rights, 9
U.S. Department of Health, Education and Welfare, 271, 275, 279
U.S. National Center for Health Statistics, 26, 28, 34
U.S. Public Health Service, 6, 29, 84, 87, 106, 195, 211
  Chicago, 84

V

V.D. Fact Sheet, 48, 61
Veddoids, 50